改訂版

やっておきたい

英語長文

700

［問題編］

河合塾講師

杉山 俊一

塚越 友幸

山下 博子

［共著］

河合出版

河合塾
SERIES

改訂版

やっておきたい

英語長文

700

［問題編］

河合塾講師

杉山 俊一
塚越 友幸
山下 博子

［共著］

河合出版

次の英文を読んで，設問に答えなさい。

　Globalization is the process in which individual lives and local communities are affected by economic and cultural forces that operate worldwide. In effect, it is the process of the world becoming a single place. Globalism is the perception of the world as a function or result of the processes of globalization upon local
5 communities.

　The word "global" has had a rapid rise since the mid-1980s, up until which time the word "international" was preferred. The rise of the word "international" itself in the eighteenth century indicated the growing importance of territorial states in organizing social relations. It can be defined as an early consequence
10 of the worldwide perspective of European imperialism. Similarly the rapidly increasing interest in globalization reflects a changing organization of worldwide social relations. (1)The nation has begun to have a decreasing importance as individuals and communities, gaining access to globally shared knowledge and culture, are affected by economic realities that come and go over the boundaries
15 of the state. The basic structure of globalization is nationalism on which the concept of internationalism is based. Globalization occurs when people in a national framework are affected by global economy and communication.

　Part of the complexity of globalism comes from the different ways in which globalization is approached. Some analysts embrace it enthusiastically as a
20 positive feature of a changing world in which access to technology, information, services and markets will be of benefit to local communities. They believe that, by globalization, dominant forms of social organization will lead to universal prosperity, peace, and freedom. They even expect that perception of a global environment will lead to a global ecological concern. For (2a)this group, globalism
25 is a term for values which treat global issues as a matter of personal and collective responsibility.

　Others reject it as a form of domination by advanced countries over developing ones, in which individual distinctions of culture and society become erased by an increasingly homogeneous global culture while local economies are more firmly incorporated into a system of global capital. For (2b) this group, globalism is a 30 political doctrine which provides, explains, and justifies an interlocking system of world trade. It has ideological overtones of historical inevitability, and (3) its attendant myths function as a gospel of the global market. The chief argument against globalization is that global culture and global economy did not spontaneously spring up but originated in the centers of capitalist power which 35 still try to sustain their own economic system. According to this group, in short, the benefits of globalization vary too much from country to country.

(2c) Proponents of critical globalism take a disinterested view of the process, simply examining its processes and effects. Critical globalism refers to the critical engagement with globalization processes, neither blocking them out nor 40 celebrating globalization. Thus, while critical globalists see that globalization has often sustained poverty, widened material inequalities, increased ecological degradation, sustained militarism, fragmented communities, marginalized minority groups, fed intolerance, and deepened crises of democracy, they also see that it has had a positive effect on the great rise of the average individual income since 1945, 45 reducing the population in miserable poverty, increasing ecological consciousness, and facilitating disarmament.

Academically, globalization covers such disciplines as international relations, political geography, economics, sociology, communication studies, agricultural, ecological, and cultural studies. It addresses the (4a) influence (though not 50 the status) of the nation-state in the world political order and the (4b) influence of multinational corporations. Globalization also means easy transportation all over the world, transnational company operations, the changing pattern of world employment, or global environmental risk. Indeed, there are compelling reasons for thinking globally where the environment is concerned. As a famous scholar 55 puts it, (5) "When the ill winds of *Chernobyl came our way, they did not pause at the frontier, produce their passports and say, 'Can I rain on your territory now?'"

(注)　Chernobyl：チェルノブイリ(旧ソ連のこの町の原子力発電所で1986年に放射能漏れの大事故が発生)

(同志社大)

問1　下線部(1)を日本語に訳しなさい。

問2　下線部(2a)〜(2c)の説明として最も適当なものを，次のア〜オからそれぞれ1つずつ選びなさい。

ア．They oppose globalization, as they think it sustains the domination of developed countries over developing countries.

イ．They are afraid that globalization will weaken advanced countries' political and economic predominance as developing ones gain power.

ウ．They see both merits and demerits of globalization, so they don't approve or disapprove of it.

エ．They think that globalization will contribute to worldwide peace and prosperity.

オ．They try to understand globalization only from an ecological point of view.

問3　下線部(3)の内容として最も適当なものを，次のア〜エから1つ選びなさい。

ア．globalists use the Bible to support their argument

イ．historians reject globalism as an utter myth

ウ．religion must take responsibility for globalization

エ．the illusions embedded in globalism serve to justify world trade

問4　空所(4a)(4b)に入れるのに最も適当な組み合わせを，次のア〜エから1つ選びなさい。

ア．increasing — increasing　　　イ．decreasing — decreasing

ウ．increasing — decreasing　　　エ．decreasing — increasing

問5　下線部(5)の引用はどのようなことを言うためのものか。本文に即して30字以内の日本語で述べなさい。

4

次の英文を読んで，設問に答えなさい。

A particular problem directly related to continuing population growth is growing global food insecurity. For a variety of reasons the demand for food by the consumer has begun to outrun the capacity to provide. Where all attention was previously focused on population growth as the sole source of demand on available food stocks, today an equally important source of demand has become ⁵ apparent and that is (1). As per capita income increases, purchasing power climbs and with it a demand for higher quality foods, especially foods of animal origin such as meat, eggs, milk and milk products. Eating meat can be considered an (2) way of utilizing grain. In the United States it takes three pounds of grain to produce a pound of *poultry; 5 : 1 is the ratio for pork, and ¹⁰ 10 : 1 for beef. In the end, Americans eat eighty percent of all the grain they consume indirectly, first using it for feed and then consuming the meat. On the basis of these data, Americans consume the equivalent of one ton of grain a year while inhabitants of poorer countries consume one fifth as much. Outside our borders, other nations with growing economies but without comparable agriculture ¹⁵ have also increased their appetites for animal protein. Hence, sixty percent of North American agricultural sales has been to nations whose people are already rather well fed. At this time, the approximately one billion people of the developed world feed enough grain to their livestock and poultry to provide minimal nutritional requirements to another 2 billion people. ₍₃₎Over the last twenty ²⁰ years, the rich minority of the world has doubled its meat consumption. This is, however, not due to eating twice as much meat per capita, although there has been some rise here. Rather, there are twice as many people with the money to buy a higher quality protein-rich diet. The net result is that while world population has been growing at 1.6 percent and agricultural production at 2.5 ²⁵ percent, world demand for food has been increasing at 3 percent per year.

It is to our advantage and the world's as well that the United States grain harvests in recent years have resulted in enormous yields. Overflowing *granaries and low grain prices are the mark of this high productivity. But the great increases

30 in food production have not occurred where populations are growing the fastest. Gains in production require modern energy-intensive methods combining irrigation, pesticides, herbicides, fertilizers, genetics, and mechanization. One reason, among several, why (4) is because their farmers have not had access to appropriate technologies, such as sufficient fertilizers, irrigation, improved seeds, pesticides,

35 storage facilities, and transportation. The world's poor are thus driven to world food markets to supplement their needs. (5)However, they must compete there with richer nations whose own increased demands have forced the price of grain upward. With food prices rising beyond their purchasing power, the poor countries can buy less and less with their precious dollars.

40 According to some estimates, world agriculture could produce enough to feed up to 30 billion people. What appears to be a food shortage may, in fact, be an uneven worldwide distribution of economic power; we have the producer nations with surpluses to sell, the affluent consumer nations who have money to buy, and the low income consumer countries that cannot effectively compete in the world

45 food markets. (6)These differentials represent an ever-growing number of hungry people. Thus there is famine in some parts of the world, most notably on the Indian subcontinent and some countries of Africa and Latin America, and an overabundance of food in a number of others.

(注)　poultry：家禽(ニワトリ，アヒルなど)，家禽の肉　　granary：穀物倉庫

（三重大）

問1　空所(1)に入れるのに最も適当なものを，次のア～エから1つ選びなさい。

　　ア．ecology　　　イ．famine　　　ウ．affluence　　　エ．nourishment

問2　空所(2)に入れるのに最も適当なものを，次のア～エから1つ選びなさい。

　　ア．ethical　　　イ．inefficient　　　ウ．effective　　　エ．ideal

問3　下線部(3)の理由を40字以内の日本語で説明しなさい。

問4　空所(　4　)に入れるのに最も適当なものを，次のア〜エから1つ選びなさい。

　　ア．poor countries have managed to produce enough food
　　イ．poor countries have lagged behind in food production
　　ウ．rich countries have a lot of food surplus
　　エ．rich countries have been suffering from food shortages

問5　下線部(5)を，they および there の内容を明らかにして日本語に訳しなさい。

問6　下線部(6)の内容を80字以内の日本語で具体的に述べなさい。

次の英文を読んで，設問に答えなさい。

Primary education in Britain begins at the age of five. Parents have a responsibility to educate their children but not always in schools. And yet, until recently, home schooling was associated with zealous parents having eccentric ideas. Today, however, dinner-table conversations among middle-class parents 5 who are conscious of their children's education often lead to debate about the (1a) pros and cons of educating children at home.

A depressing catalogue of complaints — large classes, bullying and school violence, teaching standards, and despair with the incessant pressure of examinations — has led many parents to think the unthinkable. It is estimated 10 that 140,000 children, about 1.5% of the school population, are home-schooled in Britain, a growth of about 10% during the past year. About half of these children have been withdrawn from school; (2) the rest were home-schooled from the start.

So (3) why are more parents choosing this option? The new generation of home teachers tends to be motivated more by fears that their children are not thriving 15 in conventional schools. A mother of a seven-year-old daughter in an industrial town, for example, is pragmatic about her decision to take her daughter out of her local primary school. "Her teachers lacked the ability to stimulate and encourage her," claims she, (1b) who is not committed to home schooling on principle. "I would put her back in the system if there was a decent school in 20 this area."

The fear of bullying is also often raised. (4) The perception that schools are unsafe places drives many parents to the conclusion that they should educate at home, even if only for six months until the bullying is resolved. Another mother, who is also representative of a home schooling support group, says that 25 the erosion of classroom discipline means that many schools resemble a "war zone." She believes that it is now group pressure rather than teachers that dominates the classroom.

Some parents worry that children who are either specially gifted or have learning difficulties are often overlooked within a highly bureaucratic school system. A mother, who is as well an author of a book on a woman's role at home, has decided to school her daughters at home throughout the primary years. She argues that schools often "fail to respond to the (5a) needs of children."

The growth of home education is not simply a reflection of the unhappy state of the British education system. It can also reflect the fact that modern-day parents are more concerned with the task of child-raising than ever before. Our overprotective parenting has led to a steady expansion of the amount of time mothers and fathers spend looking after their children and a corresponding reduction in the freedom children are given to explore their world with one another. Home schooling takes this one step further.

In addition, it is surprisingly easy to begin home schooling. Parents do not even need permission from the local education authority to educate their families at home. However, those who withdraw their child from school in England and Wales need to inform the head of their education authority. After this, parents can expect education officers to inquire about the arrangements they are making.

Most authorities (1c) take a fairly hands-off attitude. The representative of a home schooling support group notes that home-educating families are visited once a year for a half-hour session. She found these visits useful, since they affirmed that what she was teaching was on the (5b) track. There is also an elaborate network of support available to those opting to home-educate. Materials and advice for different levels of teaching are readily available on the Internet as well as in books and other publications. Many parents join local support groups.

In principle, there is no reason children cannot be successfully educated at home, although it is more (5c) as they get older. While there are some successful cases, few parents are equipped to teach mathematics and science beyond a basic level. Others might ask, "Do children educated at home gain the social skills necessary to relate to their age group and the outside world?" Most supporters of home schooling say yes but (1d) sound a little defensive on this subject. One supporter says: "We spend a considerable amount of time scheduling group activities for the children!"

So what's the downside of home education? It is the loss of free time for the home teacher. That was why a mother, who lives in south London, (1e) packed in her experiment. She removed her twelve-year-old and thirteen-year-old from their state schools because of concern about their education, but gave up home schooling after just over a year. "One year of home teaching finished me off," she recalls. Her solution was to move near a "good school."

Home schooling is time-consuming if it is done properly, and leaves little space to run a career, look after other children, or run a home. Since time is the one thing most modern-day adults lack, it seems (5d) that despite its growth home teaching will be used only by a small minority of parents. Indeed, many children are taken out of schools for only short periods of time before their parents resume their careers.

（同志社大）

問1 下線部(1a)～(1e)とほぼ同じ意味を表すものを，次のア～エから1つずつ選びなさい。

(1a) ア．theory and practice 　　イ．advantages and disadvantages
　　 ウ．ideal and reality 　　　　エ．quality and quantity

(1b) ア．who does not believe home schooling is always the best system
　　 イ．who is against teaching moral discipline at home
　　 ウ．who is not involved in primary education at home
　　 エ．who puts the idea of home schooling in practice

(1c) ア．fully support home-schooling families
　　 イ．never get in touch
　　 ウ．don't want to intervene too much
　　 エ．have a negative view

(1d) ア．give the impression that they are experts on the subject
　　 イ．listen to some apologies for home schooling
　　 ウ．say that mathematics and science are necessary subjects to learn
　　 エ．seem to lack confidence in developing their children's social skills

(1e) ア．cleared away her laboratory
　　 イ．gave up teaching at school
　　 ウ．finished her group activities
　　 エ．quit teaching her children at home

問2 下線部(2)の内容として最も適当なものを，次のア～エから1つ選びなさい。

　　 ア．about 70,000 children 　　　イ．about 14,000 children
　　 ウ．about 7,000 children 　　　　エ．about 2,100 children

問3　下線部(3)に対する理由として，学校制度以外に起因するものを30字以内の日本語で述べなさい。

問4　下線部(4)を日本語に訳しなさい。

問5　空所(5a)～(5d)に入れるのに最も適当なものを，次のア～エから1つずつ選びなさい。

　　ア．difficult　　　　イ．individual　　　ウ．likely　　　　エ．right

問6　本文の内容と一致しないものを，次のア～オから1つ選びなさい。

　　ア．Until recently it was strange for parents to take their children out of school to educate them at home.

　　イ．A mother who is worried about school violence insists that teachers no longer have control over their classes.

　　ウ．Overprotective child-raising has resulted in freedom for children to explore the world on their own.

　　エ．In addition to books and publications, there are a lot of helpful materials for home teachers on the Internet.

　　オ．When parents want to teach children at home properly, there is little time left for them to pursue a career, take care of other children, or keep house.

次の英文を読んで，設問に答えなさい。

The concept of retirement is a modern one. In the 1870s, the German statesman Bismarck introduced 65 as the age at which citizens could stop working and receive a pension. This was a humane initiative at a time when work usually meant heavy manual labor and life expectancy was much lower than
5 it is now. The typical retirement age for men has been set at around 65 in most developed countries since the Second World War. (Though women live longer, their retirement age has generally been set rather lower.) But in recent years, people have been retiring, willingly or unwillingly, much earlier — as young as 50 in some cases — mainly because many companies have been trying
10 to reduce the size of their workforce. Some workers have thus been able to look forward to many years of retirement. This, however, is about to change. The reason is (1).

During the twentieth century life expectancies around the world increased by one third. (2)Today, a girl born in a developed country can expect to live well into
15 her 80s, and a boy until his early 80s. Meanwhile, since the beginning of the 1950s global birth rates have halved. The populations of developing countries will keep growing for several more decades because of the numbers of young people still to reach childbearing age, but the populations of Europe and the rich countries of Asia will shrink and age. The main consequence will be (3).
20 At present in developed countries there are about three workers for every pensioner. As the babyboomer generation begins to hit retirement age, this ratio will fall dramatically. By 2030 it is expected to average 1.5 to one, and in Germany and Italy it will be one to one or lower. A distinguished economist has recently written that "we are confronting such great changes in terms of
25 population that they could redefine economic and political systems in the developed countries over the next generation."

(4)With unemployment in the USA and some European countries hitting near record lows and significant skills shortages in some areas, a strong push to retain older workers is developing. However, this will require big shifts in attitudes among both employees and employers. A recent Australian survey found that, 30 when looking to fill senior management jobs, 60% of companies still preferred people in their 30s, and 65% of companies said employees over 50 would be the first to go. Governments are just beginning to take positive action to counter (5)these prejudices. In Japan, the government is providing financial help to companies to encourage them to retain older workers. In Britain, where early 35 retirement is estimated to cost around $27 billion a year, a major effort is being made to help older unemployed people get back into jobs. The British government minister in charge of employment has declared that age discrimination is "bad for the economy and unfair to the individual."

Some companies are now realizing that getting rid of their older workers was, 40 in fact, a false economy. Older workers have lower rates of *absenteeism and stay in a job longer, which saves money on recruitment and training. Also some companies have discovered that older workers have more respect for their firms' values and traditions. British Telecom recently became the first company in Britain to raise the retirement age for its workers to 70. In the Netherlands, 45 where unemployment is at a 20-year low, a job agency specializing in recruiting workers over the age of 65 is finding that demand for its services is booming.

Not all older people want to be in the workforce, of course. But in a survey in the USA, 80% of babyboomers reported that they intended to continue working after they are 65, at least part time. Only 13% said they did not ever want to lift 50 a finger again. The issue is thus not only one of economic efficiency, but also of the health and well-being of the fastest-growing sector of the population. Though we often complain about them, for most of us, our places of work are where we find conversation, stimulation, friendship — and a reason to get up in the morning. (6)When we are 65, not only will they still need us, but we will also 55 need them.

（注）　absenteeism：正当な理由もなくたびたび仕事を休むこと

（早稲田大）

問1　空所(1)に入れるのに最も適当なものを，次のア～エから1つ選びなさい。

　　ア．changes in employment law

　　イ．low unemployment rates

　　ウ．the aging of populations

　　エ．the booming economy

問2　下線部(2)を日本語に訳しなさい。

問3　空所(3)に入れるのに最も適当なものを，次のア～エから1つ選びなさい。

　　ア．a decline of population

　　イ．an economic decline

　　ウ．an increased burden on pensioners

　　エ．an increased burden on workers

問4　下線部(4)を日本語に訳しなさい。

問5　下線部(5)に関して，本文に述べられている具体例を2つ，それぞれ25字以内の日本語で述べなさい。

問6　下線部(6)を they および them の内容を明らかにして日本語に訳しなさい。

問7　本文の内容と一致するものを，次のア～オから1つ選びなさい。

　　ア．It was not until the twentieth century that the system of retirement was introduced.

　　イ．It is an enormous disadvantage to retain older workers in developed countries.

　　ウ．In Britain, the government is offering financial advantage to companies who employ older workers.

　　エ．A majority of babyboomers want to continue working after 65 in America.

　　オ．There is much difference between European and American attitudes toward retirement.

次の英文を読んで，設問に答えなさい。

We have no idea what the job market will look like in fifty years. It is generally agreed that machine learning and robotics will change almost every line of work — from producing yoghurt to teaching yoga. However, there are (1)conflicting views about the nature of the change and its *imminence. Some believe that within a mere decade or two, billions of people will become 5 economically redundant. Others maintain that even in the long run, automation will keep generating new jobs and greater prosperity for all.

So are we on the verge of a terrifying upheaval, or are such forecasts yet another example of ill-founded *Luddite hysteria? It is hard to say. Fears that automation will create massive unemployment go back to the nineteenth century, 10 and so far they have never materialized. (2)Since the beginning of the Industrial Revolution, for every job lost to a machine, at least one new job was created, and the average standard of living has increased dramatically. Yet there are good reasons to think that this time it is different, and that machine learning will be a real game changer. 15

Humans have two types of abilities — physical and cognitive. In the past, machines competed with humans mainly in raw physical abilities, while humans retained an immense edge over machines in cognition. Hence, as manual jobs in agriculture and industry were automated, new service jobs emerged that required the kind of cognitive skills only humans possessed: learning, analyzing, 20 communicating and, above all, understanding human emotions. However, AI is now beginning to outperform humans in more and more of these skills, including the understanding of human emotions. (3)We don't know of any third field of activity — beyond the physical and the cognitive — where humans will always retain a secure edge. 25

It is crucial to realize that the AI revolution is not just about computers getting faster and smarter. It is fueled by breakthroughs in the life sciences and the social sciences as well. The better we understand the biochemical mechanisms that form the base for human emotions, desires and choices, the better computers can become at analyzing human behavior, predicting human decisions, and replacing human drivers, bankers and lawyers.

In the last few decades, research in areas such as neuroscience and behavioral economics have allowed scientists to analyze humans, and in particular to gain a much better understanding of how humans make decisions. (4)It turned out that our choices of everything from food to mates result not from some mysterious free will, but rather from billions of neurons that calculate probabilities within a split second. What we boast about as 'human intuition' is in reality 'pattern recognition'. Good drivers, bankers and lawyers don't have magical intuitions about traffic, investment or negotiation — rather, by recognizing recurring patterns, they spot and try to avoid careless pedestrians, untrustworthy borrowers and dishonest clients. It also turned out that the biochemical algorithms of the human brain are (5a) perfect. They rely on *heuristics, shortcuts and outdated circuits adapted to the African savannah rather than to the urban jungle. No wonder that even good drivers, bankers and lawyers sometimes make stupid mistakes.

This means that AI can outperform humans in tasks that supposedly demand 'intuition'. If you think AI needs to compete against the human soul in terms of mystical hunches — that sounds impossible. But if AI really needs to compete against neural networks in calculating probabilities and recognizing patterns — that sounds far less difficult.

In particular, AI can be better at jobs that demand intuitions about other people. Many lines of work — such as driving a vehicle in a street full of pedestrians, lending money to strangers, and negotiating a business deal — require the ability to correctly assess the emotions and desires of other people. Is that kid about to jump onto the road? Does the man in the suit intend to take my money and disappear? Will that lawyer act on his threats, or is he just bluffing? As long as it was thought that such emotions and desires were generated by an immaterial spirit, it seemed obvious that computers would never be able to replace human drivers, bankers and lawyers. For how can a computer understand the divinely created human spirit? Yet if these emotions and desires are in fact (5b) biochemical algorithms, there is no reason why computers cannot decipher these algorithms — and do so far better than any Homo sapiens.

A driver predicting the intentions of a pedestrian, a banker assessing the

credibility of a potential borrower, and a lawyer judging the mood at the 65
negotiation table don't rely on witchcraft. Rather, their brains are recognizing
biochemical patterns by analyzing facial expressions, tones, hand movements, and
even body odors. (6)[do / sensors / the / equipped / an / could / with / AI / right]
all that far more accurately and reliably than a human.

(注)　imminence：切迫　　　Luddite：19世紀初頭のイギリスで機械化に反対した労働者
　　　heuristics：経験則

（東京農工大）

問1　下線部(1)の内容を60字以内の日本語で述べなさい。

問2　下線部(2)を日本語に訳しなさい。

問3　下線部(3)の内容として最も適当なものを，次のア～エから1つ選びなさい。

　ア．We are not sure that AI possesses an ability that is superior to humans,
　　both physically and cognitively.

　イ．Humans can remain in a safe position by using both their physical and
　　cognitive abilities.

　ウ．Humans currently have not found a field of activity where we can
　　outperform AI.

　エ．It is very difficult for us to find a field of activity in which AI will be
　　able to defeat humans.

問4　下線部(4)を日本語に訳しなさい。

問5　空所（　5a　）（　5b　）に入れるのに最も適当なものを，次のア～エから1つず
　　つ選びなさい。

　ア．all the more　　　　　　　　　イ．far from
　ウ．all the time　　　　　　　　　エ．no more than

問6　下線部(6)の語を文意が通るように並べ換えなさい。ただし，文頭に来るべき語
　　も小文字で示してある。

問7　本文で筆者が主張している内容に最も近いものを，次のア～エから１つ選びな
さい。

ア．AI will have various kinds of emotions and become human-like.

イ．AI will take control of most of human decision making in fifty years.

ウ．Humans may not be able to compete cognitively with AI in the future.

エ．Humans need to fight against AI in order to avoid being conquered.

次の英文を読んで，設問に答えなさい。

By the 1920s it was thought that no corner of the earth fit for human habitation had remained unexplored. (1)New Guinea, the world's second largest island, was no exception. The European missionaries, planters, and administrators clung to its coastal lowlands, convinced that no one could live in the treacherous mountain range that ran in a solid line down the middle of the island. But the mountains visible from each coast in fact belonged to two ranges, not one, and between them was a mildly warm *plateau crossed by many fertile valleys. A million Stone Age people lived in those highlands, isolated from the rest of the world for forty thousand years. (2)The veil would not be lifted until gold was discovered in a *tributary of one of the main rivers. The gold rush that followed attracted many prospectors, including Michael Leahy, an Australian who on May 26, 1930 set out to look for gold in the mountains with a fellow prospector and a group of native lowland people hired as carriers. After climbing the heights, Leahy was amazed to see grassy open country on the other side. (3)By nightfall his amazement turned to alarm, because there were points of light in the distance, obvious signs that the valley was populated. After a sleepless night in which Leahy and his party loaded their weapons and assembled a crude bomb, they made their first contact with (4)the highlanders. The astonishment was mutual. Leahy wrote in his diary:

It was a relief when the natives came in sight, the men in front armed with bows and arrows, the women behind bringing stalks of sugarcane. When he saw the women, one of the native carriers told me at once that there would be no fight. We waved to them to come on, which they did cautiously, stopping every few yards to look us over. When a few of them finally got up courage to approach, we could see that they were utterly thunderstruck by our appearance. When I took off my hat, (5)[nearest / backed / me / those / away / to] in terror. One old man came forward with open mouth, and touched me to see if I was real. Then he knelt down, and rubbed his hands over my bare

legs, possibly to find if they were painted, and grabbed me around the knees
30 and hugged them, rubbing his bushy head against me. The women and
children gradually got up courage to approach also, and presently the camp
was swarming with the lot of them, all running about and jabbering at once,
pointing to everything that was new to them.

That "jabbering" was language — an unfamiliar language, one of eight hundred
35 different ones that would be discovered among the isolated highlanders right up
through the 1960s. Leahy's first contact repeated a scene that must have taken
place hundreds of times in human history, whenever one people first encountered
another. All of them, as far as we know, already had language. No mute tribe
has ever been discovered, and (6)there is no record that a region has served as a
40 "cradle" of language from which it spread to previously languageless groups.

As in every other case, the language spoken by Leahy's hosts turned out to be
no mere jabber but a medium that could express abstract concepts, invisible
entities, and complex trains of reasoning. The highlanders consulted each other
intensively, trying to agree upon the nature of the light-skinned beings. The
45 leading opinion was that they were ancestors that came back to this world with
renewed bodies or other spirits in human form, perhaps one that turned back
into skeletons at night. They agreed upon an empirical test that would settle the
matter. "One of our people hid," recalls one of the highlanders, "and watched
them going to *excrete. He came back and said, 'Those men from heaven went
50 to excrete over there.' Once they had left many men went to take a look.
When they saw that it smelt bad, they said, 'Their skin might be different, but
their shit smells bad like ours.'"

(7)[a discovery / the universality / that / of complex language / fills / is / linguists]
with awe, and is the first reason to suspect that language is not just any cultural
55 invention but the product of a special human instinct. Cultural inventions vary
widely in their sophistication from society to society; within a society, the
inventions are generally at the same level of sophistication. Some groups count
by carving lines on bone and cook on fires lit by spinning sticks in logs; others
use computers and microwave ovens. (8)Language, however, ruins this correlation.
60 There are Stone Age societies, but there is no such thing as a Stone Age
language. Early in the last century the anthropological linguist Edward Sapir
wrote, "When it comes to linguistic form, Plato walks with the Macedonian

swineherd, *Confucius with the headhunting savage of *Assam."

（注）　plateau：高原　　tributary：（川の）支流　　excrete：排泄する

　　　Confucius：孔子　　Assam：インド北東部の州

(From *The Language Instinct* by Steven Pinker published by Penguin.　Copyright © 1994 Steven Pinker.　Reprinted by permission of Penguin Books Limited.）

（明治大）

問1　下線部(1)の内容として最も適当なものを，次のア～エから1つ選びなさい。

　　ア．There were inhabitable places in New Guinea.

　　イ．New Guinea had remained unexplored.

　　ウ．New Guinea had been explored.

　　エ．New Guinea was not fit for human habitation.

問2　下線部(2)の内容として最も適当なものを，次のア～エから1つ選びなさい。

　　ア．金の発見にもかかわらず，ニューギニアの高地に人が住んでいることが明らかにならなかった。

　　イ．ニューギニアで金が発見された後，すぐにゴールドラッシュが続いた。

　　ウ．金が発見されてはじめて，ニューギニアの高地にも人々がたくさん暮らしていることがわかった。

　　エ．ニューギニアの高地で石器時代が4万年続いた後，金が発見された。

問3　下線部(3)を日本語に訳しなさい。

問4　下線部(4)の the highlanders が話していた言語はどのようなものであったか。本文に即して80字以内の日本語で述べなさい。

問5　下線部(5)の語を文意が通るように並べ換えなさい。

問6　下線部(6)を日本語に訳しなさい。

問7　下線部(7)の語（句）を文意が通るように並べ換えなさい。ただし，文頭にくるべき語も小文字で始められている。

問8　下線部(8)の内容を60字以内の日本語で述べなさい。

次の英文を読んで，設問に答えなさい。

As you read this sentence, you are one of approximately 1.6 billion people who will use English in some form today. Although English is the mother tongue of only 380 million people, it is the language of *the lion's share of the world's books, academic papers, newspapers, and magazines. American radio, television, 5 and *blockbuster films export English-language pop culture worldwide. Whether we regard the spread of English as *benign globalization or linguistic imperialism, its expansive reach is undeniable.

Yet professional linguists hesitate to predict far into the future the further globalization of English. Historically, languages have risen and fallen with the 10 military, economic, cultural, or religious powers that supported them. Beyond the ebb and flow of history, there are other reasons to suppose that (1)the English language will eventually wane in influence. For one, English actually reaches, and is then utilized by, only a small and atypically fortunate minority. Furthermore, the kinds of interactions identified with globalization, from trade to 15 communication, have also encouraged regionalization and with it the spread of regional languages. Finally, the spread of English and regional languages collectively have created pressure on small communities, producing pockets of local-language revival resistant to global change.

Globalization has done little to change the reality that, regardless of location, 20 the spread of English is closely linked to social class, age, gender, and profession. Just because a wide array of young people around the world may be able to sing along to a new Madonna song does not mean that they can hold a simple conversation in English, or even understand what Madonna is saying. The brief formal educational contact that most learners have with English is 25 (2) lasting literacy, fluency, or even comprehension.

Indeed, for all the enthusiasm generated by grand-scale globalization, it is the growth in regional interactions — trade, travel, the spread of religions, interethnic marriages — that touches the widest array of local populations. These interactions promote the spread of regional languages. Mandarin Chinese is spreading

throughout China and in some of its southern neighbors. Spanish is spreading in 30
the Americas. And Arabic is spreading in North Africa and Southeast Asia both
as the language of Islam and as an important language of regional trade. The
importance of regional languages should increase steadily in the near future.

Even if the end result of globalization is to make the world smaller, its scope
seems to foster the need for more intimate local connections among many 35
individuals. In most communities, (3) serves a strong symbolic function as
a clear mark of "authenticity." Authenticity reflects a perceived line from a
culturally idealized past to the present, carried by the language and traditions
associated with the community's origins. (4)It amounts to a central core of cultural
beliefs and interpretations that are not only resistant to globalization but are 40
actually reinforced by the "threat" that globalization seems to present to these
historical values. Scholars may argue that cultural identities change over time in
response to specific reward systems. But locals often resist such explanations
and defend authenticity and local mother tongues against the perceived threat of
globalization with near religious *ardor.   45

As a result, never before in history (5)[there are / been / have / as / as many /
there / standardized languages] today: roughly 1,200. Many smaller languages,
even those with far fewer than one million speakers, have benefited from state-
sponsored or voluntary preservation movements. In the Basque, Catalan, and
Galician regions of Spain, such movements are fiercely political and frequently 50
involve *staunch resistance to the Spanish government over political and linguistic
rights.

In addition to invoking the (6a) importance of local roots, people who
encourage local languages defend continuing to use them on (6b) grounds.
Local tongues foster higher levels of school success, higher degrees of participation 55
in local government, more informed citizenship, and better knowledge of one's
own culture, history, and faith. *Navajo children who were schooled initially in
Navajo were found to have higher reading competency in English than those who
were first schooled in English. Governments and relief agencies can also use
local languages to spread information about industrial and agricultural techniques 60
as well as modern health care to diverse audiences. Development workers in
West Africa, for example, have found that (7)the best way to teach the vast
number of farmers with little or no formal education how to sow and rotate crops
for higher yields is in these local tongues. The world's practical reliance on local

65 languages today is every bit as great as the identity roles these languages fulfill.

What is to become of English? There is no reason to assume that English will always be as necessary as it is today, particularly after its regional rivals experience their own *growth spurts. (8)<u>Civilization will not sink into the sea if and when that happens.</u> The decline of the use of English around the world does
70 not mean the values associated today with its spread must decline. Ultimately, democracy, international trade, and economic development can flourish in any tongue.

(注)　the lion's share：最も大きい部分　　blockbuster：大ヒット作の　　benign：恵み深い
　　　ardor：情熱　　staunch：頑強な　　Navajo：ナバホ族(北米先住民の一部族)，ナバホ語
　　　growth spurt：急成長

(Used with permission of Foreign Policy, from The New Linguistic Order, Joshua A. Fishman, No.113, Winter 1998–1999, permission conveyed through Copyright clearance Center, Inc.)

（明治学院大）

問1　下線部(1)の理由として本文中に<u>述べられていない</u>ものを，次のア～オから1つ選びなさい。

　ア．Pressure from the spread of English encourages the survival of local languages.

　イ．A regional language will replace English as an international language.

　ウ．It is only a small percentage of people in society who actually use English.

　エ．Language can lose its influence as the powers that support it decline.

　オ．The interactions generated by globalization promote the spread of regional languages.

問2　空所(　2　)に入れるのに最も適当なものを，次のア～エから1つ選びなさい。

　ア．enough to acquire

　イ．too limited to produce

　ウ．so intensive that they never lose

　エ．encouraged because it brings them

問3　空所(　3　)に入れるのに最も適当なものを，次のア〜エから1つ選びなさい。

　　ア．the English language　　　　　イ．the global language
　　ウ．the regional language　　　　　エ．the local language

問4　下線部(4)を日本語に訳しなさい。

問5　下線部(5)の語(句)を文意が通るように並べ換えなさい。

問6　空所(　6a　)(　6b　)に入れるのに最も適当な組み合わせを，次のア〜エから1つ選びなさい。

　　ア．subjective — practical　　　　イ．practical — subjective
　　ウ．theoretical — political　　　　エ．political — theoretical

問7　下線部(7)を日本語に訳しなさい。

問8　下線部(8)の理由を30字以内の日本語で述べなさい。

次の英文を読んで，設問に答えなさい。

I am on a bus traveling through the desert between Kerman and Yazd when we pull over to a checkpoint. Checkpoints are common along Iranian highways and I've grown accustomed to stopping every hundred miles or so to watch the driver climb out, papers in hand. Sometimes a guard in a dark green uniform
5 enters the bus and walks up and down the aisle, eyes flicking from side to side, pistol gleaming in the shadowed interior light.

This is one of those times. The bus falls silent as a young guard enters, and we all determinedly stare straight ahead, as if by our pretending to ignore the guard, he will ignore us. We listen to his footfalls sound down the Persian
10 carpet that lines the aisle, turn, and come back again. He reaches the front of the bus and makes a half-turn toward the door. But then, (1)just as we begin a collective deep breath, he surprises us by completing his turn and starting down the aisle again, this time to tap various passengers on the shoulder. They gather their belongings together and move slowly out of the bus and up the steps of a
15 cement block building.

I sit frozen, hoping that the guard will not notice me and the blond hair sticking out of my *rusari*, or head scarf. I've seen guards pull passengers off buses before, and although it never seems to be anything serious — the passengers always return within five or ten minutes — (2)I'd just as soon remain
20 in my seat.

(3)The guard climbs out of the bus and I relax, wondering what, if anything, he is looking for. I've been told that these searches are usually about drugs and smuggling, but to me, they seem to be more about the display of power.

The guard is back, and instinctively, I know why. He points to me.
25 Me? I gesture, still not completely convinced that he wants me. After two months in Iran, I've learned that — contrary to (4)what I had expected — foreigners are seldom bothered here.

You, he nods.

Copying my fellow passengers, I gather my belongings together and stand up.

Everyone is staring at me — as usual, I am the only foreigner on the bus.   30

I climb out, nearly falling over my long black raincoat — it or something $_{(5)}$[all / being / for / required / similar] women in public in Iran. My heart is knocking against my chest. The guard and one of his colleagues are waiting for me on the steps of the guardhouse. At their feet is my bag, which they've dragged out of the belly of the bus. It looks like a fat green watermelon.   35

'Passport,' the young guard barks in Persian.

I hand him my crisp, dark blue document, suddenly feeling that *United States of America* is printed across the front much too boldly. I remember someone back home (6) entering Iran. Too late now.

'Visa?'   40

I show him the appropriate page in my passport.

'Where are you coming from?' His Persian has a strange accent that I haven't heard before.

'Kerman,' I say.

'Where are you going to?'   45

'Yazd.'

'Tourist?'

I nod, thinking there's no need to complicate matters by telling him that I'm here in Iran to write a *safarnameh*, the Persian word for travelogue or, literally, 'travel letter.' But then immediately (7). My visa says *Journalist*.   50

Slowly, the young guard flips through the pages of my passport, examining the immigration stamps and the rules and regulations listed in the back. He studies my picture long and hard, and then passes my passport to his unsmiling colleague, who asks me the same questions I've just been asked.

'Where are you coming from?'   55

'Kerman.'

'Where are you going to?'

'Yazd.'

'Tourist?'

I nod again. I can't change my answer now.   60

The second guard hands my passport back to the first, who reluctantly hands it back to me. I look at his smooth boyish face and wonder if he's old enough to shave.

'Is this your suitcase?' he says, looking at my bag.

65   'Yes,' I say, and move to open it.

He (8   ) his head.

All of the other passengers are now back on the bus, and I wonder how much longer the guards will keep me. What will happen, I worry, if the bus leaves without me? We're out in the middle of the desert; there are no other buildings
70 in sight. Hardened dust-white plains, broken only by thin grass, stretch in all directions. The sky is a pale metallic dome sucking the color and moisture out of the landscape.

Clearing his throat, the first guard stares at me intently. His eyes are an unusual smoke blue, framed by long lashes. They're the same eyes I've noticed
75 before on more than a few Iranians. He looks at his colleague and they whisper together. Sweat is slipping down their foreheads, and down mine.

(9)Then the first guard straightens his shoulders, takes a deep breath, and blushes. 'Thank you,' he says carefully in stiff, self-conscious English. 'Nice to meet you.'

80   'Hello.' The second guard is now blushing as furiously as the first. 'How are you?' He falls back into Persian, only some of which I understand. 'We will never forget this day. You are the first American we have met. Welcome to the Islamic Republic of Iran. Go with Allah.'

(東京大)

問1　下線部(1)を日本語に訳しなさい。

問2　下線部(2)とほぼ同じ意味を表すものを，次のア〜エから１つ選びなさい。

   ア．I hope I will be allowed to remain seated

   イ．In no time I take a seat and remain there

   ウ．I hope I will not be out of my seat for long

   エ．Quickly, I make up my mind to remain seated

問3　下線部(3)を日本語に訳しなさい。

問4　下線部(4)の内容を25字以内の日本語で述べなさい。

問5　下線部(5)の語を文意が通るように並べ換えなさい。

問6　空所(　6　)に入れるのに最も適当なものを，次のア～エから1つ選びなさい。

　　ア．warning me not to disobey the guards after

　　イ．advising me to learn some basic Persian before

　　ウ．warning me to put a cover on my passport before

　　エ．advising me not to forget to carry my passport after

問7　空所(　7　)に入れるのに最も適当なものを，次のア～エから1つ選びなさい。

　　ア．I wish I were a journalist

　　イ．I wonder if I've done the right thing

　　ウ．I realize that I look too much like a tourist

　　エ．I realize I should have said 'tourist' in English

問8　空所(　8　)に入れるのに最も適当なものを，次のア～エから1つ選びなさい。

　　ア．opens　　　　イ．shows　　　　ウ．nods　　　　エ．shakes

問9　下線部(9)の理由として最も適当なものを，次のア～エから1つ選びなさい。

　　ア．It is too hot to stand outside.

　　イ．He has never talked to a woman before.

　　ウ．He is ashamed that his Persian has a strong accent.

　　エ．It is the first time he has spoken to an American in English.

問10　本文の内容と一致するものを，次のア～オから1つ選びなさい。

　　ア．When the guard enters the author's bus, the passengers look at him in surprise.

　　イ．The guards keep the author for such a long time that the bus leaves without her.

　　ウ．Except for the author, there are no foreigners on the bus.

　　エ．The second guard speaks to the author in fluent English.

　　オ．The guard tells the author to pull her bag out of the belly of the bus.

次の英文を読んで，設問に答えなさい。

Culture is a set of shared ideals, values, and standards of behavior; (1) it is the common element that allows the members of a society to correctly interpret each other's actions and gives meaning to their lives. Because they share a common culture, people can predict how others are most likely to behave in a certain
5 circumstance and react accordingly. A group of people from different cultures, deserted on an uninhabited island for a period of time, might appear to become a sort of society. They would have a common interest — (2) — and would develop techniques for living and working together. Each of the members of this group, however, would retain his or her own identity and cultural background,
10 and the group would break up easily as soon as its members were rescued from the island. The group would have been merely a collection of individuals without a unified cultural identity. Society may be defined as a group of people who not only are dependent on each other for survival but also share a common culture. How these people depend on each other can be seen in such things as their
15 economic systems and their family relationships; moreover, members of society are held together by a sense of common identity. The rule-governed relationships that hold a society together, with all their rights, duties, and obligations, are known as its social structure.

(3) Culture and society are two closely related concepts, and anthropologists study
20 both. Obviously, there can be no culture without a society, just as there can be no society without individuals. Conversely, there are no known human societies that do not exhibit culture. Some other species of animals, however, do lead a social existence. Ants and bees, for example, instinctively cooperate in a manner that clearly indicates a degree of social organization, yet this instinctive behavior
25 is not a culture. One can, therefore, have a society (but not a human society) without a culture, even though one cannot have a culture without a society.

While a culture is shared by members of a society, it is important to realize that (4) is uniform. For one thing, no one has exactly the same version of his or her culture. Beyond such individual variation, however, there is bound to

be some further variation within a culture. At the very least, in any human 30
society, there is some difference between the roles of men and women. This
stems from the fact that women give birth but men do not, and that there are
obvious differences between male and female bodies. What every culture does is
to give meaning to these differences by explaining them and deciding what is to
be done about (5)them. Every culture also determines how these two different 35
kinds of people should relate to one another and to the world at large. Since
each culture does this in its own way, there is tremendous variation from one
society to another. Anthropologists use the term "gender" to refer to the cultural
systems and meanings assigned to the biological difference between the sexes.
Thus, though one's "sex" is biologically determined, one's sexual identity or 40
gender is culturally constructed.

The distinction between sex, which is biological, and gender, which is cultural,
is an important one. Presumably, gender differences are as old as human culture
— about 2.5 million years — and arose from the biological differences between
early human males and females. Early human males were about twice the size 45
of females, just as males are today among such species as gorillas and orangutans,
which are related to humans. In the course of human evolution, however, the
biological differences between the two sexes were radically reduced. (6)Thus, apart
from differences directly related to reproduction, whatever biological basis there
once was for gender role differences has largely disappeared. Nevertheless, 50
cultures have maintained some distinctions of gender roles ever since, although
(7)these are far greater in some societies than in others. Strangely enough,
gender differences were more extreme in late 19th and early 20th century
Western societies, where women were expected to submit completely to male
authority, than they are among most historically known pre-agricultural peoples 55
whose ways of life resemble those of the late Stone Age ancestors of Western
peoples. Among them, relations between men and women tend to be
characterized by a spirit of equality, and although they may not typically carry
out the same tasks, such arrangements tend to be flexible. (8)In other words,
differences between the behavior of men and women in Western societies today, 60
which are thought by many to be rooted in human biology, are not so rooted at
all. Rather, they appear to have been recently elaborated in the course of history.

In addition to cultural variation associated with gender, there will also be some
related to differences in age. In any society, children are not expected to behave

as adults, and the reverse is equally true. But then, who is a child and who is
an adult? Again, although the age differences are natural, (9) give their
own meaning to the human life cycle. In the United States, for example,
individuals are not regarded as adults until the age of 21; in many others,
adulthood begins earlier. Often, <u>it is not tied so much to age as it is to</u>
₍₁₀₎
<u>passage through certain established rituals.</u>

（Cengage Learning Inc.　Reproduced by permission.　www.cengage.com/permissions）

（同志社大）

問1　下線部(1)を日本語に訳しなさい。

問2　空所（　2　）に入れるのに最も適当な1語を第1段落から探して答えなさい。

問3　下線部(3)に関して，人間と他の動物との違いを60字以内の日本語で述べなさい。

問4　空所（　4　）に入れるのに最も適当なものを，次のア～エから1つ選びなさい。

　　ア．nothing　　　　イ．anything　　　　ウ．not everything　　　エ．everything

問5　下線部(5)の内容として最も適当なものを，次のア～エから1つ選びなさい。

　　ア．biological differences between the sexes

　　イ．men and women

　　ウ．historical changes within a culture

　　エ．cultural differences

問6　下線部(6)を日本語に訳しなさい。

問7　下線部(7)の理由を70字以内の日本語で述べなさい。

問8　下線部(8)を日本語に訳しなさい。

問9　空所（　9　）に入れるのに最も適当なものを，次のア～エから1つ選びなさい。

　　ア．gender roles　　　　　　　　イ．individuals

　　ウ．cultures　　　　　　　　　　エ．biological differences

問10　下線部(10)を it の内容を明らかにして日本語に訳しなさい。

10

次の英文を読んで，設問に答えなさい。

Many people believe that nature's value cannot be put into dollars and cents. That is, they value the natural world for its own sake, regardless of what services or benefits it provides for humans. Yet this notion is fundamentally (1a) at odds with the economic system we've created.

We live in a world that is increasingly dominated by a global economy, where 5 it is assumed that everything of value has a price tag attached. If something can't be quantified and sold, it is considered (2a). The president of a forest company once said to me, "A tree has no value until it's cut down. Then it adds value to the economy."

So how do we (1b) reconcile our economy with ecology? The Earth provides us 10 with essential natural services like air and water purification and climate stability, but these aren't part of our economy because we've always assumed such things are free.

But natural services are only free when the ecosystems that maintain them are healthy. Today, with our growing population and increasing demands on 15 ecosystems, we're degrading them more and more. Unfortunately, remedial activities and products like air filters, bottled water, eye drops and other things we need to combat degraded services all add to the GDP, which economists call growth. Something is terribly wrong with our economic system when (3) poor environmental health and reduced quality of life are actually good for the 20 economy!

But (4) [on / tag / what / did / we / if / price / put / a] things like clean air and water? If we assigned a monetary value to natural systems and functions, would we be more inclined to conserve them? Yes, according to an international group of ecologists writing in the latest edition of the journal *Science*. 25

The group argues that humanity will continue to degrade natural systems until we realize that the costs to repair or replace them are (2b). So we must find a way to place a dollar value on all ecosystem assets — natural resources such as fish or timber, life-support processes such as water purification and

33

30 pollination, and life-enriching conditions like beauty and recreation.

Most of these assets, with the exception of natural resources, we already exploit but do not trade in the marketplace because they are difficult to price. But (5)this is changing. For example, this spring an Australian organization became the first conservation group to be listed on a stock exchange. The company 35 buys and restores native wildlife and vegetation, (2c) earning income from tourism and wildlife sales.

In New York City, officials recently decided to buy land around watersheds and let the forest and soil organisms filter water instead of building a massive new filtration plant. Until recently, this potential to use natural services rather than 40 technology to solve problems has been largely (2d), even though natural approaches may provide greater benefits to communities such as lower costs, reduced flooding and soil erosion and aesthetic benefits.

In Canada, forests are primarily valued for the timber they provide. But this leads to conflicts. For instance, a recent report from the Department of Fisheries 45 and Oceans found that logging roads in British Columbia continue to (6a) fish-bearing streams, even though legislation is supposed to (6b) them. In fact, our forests provide many services that, if assigned a monetary value, could completely change the way we use them.

As just one species out of perhaps 15 million, the notion of assigning value to 50 everything on Earth solely for its utility to humans may seem like an act of incredible arrogance. But the harsh reality of today's world is that money talks and economies are a central preoccupation. At the very least, assigning monetary value to ecosystem services may force us to take a hard look at all that nature provides. Maybe then we'll stop taking (7)it for granted.

(*The Big Picture: Reflections on Science, Humanity, and a Quickly Changing Planet* by David Suzuki and Dave Robert Taylor is reprinted with permission from Greystone Books Ltd.)

(大阪大)

問1 　下線部(1a)(1b)とほぼ同じ意味を表すものを，それぞれ次のア～エから1つずつ選びなさい。

(1a) 　ア．in opposition to 　　　　イ．in favor of
　　　ウ．in accordance with 　　　エ．as important as

(1b) 　ア．adapt 　　イ．console 　　ウ．harmonize 　　エ．treat

34

問2　空所（ 2a ）〜（ 2d ）に入れるのに最も適当なものを，それぞれ次のア〜エから1つずつ選びなさい。

（ 2a ）　ア．superior　　　　　　イ．worthless
　　　　　ウ．inferior　　　　　　エ．comprehensible

（ 2b ）　ア．reasonable　　　　　イ．enormous
　　　　　ウ．low　　　　　　　　エ．ignorable

（ 2c ）　ア．while　　　　　　　イ．toward
　　　　　ウ．without　　　　　　エ．unless

（ 2d ）　ア．practiced　　　　　　イ．attempted
　　　　　ウ．overlooked　　　　　エ．discussed

問3　下線部(3)の理由を40字以内の日本語で説明しなさい。

問4　下線部(4)の語を文意が通るように並べ換えなさい。

問5　下線部(5)の内容を60字以内の日本語で説明しなさい。

問6　空所（ 6a ）（ 6b ）に入る最も適当な組み合わせを，次のア〜エから1つ選びなさい。

ア．protect — devastate　　　　イ．devastate — protect
ウ．expand — narrow　　　　　エ．narrow — expand

問7　下線部(7)の内容を15字以内の日本語で説明しなさい。

問8　本文の内容と一致するものを，次のア〜エから1つ選びなさい。

ア．We must prevent the growth of the global economy at any cost because it is destructive to the environment.

イ．One way to protect the environment is to look at nature from an economic viewpoint, although it is rather unfortunate that we have to do so.

ウ．Ecology-related problems should be addressed even at the expense of our economic system.

エ．Technology is always expected to solve ecological problems because it can provide better services to communities at lower costs.

次の英文を読んで，設問に答えなさい。

Electric light is transforming our world. Around 80% of the global population now lives in places where night skies are polluted with artificial light. A third of humanity can no longer see the Milky Way. But (1) light at night has deeper effects. In humans, nocturnal light pollution has been linked to sleep disorders,
5 depression, obesity and even some types of cancer. Studies have shown that nocturnal animals modify their behavior even with slight changes in night-time light levels. *Dung beetles become disoriented when navigating landscapes if light pollution prevents them from seeing the stars. Light can also change how species interact with each other. Insects such as moths are more vulnerable to
10 being eaten by bats when light reduces how effective they are at evading predators.

Relatively little is known about how marine and coastal creatures cope. *Clownfish exposed to light pollution fail to reproduce properly, as they need darkness for their eggs to hatch. Other fish stay active at night when there's
15 too much light, emerging more quickly from their hiding places during the day and increasing their exposure to predators. These effects have been observed under direct artificial light from coastal homes, promenades, boats and harbors, which might suggest the effects of light pollution on nocturnal ocean life are quite limited.

20 However, when light from street lamps is emitted upwards, it's scattered in the atmosphere and reflected back to the ground. Anyone out in the countryside at night will notice this effect as a glow in the sky above a distant city or town. This form of light pollution is known as (2) artificial skyglow, and it's about 100 times dimmer than that from direct light, but it is much more widespread. It's
25 currently detectable above a quarter of the world's coastline, and from there it can extend hundreds of kilometers out to sea. Humans aren't well adapted to seeing at night, which might make the effects of skyglow seem (3a). But many marine and coastal organisms are highly (3b) to low light. Skyglow could be changing the way they perceive the night sky, and ultimately affecting

their lives.

We tested this idea using the tiny *sand hopper, a coastal *crustacean which is known to use the moon to guide its nightly food-seeking trips. Less than one inch long, sand hoppers are commonly found across Europe's sandy beaches and named for their ability to jump several inches in the air. They bury themselves in the sand during the day and emerge to feed on rotting seaweed at night. 35 They play an important role in their ecosystem by breaking down and recycling nutrients from stranded algae on the beach.

In (4)our study, we recreated the effects of artificial skyglow using a white LED light in a diffusing sphere that threw an even and dim layer of light over a beach across 19 nights. During clear nights with a full moon, sand hoppers 40 would naturally migrate towards the shore where they would encounter seaweed. Under our artificial skyglow, their movement was much more random.

They migrated less often, missing out on feeding opportunities, which due to their role as recyclers, could have wider effects on the ecosystem. Artificial skyglow changes the way sand hoppers use the moon to navigate. But since 45 using the moon and stars as a (5) is a common trait among a diverse range of sea and land animals, including seals, birds, reptiles, amphibians and insects, many more organisms are likely to be vulnerable to skyglow. And there's evidence that the Earth at night is getting brighter. Scientists found that Earth's artificially lit outdoor areas increased by 2.2% each year. 50

As researchers, we aim to uncover how light pollution is affecting coastal and marine ecosystems, by focusing on how it affects the development of different animals and interactions between species. (6)Only by understanding if, when and how light pollution affects nocturnal life can we find ways to moderate the impact. 55

(注)　dung beetle：フンコロガシ　　clownfish：クマノミ　　sand hopper：ハマトビムシ
　　　crustacean：甲殻類

(Svenja Tidau, Daniela Torres Diaz, Stuart Jenkins, The Moon And Stars Are A Compass For Nocturnal Animals — But Light Pollution Is Leading Them Astray, The Conversation)

（神戸大）

問 1　下線部(1)について，人間以外の生物への影響として本文中に<u>述べられていない</u>ものを，次のア〜エから 1 つ選びなさい。

　　ア．Bats fail to evade predators effectively when eating moths.

　　イ．Clownfish experience problems breeding at night.

　　ウ．Dung beetles get confused and don't know where to go.

　　エ．Fish face a greater risk of being eaten by other fish that prey on them.

問 2　下線部(2)はどのような光害か，40字以内の日本語で述べなさい。

問 3　空所（ 3a ）（ 3b ）に入れるのに最も適当な組み合わせを，次のア〜エから 1 つ選びなさい。

　　ア．attractive —— insensitive　　　　イ．insignificant —— resistant

　　イ．invisible —— attracted　　　　　エ．negligible —— sensitive

問 4　下線部(4)の結果，ハマトビムシについてわかったことを，具体的に50字以内の日本語で述べなさい。

問 5　空所（ 5 ）に入れるのに最も適当なものを，次のア〜エから 1 つ選びなさい。

　　ア．binocular　　　イ．magnet　　　ウ．compass　　　エ．telescope

問 6　下線部(6)を日本語に訳しなさい。

次の英文を読んで，設問に答えなさい。

Almost everyone has heard about global warming and how it could cause damage to our environment. Recent measurements of the oceans show that this warming is causing the sea level to rise by several millimeters every decade. Many island nations are concerned that within a century or so their homes will disappear under water. Moreover, this rise in temperature together with pollution 5 and the loss of natural habitat is said to be causing a huge loss in the diversity of life on Earth.

When we think of changes like this, we call them disasters, and believe that they are exceptional events in the life of our planet. This rise in temperature, however, is just one of many drastic changes in the Earth's existence, and as we 10 shall see, some of these changes are even (　1　) for life.

Perhaps the most famous disaster in the Earth's existence occurred 65 million years ago when it is thought that an *asteroid hit the Earth, causing the dinosaurs to go extinct. Although this was a disaster for the dinosaurs, it turned out to be good news for humans. It is almost certain that if the asteroid had 15 not struck the Earth, you would not be reading this passage now. This shows us that disasters can sometimes have a happy ending.

Although global warming has become a real concern, it is interesting to note that over the past one million years, the Earth's temperature has cooled down several times during ice ages. These changes in temperature were also 20 disastrous for some species, but (2) they may have actually helped humans spread around the world. When the glaciers grew in size, the level of the sea fell and this may have made it possible for humans to reach new lands. For example, perhaps early Asians crossed into North America via a land bridge which no longer exists. 25

Smaller disasters, such as forest fires and volcanoes, may also be helpful. (3) Often we hear stories of forest fires which destroy huge numbers of trees and all the animal life that they contain. When this happens we feel it is a shame that so much nature has been lost. However, it is now known that fires are actually necessary. Without fires, the tallest trees take all the sunlight, which creates very little diversity. However, diversity is important in any ecosystem. Without diversity, one disease could easily kill most life. *Erupting volcanoes are another type of disaster which often causes death and destruction, yet once again, they bring great benefits. The soil around volcanoes is usually very rich, which improves the quality of life for farmers and those living near them.

Perhaps the greatest disaster for life in the existence of the Earth is one that we seldom think about. Two billion years ago, there was no oxygen on the Earth, and all forms of life consisted of creatures so tiny that they would be invisible to the human eye. Gradually, these creatures began producing oxygen as a waste product, just as plants do now. However, at that time, for most life, oxygen was poisonous. As oxygen increased from 0% of our atmosphere two billion years ago, to the present 21%, species were forced to (4). Naturally, many species must have died in the poisonous atmosphere; however, some managed to adapt, and these were our ancestors. While it may seem difficult to believe that oxygen can be poisonous to life, this shows us how disasters can produce strange and unpredictable results.

The present disaster, which is happening before our eyes, is interesting because it is being caused by humans. Unlike past disasters, global warming is unique in that it is not natural. At this point, no one knows what the outcome of this environmental destruction will be. (5)By studying disasters in the past, it is possible to predict that the big changes occurring in today's environment will force humans to change if they are to survive.

This discussion of disasters is probably both good news and bad news. The good news is that in all previous disasters, no matter how destructive they have been, some form of life has always survived. This means that there is a very good chance that global warming caused by humans may even be beneficial for some microscopic forms of life which can evolve quickly. (6)Unfortunately, species that thrive in warmth include things like bacteria that can often cause disease. This leads us to the bad news, which suggests that this present disaster is almost certainly bad for large species, like humans, which cannot evolve quickly. With temperatures rising so quickly, humans may not be able to adapt quickly enough to the new conditions on Earth.

Although it seems cruel to say so, the extinction of humans would probably be good news for our planet. Our selfish behavior, which has led to the extinction

of so many species, is obviously not good for life. The present disaster caused 65
by humans may just be part of a cycle of destruction and rebirth that our planet
has experienced for billions of years.

(注) asteroid：小惑星   erupt：噴火する

（青山学院大）

問1 空所（ 1 ）に入れるのに最も適当なものを，次のア～エから1つ選びなさ
い。

　ア．fatal and tragic

　イ．helpful and necessary

　ウ．interesting but unnecessary

　エ．vital but frightening

問2 下線部(2)の内容を20字以内の日本語で述べなさい。

問3 下線部(3)を日本語に訳しなさい。

問4 空所（ 4 ）に入れるのに最も適当なものを，次のア～エから1つ選びなさ
い。

　ア．die　　　　　　イ．evolve　　　　　ウ．reproduce　　　エ．retreat

問5 下線部(5)を日本語に訳しなさい。

問6 下線部(6)で，なぜ筆者は Unfortunately と言っているのか。本文に即して70字
以内の日本語で述べなさい。

次の英文を読んで，設問に答えなさい。

The natural curiosity of scientists has often led them into controversial areas. When that curiosity is backed up by the resources of rich drug companies and is directed towards the secrets of life itself, however, it becomes a potential time bomb. Genetic research is racing ahead without giving society time to establish 5 the *parameters of acceptability.

Cloning is one of the most controversial aspects of genetic engineering. When an animal is cloned, a twin is created. So far, the process has succeeded only with sheep, mice, cows and pigs, but several researchers have announced plans to clone human beings. This has already been made illegal in Germany, and is 10 likely to be banned in all Western countries soon. (1)Opponents of human cloning tend to emphasize the risks of children being born with severe defects, but there is also a fear that the technique, once perfected, will be abused in various ways, together with a sense that the creation of life is something sacred, and should be left to God. Where the cloning of animals is concerned, however, (2). 15 American scientists managed to clone a gaur, an endangered Asian species of ox, by implanting a gaur embryo into the womb of a cow. Although the baby died two days later, its birth was hailed as a major breakthrough which could benefit not only endangered species such as pandas and tigers but even species which have already died out. When the last bucardo (a mountain goat) died recently, 20 scientists removed some cells in order to produce clones. Some Japanese researchers are even more ambitious: they hope to clone a mammoth, using DNA extracted from cells taken from a frozen mammoth *carcass in Siberia or Alaska and inserted into the womb of a living elephant.

Another use of genetic engineering is in gene therapy. Many diseases occur 25 because a particular gene is missing or defective. Researchers in Philadelphia have found a way to restore such genes by attaching normal genes to a harmless virus and then infecting the patient. (3)A similar technique has already been used to cure a certain kind of blindness in dogs and may easily be adapted to cure humans too.

Now that researchers can identify missing or defective genes, it is possible to 30 predict illnesses long before symptoms appear. (4)<u>While this enables people to take preventive action, by making appropriate changes to their lifestyles or diets, it also gives insurance companies the chance to identify bad risks</u>. An above-average risk of breast cancer, for example, can be discovered through genetic testing; and some insurance companies now insist that female applicants reveal 35 the results of such tests, and raise their fees to cover the increased risk. Once insurance companies demand such information as a matter of course, potential employers will no doubt follow suit, rejecting high-risk job applicants.

Of all the applications of genetic engineering, the one which has most outraged the public is the genetic modification of food crops and livestock. In 1996, the 40 first genetically-modified tomatoes reached the market. This was followed by potatoes and other crops such as corn, soybeans and rapeseed containing genes enabling them to kill insects or to withstand heavy doses of *herbicides; and by genetically altered livestock, such as pigs with genes that made them grow bigger and heavier, cows genetically altered to produce more milk, and salmon with 45 growth-accelerating genes. A few people questioned the safety of these products and were assured by industry and government officials that they were absolutely no different from ordinary food products. Questions about their effects on the environment were also (5)<u>brushed aside</u>. By 1999, the US Food and Drug Administration had approved 44 genetically modified crops, including a third of all 50 corn and a half of all soybeans grown in the US.

In Europe, however, there was growing resentment at the way *GM foods had been forced on the public. Consumers began demanding labels that allowed them to distinguish between GM and non-GM products; when the Americans refused to sell them separately, British supermarkets stopped buying their corn and 55 soybeans. Environmentalists wanted proof that modified crops would not harm other species; on the contrary, they heard reports from Cornell University of a drastic decline in the *monarch butterfly population related to pollen from GM corn. Then came the announcement that US *agribusinesses had developed a 'terminator' gene which could be inserted into their seeds to ensure that farmers 60 could not follow the traditional practice of taking seeds from their own crops for use the following year. Development agencies were furious: if such seeds were marketed to developing countries, farmers would become (6) American agribusinesses. The resulting bad publicity led to a hasty denial by the

65 producers of any plan to market such seeds.

(7)<u>The harmful effects</u> of genetically modified crops on the environment are gradually appearing: the disappearance of benevolent insects; the growth of herbicide-resistant weeds; the contamination of nearby organic farms. Health problems have also surfaced, including a reported increase in allergies and a
70 decrease in the effectiveness of antibiotic drugs. If, as seems likely, more serious problems develop in due course, there will be huge lawsuits, and some biotech companies may go bankrupt. However, the system which has allowed them to gamble with our health and environment will remain: a system in which priority is given (8   ).

（注）　parameter：範囲　　carcass：死体　　herbicide：除草剤

　　　　GM：遺伝子組み換えの（＝genetically modified）

　　　　monarch butterfly：オオカバマダラチョウ　　agribusiness：農業関連産業

（青山学院大）

問1　下線部(1)を日本語に訳しなさい。

問2　空所(　2　)に入れるのに最も適当なものを，次のア～エから1つ選びなさい。

　　ア．there is stronger hostility

　　イ．everyone strongly disagrees with the idea

　　ウ．it is banned by the government

　　エ．there is much less opposition

問3　下線部(3)の内容を60字以内の日本語で述べなさい。

問4　下線部(4)を日本語に訳しなさい。

問5　下線部(5)とほぼ同じ意味を表すものを，次のア～エから1つ選びなさい。

　　ア．talked about seriously

　　イ．paid no attention to

　　ウ．thought over

　　エ．given careful consideration to

問6 空所（ 6 ）に入れるのに最も適当なものを，次のア～エから1つ選びなさい。
　　ア．totally dependent on
　　イ．quite familiar with
　　ウ．completely free from
　　エ．much superior to

問7 下線部(7)に<u>含まれないもの</u>を，次のア～エから1つ選びなさい。
　　ア．抗生物質の有効性の低下
　　イ．近隣地域での土壌流出
　　ウ．除草剤に強い雑草の繁茂
　　エ．益虫の消失

問8 空所（ 8 ）に入れるのに最も適当なものを，次のア～エから1つ選びなさい。
　　ア．to safety and social responsibility rather than to technological development and profits
　　イ．neither to safety and social responsibility nor to technological development and profits
　　ウ．to technological development and profits rather than to safety and social responsibility
　　エ．not so much to technological development and profits as to safety and social responsibility

次の英文を読んで，設問に答えなさい。

Natural and inevitable (1a) it may be, death confuses us nowadays. All too often, dying seems like a mysterious process full of difficult decisions, like the dilemma Michele Finn faced after she decided to have her severely brain-damaged husband's feeding tube withdrawn, allowing him to die.

5　(2)So complex and painful are the medical and ethical questions surrounding such an event that it is easy to overlook the fact that, until recently, we had a single, simple medical understanding of death: we accepted that people died when their hearts stopped beating and they stopped breathing. It is the absence of those signs that doctors still use to decide death about 90 percent of the time in
10 hospitals today. Since the late 20th century, though, medical advances have undermined (3)this simple understanding and forced physicians to look beyond the heart for an additional means of defining the end of life.

(1b) doctors are able to keep a patient's heart beating mechanically or replace a damaged heart with a new one, we have turned to the brain as a place
15 to decide death. The brain cannot be transplanted or replaced by any machine; without a working brain, people cannot breathe or maintain their blood pressure; they also lose the traits that we commonly associate with humanness, such as their ability to communicate, as well as any awareness of their surroundings. Although widely accepted in medical practice, (4)the concept of brain death has
20 *spawned a host of medical, legal, ethical and philosophical debates, and recently has come under attack by different religious or political groups. Some say that defining death should not be left to physicians, that the death of the brain is not the same as the death of a person; others resist any definition of death that is based on science and technology.

25　The first challenge came in the late '50s with the invention of life-support machines that could keep the heart beating. According to the traditional way of thinking about death, patients who are supported by this kind of machine are (5a), but they (5b) recover from severe brain damage, which means they will never again be aware of their surroundings, recognize or respond to their loved ones, or have any thoughts or emotions.   30

There is a second challenge arising from the medical and technological advances. A dying person may be a potential donor of vital organs such as the heart or lungs. If a surgeon operates quickly enough, a heart that has stopped in one body can be removed and transplanted into another, where it can return to normal working — possibly for many years. The stopping of the heart, then, 35 is not a satisfactory way of deciding death.

It is important to understand that brain damage is not an all-or-nothing state, though. Some patients cannot move but can breathe or their hearts still keep pumping. Others have lost any brain working, and can be maintained solely by machines. The distinction between the two conditions is important: withdrawing 40 life support in a hopelessly brain-damaged person, (1c) in the first condition, will result in brain death, but that person is not actually brain dead at the time the decision is made; in the second condition, the patient is already brain dead.

(6)The importance of this distinction is evident not only for doctors treating brain-damaged patients and for families who need to understand their loved one's 45 condition, but also in the question of supplying organs for transplant patients. Since transplantation techniques were first developed, it has been clear there would be more potential recipients than donors. The primary responsibility of the potential donor's medical team is proper care of that patient and the patient's family. Until a patient is declared brain dead, absolutely no steps should be 50 taken to preserve organs for donation, (1d) the patient has declared his or her wishes to donate organs or carries a donor card. (7), the basis for deciding to stop life-support machines and to remove organs for transplant would be vague, subjective, and likely to change often.

(注)　spawn：を生む

(中央大)

問1　空所(1a)～(1d)に入れるのに最も適当なものを，次のア～エからそれ
　　ぞれ1つずつ選びなさい。ただし，同じものを2度選んではならない。なお，文
　　頭に入るものも小文字で始められている。
　　　ア．as　　　　　　　イ．even if　　　　ウ．now that　　　エ．though
問2　下線部(2)を日本語に訳しなさい。
問3　下線部(3)の内容を30字以内の日本語で述べなさい。

問4　下線部(4)が生まれた背景にある医学の進歩を2つ，それぞれ10字以内の日本語で述べなさい。

問5　空所（　5a　）（　5b　）に入れるのに最も適当な組み合わせを，次のア〜エから1つ選びなさい。

　　　ア．still alive — can　　　　　　　　イ．still alive — cannot

　　　ウ．already dead — can　　　　　　　エ．already dead — cannot

問6　下線部(6)を日本語に訳しなさい。

問7　空所（　7　）に入れるのに最も適当なものを，次のア〜エから1つ選びなさい。

　　　ア．Without clear guidelines for brain death

　　　イ．With more potential recipients than donors

　　　ウ．In spite of strict restriction on transplants

　　　エ．Thanks to improved transplantation techniques

次の英文を読んで，設問に答えなさい。

What was the greatest scientific discovery of the 20th century? Nuclear energy? The structure of DNA? The theory of digital computation? The Big Bang? It was an exceptional century of discovery. How do we choose one discovery over any other?

The physician Lewis Thomas made a choice. He bluntly asserts: "The greatest 5 of all the accomplishments of 20th-century science has been the discovery of human ignorance."

The science writer Timothy Ferris agrees: "Our ignorance, of course, has always been with us, and always will be. What is new is our awareness of it, and (1)it is this, more than anything else, that marks the coming of age of our 10 species."

It is an odd, unsettling thought that the greatest discovery of the last century should be the confirmation of our ignorance. How did such a thing come about? The discovery of our ignorance followed inevitably from (2).

I begin my course in astronomy at Stonehill College holding in my hands a 16- 15 inch clear *acrylic celestial globe *spangled with stars. A smaller *terrestrial globe is at the center, and a tiny yellow ball representing the sun circles between Earth and sky. This tidy cosmos of *concentric spheres was invented thousands of years ago to account for the apparent motions of sun, moon, and stars, and for that task it still works pretty well. 20

When we thought we lived in such a universe, we could believe that a complete catalog of its contents was possible. The universe was proportioned to the human scale, created specifically for our home. Presumably, since it was made for us, the universe contained (3) beyond the understanding of the human mind. 25

Then, in the winter of 1610, Galileo turned his newly-crafted telescope to the Milky Way and saw stars in uncountable numbers, stars that served no apparent purpose in the human scheme of things since they could not be seen by human eyes. It was an ominous hint of the *cascading discoveries to come.

30 I end my astronomy course with the Hubble Space Telescope's Deep Field
Photograph, a 10-day exposure of a part of the dark night sky so tiny that it
could be covered by the intersection of crossed pins held at arm's length. (4) In
this photo are contained the images of several thousand galaxies, each galaxy
consisting of hundreds of billions of stars and planet systems. A survey of the
35 bowl of *the Big Dipper at the same scale would show 40 million galaxies.

Galaxies as numerous as snowflakes in a storm! Each with uncountable
planets, strange geographies, perhaps life forms, intelligent beings. To live in
such a universe is to admit that the human mind singly or collectively will never
be in possession of final knowledge.

40 Ferris quotes the philosopher Karl Popper: "The more we learn about the
world, and the deeper our learning, the more conscious, specific, and clear will
be our knowledge of what we do not know, our knowledge of our ignorance.
For this, indeed, is the main source of our ignorance — the fact that our
knowledge can be only (5a), while our ignorance must necessarily be
45 (5b)."

How do we react to this new and humbling knowledge? That depends, I
suppose, on our temperaments. Some of us are frightened by the vast spaces of
our ignorance, and seek refuge in the human-centered universe of the acrylic star
globe. Others are inspired by the opportunities for further discovery, for the new
50 vistas that will surely open before us.

It is the latter frame of mind that (6) science. The physicist Heinz
Pagels wrote: "The capacity to tolerate complexity and welcome contradiction, not
the need for simplicity and certainty, is the attribute of an explorer. Centuries
ago, when some people suspended their search for absolute truth and began
55 instead to ask how things worked, modern science was born. Curiously, it was
by abandoning the search for absolute truth that science began to make progress,
opening the material universe to human exploration."

The discovery of our ignorance should not be conceived as a negative thing.
Ignorance is a vessel waiting to be filled, permission for growth, a foundation for
60 the electrifying encounter with mystery.

Now we can claim with optimism that (7) we know both more and less than we
knew at the beginning of the last century: more because our inventory of
knowledge has been greatly expanded, less because the scope of our ignorance
has been even more greatly realized.

Timothy Ferris writes: "No thinking man or woman ought really to want to ⁶⁵ know everything, for when knowledge and its analysis is complete, thinking stops."

(注) acrylic celestial globe：アクリル製の天球儀　　spangle：(光る物)をちりばめる

terrestrial globe：地球儀　　concentric：同心の，中心を同じくする

cascading：滝のように降り注ぐ　　the Big Dipper：北斗七星

(Chet Raymo, The discovery of ignorance, Science Musings, The Boston Globe)

（千葉大）

問1　下線部(1)を this の内容を明らかにして日本語に訳しなさい。

問2　空所（　2　）に入れるのに最も適当なものを，次のア〜エから1つ選びなさい。

　　ア．the discovery of the structure of DNA

　　イ．discoveries of the vastness of the universe

　　ウ．the idea that Earth was at the center of the universe

　　エ．the explanation of the motions of stars

問3　空所（　3　）に入れるのに最も適当なものを，次のア〜エから1つ選びなさい。

　　ア．all　　　　　　イ．much　　　　　ウ．something　　　エ．nothing

問4　下線部(4)を日本語に訳しなさい。

問5　空所（　5a　）（　5b　）に入れるのに最も適当な組み合わせを，次のア〜エから1つ選びなさい。

　　ア．finite — infinite　　　　　　イ．infinite — finite

　　ウ．conscious — unconscious　　　エ．unconscious — conscious

問6　空所（　6　）に入れるのに最も適当なものを，次のア〜エから1つ選びなさい。

　　ア．simplifies　　イ．drives　　　ウ．denies　　　　エ．contradicts

問7　下線部(7)はどういうことなのか，日本語で説明しなさい。

河合塾
SERIES

改訂版

やっておきたい

英語長文

700

[解答・解説編]

河合塾講師

杉山 俊一
塚越 友幸
山下 博子

[共著]

河合出版

はじめに

　大学の入試問題では、読解問題が最も大きな割合を占めていますし，その割合はますます高くなっています。読解問題を解けるようにすることは，受験を突破するうえで避けては通ることができません。それでは，読解問題を解くためには，どのような力が必要なのでしょうか。語い力に加えて，一文一文の構造を正確に捉え，内容を把握する力が必要です。さらに，複数の文が集まって文章が構成されている以上，文と文のつながり，すなわち文脈を読み取る力も必要です。また，今日的な話題が出題されることが増えています。そうした話題について知っておくことも，内容を理解するためには大切です。

　こうした力をつけるためには，何よりも良い英文を読み，良い問題を解くことです。そこで，これまでに出題された問題の中から，英文の長さと難易度を基準に繰り返し読むに値する英文を選び，4 冊の問題集にまとめました。設問は，ある文章に対して問うべきこと—内容の理解と英語の理解—という観点から，ほぼ全面的に作り変えてあります。

　やっておきたい英語長文700は，**600語**から**900語程度**のやや難から難レベルの英文15題で構成されています。難関大学の入試を突破できるゆるぎない読解力の完成を目指します。また，よく出題されるテーマが網羅されるように英文を選び，**Topic**として背景知識の解説も加えてあります。

	words		level	
	0　200　400　600　800　1000　1600		易　　　標準　　　難	
やっておきたい英語長文300				
やっておきたい英語長文500				
やっておきたい英語長文700				
やっておきたい英語長文1000				

　本書が皆さんの想いの実現に向けて，役に立つことを願ってやみません。それでは，問題1にトライしてみましょう。

　最後に，本書を改訂するにあたり，Kathryn A. Craft 先生に英文校閲を行っていただきました。この場を借りて御礼申し上げます。

著者記す

本書の使い方

1　問題には語数と標準解答時間を示してあります。標準解答時間を目標に問題を解いてください。

2　解説には，解答と設問解説，要約，構文・語句解説があります。設問解説を読み，解答を確認してください。設問解説中の第1・2段落第5文といった表記は，構文・語句解説の番号に対応しています。

3　構文・語句解説では，訳例と設問解説で触れなかった，構文および語句の解説があります。設問以外の箇所で理解できなかった部分を確認してください。

4　構文・語句解説では，問題文から下線を省き空所を埋めた形で英文を再録してあります。英文を繰り返し読んでもらいたいからです。こうすることが，速読の練習にもなりますし，語いの定着にもつながります。また，このときは，英文の構造よりも，内容・論旨を追うことを心がけてください。確認のために要約を活用してください。

5　英文を読む際には，音読とリスニングを組み合わせることで，リスニング力も強化できます。英語のネイティブ・スピーカーが読み上げた音声が用意されていますので，利用してください。

　音声は，パソコンやスマートフォンから下記の URL にアクセスして聴くことができます。QR コードからもアクセスできます。

https://www.kawai-publishing.jp/onsei/01/index.html

・ファイルは MP4形式の音声です。再生するには，最新版の OS をご利用ください。

また，パソコンから URL にアクセスしていただくことで，音声データのダウンロードも可能です。

※ホームページより直接スマートフォンへのダウンロードはできません。パソコンにダウンロードしていただいた上で，スマートフォンへお取り込みいただきますよう，お願いいたします。
・ファイルは ZIP 形式で圧縮されていますので，解凍ソフトが必要です。
・ファイルは MP3形式の音声です。再生するには，Windows Media Player や iTunes などの再生ソフトが必要です。
・Y701〜Y715の全15ファイル構成となっています。

＜音声データに関する注意＞
・当サイトに掲載されている音声ファイルのデータは著作権法で保護されています。本データあるいはそれを加工したものを複製・譲渡・配信・販売することはできません。また，データを使用できるのは，本教材の購入者がリスニングの学習を目的とする場合に限られます。
・お客様のパソコンやネット環境により音声を再生できない場合，当社は責任を負いかねます。ご理解とご了承をいただきますよう，お願いいたします。
・ダウンロードや配信サイトから聴くことができるのは，本書を改訂するまでの期間です。

本書で用いた記号

・（　）は省略可能な語句を表す。
・[ ]は直前の語句と書き換え可能な語句を表す。
・S は主語，O は目的語，C は補語を表す。
・A, B は名詞を表す。
・X, Y は文の中で同じ働きをするものを表す。
・*do* は動詞の原形を表す。
・to *do* は不定詞を表す。
・*doing* は動名詞または現在分詞を表す。
・*done* は過去分詞を表す。
・*one's* は主語と同じ所有格を表す。
・A's は主語と同じになるとは限らない所有格を表す。
・「自動詞＋前置詞」型の熟語は，account for A のように表す。
・「他動詞＋副詞」型の熟語は，put A off のように表す。
・他動詞は，solve「を解く」のように表す。

目　　次

Topic

① グローバル化

② 食糧問題

③ 自宅教育

④ 少子高齢化社会

⑤ AI

⑥ 言語論

⑦ 国際語としての英語

⑧ 文化論

⑨ ジェンダー論

⑩ 環境と経済

⑪ 環境汚染

⑫ 地球温暖化

⑬ 遺伝子

⑭ 脳死

⑮ 科学論

グローバル化

問1　個人や地域社会が，世界規模で共有されている知識や文化を利用できるようになり，国境を越えて行き来する経済の実体に影響を受けているため，国家は重要性を低下させるようになった。

問2　(2a)エ　　　(2b)ア　　　(2c)ウ

問3　エ. the illusions embedded in globalism serve to justify world trade

問4　エ. decreasing ── increasing

問5　環境に関する限り，地球規模で考えざるをえないということ。(28字)

▶▶▶　設問解説　◀◀◀

問1　ポイントは as が前置詞ではなく，接続詞である点。as の後に S, *doing* ..., V 〜という形が続いていることから判断する。S, *doing* ..., V は「Sは…し，〜する」と訳せばよい。that 以下は economic realities を修飾する関係代名詞節である。なお，as は理由を表している。

例　My mother, speaking with the man, remembered that she had met him before.

「母は，その男と話していて，以前会ったことがあることを思い出した」

□ have a decreasing importance「次第に低下する重要性を持つ，重要性を低下させる」

□ gain access to A「Aが利用できる」

□ globally shared knowledge and culture「世界的規模で共有されている知識や文化」shared は形容詞用法の過去分詞。　　　□ affect「に影響を与える」　　　□ boundary「境界，国境」

問2　(2a)の this group は第3段落で述べられたグローバル化賛成派のこと。第3段落第3文 They believe that, by globalization, dominant forms of social organization will lead to universal prosperity, peace, and freedom. に一致するエが(2a)の説明として適当。(2b)の this group は第4段落で述べられたグローバル化反対派のこと。第4段落第1文 Others reject it as a form of domination by advanced countries over developing ones に一致するアが(2b)の説明として適当。(2c)の Proponents of critical globalism とは，直後に take a disinterested view of the process「その過程を公平な目で見つめる」とあるように，グローバル化を肯定するのでも否定するのでもなく，批評的に捉える

立場である。したがって，ウが(2c)の説明として適当。

ア.「グローバル化は先進国による発展途上国の支配を維持すると考え，グローバル化に反対している」

イ.「グローバル化は，発展途上国が力を得るにつれ，先進国の政治的および経済的支配を弱めると懸念している」

ウ.「グローバル化のよい面と悪い面を認め，賛成も反対もしていない」

エ.「グローバル化は世界平和と繁栄に貢献すると考えている」

オ.「生態学的な観点からのみグローバル化を理解しようとしている」

□ proponent「支持者」　　□ critical「批評の／批判的な」

問3　下線部(3)は「それ(＝グローバリズム)に付随する神話は世界市場という福音として機能する」という意味。第4段落第2文および第3文の前半で，グローバル化否定派にとって，「グローバリズムとは，世界貿易を歴史的必然として正当化する政治的主義のことである」と述べられている。したがって，its attendant myths とは「グローバル化に伴う根拠のない通念」ということであり，function as a gospel of the global market とは「世界市場の絶対性を正当化することになる」ということである。

ア.「グローバル化支持者は聖書を論拠の一部に用いる」

イ.「歴史家はグローバル化はまったくの神話であるとして拒絶する」

ウ.「宗教がグローバル化に対して責任を持たなければならない」

エ.「グローバリズムに組み込まれている幻想が世界貿易を正当化するのに役立つ」

□ attendant「付随する」　　□ myth「神話／根拠のない通念」

□ function as A「Aとして機能する」　　□ gospel「福音」

問4　グローバル化とは第1段落第1文および第2段落第5文に述べられているように，「国家が重要性を低下させ」，「国境を越えて経済活動が行われる」過程である。したがって，正解はエ。

問5　論説文で，比喩・引用が何を言うためのものなのかを問う問題。「本文に即して」とある以上，本文中で述べられた部分を探せばよい。ここでは，前の文に there are compelling reasons for thinking globally where the environment is concerned とあり，「環境に関する限り，地球規模で考えざるをえないということ」を言っている。

□ come A's way「Aの方にやって来る」　　□ pause「立ち止まる」　　□ frontier「国境」

□ produce「を取り出す」　　□ territory「領土」

グローバル化は，全世界で社会間の関係の編成が変化した結果として，世界規模で作用している経済的，文化的な力によって個人の生活と地域社会が影響を受ける過程のことである。また，この過程に対しては，肯定的，否定的，中立的，学問的など様々な捉え方があるが，環境に関しては地球規模で考えざるをえない。(144字)

▶▶ 構文・語句解説 ◀◀

第1段落

¹Globalization is the process in which individual lives and local communities are affected by economic and cultural forces that operate worldwide. ²In effect, it is the process of the world becoming a single place. ³Globalism is the perception of the world as a function or result of the processes of globalization upon local communities.

¹グローバル化とは，世界規模で作用している経済的，文化的な力によって個人の生活と地域社会が影響を受ける過程である。²実際，それは世界が一つの場所になる過程なのである。³グローバリズムとは，世界を地域社会に対するグローバル化の過程の作用，あるいは結果であると認識することである。

1 □ globalization「グローバル化」　　□ operate「作用する」

2 the process of the world becoming a single place の becoming 以下は動名詞句で，the world がその意味上の主語。

□ in effect「実際には」

3 upon local communities の upon は the processes に伴う前置詞で「…に対する」という意味。

□ the perception of A as B「AをBと認識すること」

第2段落

¹The word "global" has had a rapid rise since the mid-1980s, up until which time the word "international" was preferred. ²The rise of the word "international" itself in the eighteenth century indicated the growing importance of territorial states in organizing social relations. ³It can be defined as an early consequence of the worldwide perspective of European imperialism. ⁴Similarly the rapidly increasing interest in globalization reflects a changing organization of worldwide social relations. ⁵The nation has begun to have a decreasing importance as individuals and communities, gaining access to globally shared knowledge and culture, are affected by economic realities that come and go over the

boundaries of the state. [6]The basic structure of globalization is nationalism on which the concept of internationalism is based. [7]Globalization occurs when people in a national framework are affected by global economy and communication.

[1]「グローバル」という言葉は，1980年代の半ばから急速に使われるようになったが，それまでは「国際的」という言葉が好まれていた。[2]「国際的」という言葉そのものが18世紀に使われるようになったことは，社会間の関係を編成する上で領土国家の重要性が増大していたことを示していた。[3]それは，ヨーロッパ帝国主義の世界的展望の初期の産物であると定義できるであろう。[4]同様に，グローバル化に対する関心の急速な増大は，全世界で社会間の関係の編成が変化していることを反映している。[5]個人や地域社会が，世界規模で共有されている知識や文化を利用できるようになり，国境を越えて行き来する経済の実体に影響を受けているため，国家は重要性を低下させるようになった。[6]グローバル化の基本構造は，国際主義という概念の基盤となっている国家主義である。[7]グローバル化は，国家の枠の中にいる人々が地球規模の経済やコミュニケーションに影響を受けるときに起こるのである。

1 up until ... was preferred は the mid-1980s を修飾する関係形容詞節。

　例　Please come at noon, by which time I shall be back in my office.
　　　「正午に来てください。それまでには会社に戻っていますから」

　□ up until A「Aまでは」
2 □ territorial state「領土国家」　　□ organize「を編成する」
　□ social relation「社会間の関係」
3 □ define O as C「OをCと定義する」　　□ consequence「結果」
　□ perspective「大局的な見方」　　□ imperialism「帝国主義」
4 □ reflect「を反映する」　　□ organization「編成，構成」
6 □ structure「構造」
　□ nationalism「国家主義」国家を人間社会の中で第一義的に考え，その権威と意思とに絶対の優位を認める立場。
　□ internationalism「国際主義」国家相互の協調を本位とし，世界平和を目的とする立場。
7 □ national「国家の，国民の」　　□ framework「枠組み」

―― 第3段落 ――
[1]Part of the complexity of globalism comes from the different ways in which globalization is approached. [2]Some analysts embrace it enthusiastically as a positive feature of a changing world in which access to technology, information, services and markets will be of

11

benefit to local communities. ³They believe that, by globalization, dominant forms of social organization will lead to universal prosperity, peace, and freedom. ⁴They even expect that perception of a global environment will lead to a global ecological concern. ⁵For this group, globalism is a term for values which treat global issues as a matter of personal and collective responsibility.

¹グローバリズムの複雑さは，一つにはグローバル化に対するアプローチが様々であることに起因する。²グローバル化を変化する世界の肯定的な特徴であると積極的に受け入れている識者もいる。そこでは，科学技術や，情報，サービス，市場を利用できることが地域社会にとって有益になるというのである。³こうした人々は，グローバル化によって，社会組織の最も有力な形態が世界的な繁栄，平和，自由につながると考えている。⁴世界規模の環境を認識することで，世界規模の環境に対する関心につながると期待してさえいる。⁵このグループにとって，グローバリズムとは，世界規模の問題を個人や集団の責任の問題として扱う価値観を表す言葉なのだ。

1 □ complexity「複雑さ」　　□ different A「様々なA」
2 □ analyst「〈政治・社会経済・情勢などの〉分析者」
　 □ embrace O as C「OをCとして受け入れる」　　□ enthusiastically「積極的に，熱心に」
　 □ positive「肯定的な／明白な」　　□ feature「特徴」　　□ of benefit「有益である」
3 □ dominant「最も有力な」　　□ lead to A「Aにつながる」　　□ prosperity「繁栄」
4 □ ecological concern「環境に対する関心」
5 □ term for A「Aを表す言葉」　　□ values「価値観」　　□ issue「問題」
　 □ as a matter of A「Aの問題として」　　□ collective「集団の，共同の」

─ 第4段落 ─

¹Others reject it as a form of domination by advanced countries over developing ones, in which individual distinctions of culture and society become erased by an increasingly homogeneous global culture while local economies are more firmly incorporated into a system of global capital. ²For this group, globalism is a political doctrine which provides, explains, and justifies an interlocking system of world trade. ³It has ideological overtones of historical inevitability, and its attendant myths function as a gospel of the global market. ⁴The chief argument against globalization is that global culture and global economy did not spontaneously spring up but originated in the centers of capitalist power which still try to sustain their own economic system. ⁵According to this group, in short, the benefits of

---

　¹グローバリズムを発展途上国に対する先進国の支配形態の一つであるとして拒絶する人々もいる。そこでは，文化や社会の個々の特徴がますます均質化する世界的文化によってかき消されるようになり，その一方で地域経済は世界規模の資本体制にがっちり組み込まれるというのである。²このグループにとって，グローバリズムとは，連動している世界貿易の体制を用意し，説明し，正当化する政治的な主義のことである。³それは歴史的必然性というイデオロギー的な響きを持ち，それに付随する神話は世界市場という福音として機能する。⁴グローバル化に反対する主要な論点は，世界規模の文化や世界規模の経済は自然発生的に現れたのではなく，自らの経済体制を今なお維持しようとしている資本主義大国の中心地で始まったというものである。⁵このグループによれば，要するに，グローバル化の恩恵は国によって非常に大きく異なるということである。

1 developing ones の ones は countries の代用。developing countries は「発展途上国」という意味。in which 以下は a form of domination by advanced countries over developing ones を補足説明する非制限用法の関係代名詞節。

　□ reject O as C「OをCであるとして拒絶する」

　□ domination by A over B「AがBを支配すること」

　□ advanced country「先進国」（＝developed country）　　□ distinction「特徴」

　□ erase「を消す」　　□ homogeneous「均質の」

　□ while S V ...「ところが一方…，…する一方で」

　□ incorporate A into B「AをBに組み込む」　　□ capital「資本」

2 □ doctrine「主義，信条」　　□ justify「を正当化する」　　□ interlocking「連動する」

3 □ ideological「イデオロギーの，観念上の」　　□ overtone「響き」　　□ inevitability「必然性」

4 □ argument against A「Aに反対する論点」　　□ spontaneously「自然発生的に」

　□ spring up「現れる」　　□ originate「始まる」　　□ capitalist power「資本主義大国」

　□ sustain「を維持する」

5 □ in short「要するに」　　□ benefit「恩恵，利益」　　□ vary from A to A「Aによって異なる」

── 第5段落 ──

　¹Proponents of critical globalism take a disinterested view of the process, simply examining its processes and effects. ²Critical globalism refers to the critical engagement with globalization processes, neither blocking them out nor celebrating globalization.

³Thus, while critical globalists see that globalization has often sustained poverty, widened material inequalities, increased ecological degradation, sustained militarism, fragmented communities, marginalized minority groups, fed intolerance, and deepened crises of democracy, they also see that it has had a positive effect on the great rise of the average individual income since 1945, reducing the population in miserable poverty, increasing ecological consciousness, and facilitating disarmament.

¹批評的グローバリズムを支持するものは，その過程を公平な目で見つめ，ただその過程と影響を検証する。²批評的グローバリズムとは，グローバル化の過程に対する批評的な取り組みのことであり，その過程を阻止することも，グローバル化を賛美することもない。³したがって，批評的グローバル主義者は，グローバル化がしばしば貧困を持続させ，物質的な不平等を拡大し，環境の悪化を増大し，軍国主義を持続させ，地域社会を分断し，少数派を軽視し，不寛容を助長し，民主主義の危機を深めたと理解しているが，一方で1945年以来個人の平均収入が大幅に増加したことにはっきりとした影響を与え，悲惨な貧困状態にある人々を減らし，環境に対する意識を高め，軍備縮小を促進させたと理解している。

1 simply 以下は同時動作を表す分詞構文。　　□ disinterested「公平な」

2 neither 以下は同時動作を表す分詞構文。　　□ refer to A「Aに言及する，Aを指す」
　□ engagement with A「Aに対する取り組み」　　□ block A out「Aを阻止する」
　□ celebrate「を賛美する」

3 reducing the population in miserable poverty と increasing ecological consciousness と facilitating disarmament の3つの連続・結果を表す分詞構文が and で結ばれている。
　□ see that 節「…だと理解する」　　□ material「物質的な」
　□ inequality「不平等」　　□ degradation「悪化」　　□ militarism「軍国主義」
　□ fragment「を分断する」　　□ marginalize「を軽視する，主流から追いやる」
　□ feed「を助長する」　　□ intolerance「不寛容」
　□ have a ... effect on A「Aに…な影響を与える」　　□ facilitate「を促進する」
　□ disarmament「軍備縮小」

─ 第6段落 ─

¹Academically, globalization covers such disciplines as international relations, political geography, economics, sociology, communication studies, agricultural, ecological, and cultural studies. ²It addresses the decreasing influence (though not the status) of the nation-state in the world political order and the increasing influence of multinational corporations.

³Globalization also means easy transportation all over the world, transnational company operations, the changing pattern of world employment, or global environmental risk. ⁴Indeed, there are compelling reasons for thinking globally where the environment is concerned. ⁵As a famous scholar puts it, "When the ill winds of Chernobyl came our way, they did not pause at the frontier, produce their passports and say, 'Can I rain on your territory now?'"

¹学問的には，グローバル化は，国際関係論，政治地理学，経済学，社会学，コミュニケーション論，農学，生態学，文化研究といった分野にわたるものである。²それは世界の政治秩序における国民国家の影響力（地位ではないが）の低下と，多国籍企業の影響力の増加を対象としている。³グローバル化はまた，世界中の輸送機関が便利になること，企業が国を超えて活動すること，世界の雇用形態が変化すること，世界規模の環境の危機を意味する。⁴確かに，環境に関する限り，地球規模で考えることに対しては説得力のある理由がある。⁵ある有名な学者が言っているように，「チェルノブイリの有害な風がこちらに向かって吹いたとき，風は国境で立ち止まり，パスポートを取り出して，『お宅の領土に雨を降らせてもいいかね』などと言わなかったのである」

1 □ academically「学問的に」　　□ discipline「学問分野」　　□ political geography「政治地理学」
　 □ sociology「社会学」　　□ communication studies「コミュニケーション論」
2 though not the status＝though it does not address the status
　 □ address「に取り組む，焦点を当てる」
　 □ nation-state「国民国家」主として国民の単位にまとめられた民族を基礎として，近代，特に18〜19世紀のヨーロッパに典型的に成立した統一国家。　　□ order「秩序」
　 □ multinational corporation「多国籍企業」
3 □ transportation「輸送機関」　　□ transnational「国家を超えた」
4 □ compelling「説得力のある，やむにやまれぬ」
　 □ where A be concerned「Aに関する限り」（＝as far as A be concerned）
5 □ as A put it「Aが言っているように」

　グローバル化(globalization)とは，特に冷戦(the　Cold　War)終結後，市場経済(market economy)が世界的に拡大する中で，ヒト，モノ，カネそして情報の国境を越えた移動が，地球的規模で盛んになり，政治的，経済的，あるいは文化的な境界線，障壁がボーダレス(borderless)化することによって，社会の同質化と多様化が同時に進展することをいう。金融の自由化は，経済のグローバル化を押し進め，さらにインターネット(the　Internet)をはじめとする情報通信技術(information　technology)が経済，文化，政治のグローバル化を促進する要因となった。経済的格差の是正，情報・知識の共有化，世界平和や環境問題への国際的な取り組みなどに寄与するとして，グローバル化の一層の促進を図る立場に対して，先進国，多国籍企業(multinational　corporation)による発展途上国の搾取，環境破壊，文化の画一化といった点から，グローバル化を批判する立場もある。また，グローバル化の下でも人々との生活の基盤は地域や共同体にあり，グローバル化を前提として，地域主義(regionalism)や地方分権(localization)など秩序の多層化が進むという捉え方もある → **Topic ⑦**　。本問はグローバル化の歴史的経緯，グローバリズムの様々な立場を紹介した文章であるが，賛成・反対いずれかの立場からグローバル化を論じた文章，グローバル化の個々の現象を取り上げた文章など，今後長文問題のトピックとしてさらに出題が増えることが予想される。

2 食糧問題

解 答

問1 　ウ. affluence

問2 　イ. inefficient

問3 　より高品質でタンパク質の豊富な食糧を買うお金を持つ人の数が2倍になったから。(38字)

問4 　イ. poor countries have lagged behind in food production

問5 　ところが，貧しい国々は，国内需要が増えたせいで穀物の価格が跳ね上がってしまっているより豊かな国々と世界の食糧市場で競争をしなければならない。

問6 　売ることのできる食糧余剰を持った生産国，食糧を買う金を持った裕福な消費国，世界の食糧市場でうまく競争することができない低収入の消費国の間の経済格差。(74字)

▶▶▶ **設問解説** ◀◀◀

問1 　空所(1)を含む文全体は「以前は，利用できる食糧備蓄に対する必要性の唯一の根拠として，人口増加にすべての注目が集まっていたが，今日では同様に重要な必要性の根拠が明らかになった。それは(1)である」という意味。第1段落全体で「豊かな国では，肉に対する需要が高まることで，その生産に多量の穀物を消費している」ことが述べられている。したがって，食糧の必要性の根拠として重要なのは「豊かさ」である。
　　ア.「環境，生態」イ.「飢饉」ウ.「豊かさ」エ.「栄養」

問2 　肉を食べることが穀物のどのような利用方法の1つかを考える。後ろの文で「アメリカでは1ポンドの家禽の肉を作るのに3ポンドの穀物が必要である。豚肉の場合，その割合は5対1であり，牛肉の場合は10対1である」と述べられている。つまり，「肉を作って食べるためには，その3倍から10倍の穀物を飼料として使わなければならない」ということなので，正解はイ。
　　ア.「倫理的な」イ.「非効率的な」ウ.「効果的な」エ.「理想的な」

問3 　下線部(3)は「過去20年の間に，世界の裕福な少数の国々においては，肉の消費量が2倍になった」という意味。後に続く2文の This is, however, not due to .... Rather, there are 〜. は「しかし，これは…が原因ではない。そうでは

17

なくて，〜なのだ」という意味なので，Rather, there ... protein-rich diet. の内容を制限字数に留意してまとめればよい。

□ minority「少数（派）」　　　□ double「を倍に増やす」　　　□ consumption「消費」

問4　One reason why ... is because 節は「…の１つの理由は〜である」という意味なので，空所には because 節の「農夫が適切な技術を利用する機会がなかった」ことが原因となって生じることが入る。空所(4)の前の第２段落第１〜４文では「アメリカなど豊かな国では，近代的な生産方法を用いることで，穀物の増産が可能になった」と述べられていることから，「農夫が適切な技術を利用する機会がなかった」ことから生じるのは「貧しい国々が食糧生産において遅れをとっている」ということである。
　　ア．「貧しい国々がなんとか十分な食糧を生産できている」
　　イ．「貧しい国々が食糧生産において遅れをとっている」
　　ウ．「豊かな国々が多くの食糧余剰を抱えている」
　　エ．「豊かな国々が食糧不足に悩んでいる」

問5　they が前の文の主語 The world's poor を指していると考えると，「The world's poor（＝The world's poor countries）は richer nations と競争しなければならない」という自然な文意になる。また，there は「貧しい国々と豊かな国々が競争をする場所」であることから，前の文の world food markets と考えられる。なお，whose 以下の関係代名詞節は richer nations を修飾している。

□ compete with A「Aと競争する」　　　□ nation「国／国民」　　　□ demand「需要」
□ force O upward「Oを押し上げる」

問6　下線部(6)を含む文は「このような格差は飢餓で苦しむ人々が常に増えていることを表している」という意味。前の文に「食糧不足の原因は経済力の不均衡な分布である」と述べられ，その具体的な内容がセミコロン以下に述べられている。したがって，その内容を制限字数に留意してまとめればよい。

□ differential「格差，違い」

要　約

　豊かな食糧生産国では，肉に対する需要が高まることで，その生産に多量の穀物を消費しており，余剰穀物は食糧市場を通じて豊かな消費国が購入している一方で，貧しい国は食糧増産のための技術も利用できず，食糧市場でもうまく競争ができない。食糧問題はこうした経済力の不均衡な分布により引き起こされている。(145字)

── 第1段落 ──

¹A particular problem directly related to continuing population growth is growing global food insecurity. ²For a variety of reasons the demand for food by the consumer has begun to outrun the capacity to provide. ³Where all attention was previously focused on population growth as the sole source of demand on available food stocks, today an equally important source of demand has become apparent and that is affluence. ⁴As per capita income increases, purchasing power climbs and with it a demand for higher quality foods, especially foods of animal origin such as meat, eggs, milk and milk products. ⁵Eating meat can be considered an inefficient way of utilizing grain. ⁶In the United States it takes three pounds of grain to produce a pound of poultry; 5:1 is the ratio for pork, and 10:1 for beef. ⁷In the end, Americans eat eighty percent of all the grain they consume indirectly, first using it for feed and then consuming the meat. ⁸On the basis of these data, Americans consume the equivalent of one ton of grain a year while inhabitants of poorer countries consume one fifth as much. ⁹Outside our borders, other nations with growing economies but without comparable agriculture have also increased their appetites for animal protein. ¹⁰Hence, sixty percent of North American agricultural sales has been to nations whose people are already rather well fed. ¹¹At this time, the approximately one billion people of the developed world feed enough grain to their livestock and poultry to provide minimal nutritional requirements to another 2 billion people. ¹²Over the last twenty years, the rich minority of the world has doubled its meat consumption. ¹³This is, however, not due to eating twice as much meat per capita, although there has been some rise here. ¹⁴Rather, there are twice as many people with the money to buy a higher quality protein-rich diet. ¹⁵The net result is that while world population has been growing at 1.6 percent and agricultural production at 2.5 percent, world demand for food has been increasing at 3 percent per year.

¹絶え間なく続く人口増加と直接に関連している特定の問題として，食糧の不安定性の世界的な増大がある。²様々な理由から，消費者の食糧に対する需要が供給能力を上回り始めた。³以前は，利用できる食糧備蓄に対する必要性の唯一の根拠として，人口増加にすべての注目が集まっていたが，今日では同様に重要な必要性の根拠が明らかになった。それは豊かさである。⁴1人当たりの収入が増えるにつれて購買力が高まり，それとともにより質の高い食糧，特に肉，卵，牛乳，および乳製品のような動物性の食品に対する需要が高まっている。⁵肉を食べることは穀物の非効率的な利用方法の1つと考えられる。⁶アメリカでは1ポンドの家禽の肉を作

るのに３ポンドの穀物が必要である。豚肉の場合，その割合は５対１であり，牛肉の場合は10対１である。⁷結局，アメリカ人は，自分たちが消費するすべての穀物のうち80パーセントを，まず飼料として使い，それから肉を消費することによって，間接的に食べているのである。⁸これらのデータに基づけば，アメリカ人は１年につき１トンに相当する穀物を消費していることになるが，より貧しい国々に住む人の消費量はその５分の１である。⁹アメリカ以外では，経済が成長しているのにそれに見合う農業を持たない国々においても，動物性タンパク質に対する欲求が高まってきている。¹⁰したがって，北アメリカにおける農業の売り上げの60パーセントは，国民が食糧をすでにかなり十分に供給されている国々に対するものなのである。¹¹現在，先進世界に住む約10億人の人々は，さらに20億人に最低限の栄養必要量を供給するのに十分なだけの穀物を自国の家畜や家禽に与えている。¹²過去20年の間に，世界の裕福な少数の国々においては，肉の消費量が２倍になった。¹³しかしこれは，多少増えたとはいっても，１人当たりの肉の消費量が２倍になったからではない。¹⁴そうではなくて，より質の高いタンパク質の豊富な食糧を買うお金を持った人の数が２倍になったからである。¹⁵結果的には，世界の人口が1.6パーセント，農業生産高が2.5パーセントの割合で増加してきた一方で，食糧に対する世界の需要は年３パーセントの割合で増えてきているのである。

1 □ particular「特定の，個別の」 　　□ related to A「Aと関連している」

　□ population growth「人口増加」

　□ global food insecurity「食糧の世界的な不安定さ」ここでは食糧の供給面での不安定さのこと。

2 □ a variety of A「様々なA」 　　□ demand for A by B「BのAに対する需要，要求」

　□ outrun「を上回る，より勝る」 　　□ capacity to do「…する能力」

3 □ where S V ...「…なのに，…する一方で」 　　□ previously「以前は」

　□ focus A on B「AをBに集める，集中させる」 　　□ the sole A「唯一のA」

　□ source「原因／源」 　　□ available「入手可能な，利用可能な」 　　□ stock「備蓄，蓄え」

　□ apparent「明らかな」

4 □ per capita「一人当たりの」 　　□ purchasing power「購買力」 　　□ climb「上昇する」

　□ high quality「質の高い，良質の」

5 □ utilize「を利用する」 　　□ grain「穀物」

6 10 : 1 for beef ＝ 10 : 1 is the ratio for beef

　□ it takes O to do「…するのにOを必要とする」

　□ pound「ポンド」重さの単位。１ポンドは約450グラム。 　　□ ratio「割合，率」

7 they consume は all the grain を修飾する関係代名詞節。indirectly は eat を修飾しているが，その具体的な内容は first using ... the meat の分詞構文で述べられている。

　□ in the end「結局，最終的には」 　　□ consume「を消費する」 　　□ indirectly「間接的に」

□ feed「飼料」

8 □ on the basis of A「Aに基づいて」　　　□ equivalent of A「Aに相当する量」

□ inhabitant「住民，住人」

9 with growing economies と without comparable agriculture が but で結ばれ，other nations を修飾している。

□ border「国境」　　　□ comparable「それに匹敵する，同等の」

□ appetite for A「Aに対する欲求」　　　□ animal protein「動物性タンパク質」

10 □ hence「したがって，それゆえ」　　　□ sales「売り上げ額」

□ be well fed「十分な食べ物を与えられている，栄養状態がよい」

11 □ at this time「現在，今は」　　　□ approximately「およそ，約」　　　□ billion「10億」

□ developed world「先進世界」　　　□ feed A to B「BにA〈食べ物〉を与える」

□ enough (A) to do「…するのに十分な量(のA)」　　　□ livestock「家畜」

□ minimal「最低限の」　　　□ nutritional requirement「栄養必要量」

13 here は文脈から「肉を食べることに関しては」という意味。

□ be due to A「Aのせいである，Aが原因である」

14 □ rather「〈前文の内容を否定して〉そうではなくて，いやむしろ」

□ protein-rich「タンパク質の豊富な」　　　□ diet「食品／(日常の)食事」

15 agricultural production at 2.5 percent＝agricultural production has been growing at 2.5 percent

□ net result「最終結果」　　　□ agricultural production「農業生産高」

─ 第2段落 ─

¹It is to our advantage and the world's as well that the United States grain harvests in recent years have resulted in enormous yields. ²Overflowing granaries and low grain prices are the mark of this high productivity. ³But the great increases in food production have not occurred where populations are growing the fastest. ⁴Gains in production require modern energy-intensive methods combining irrigation, pesticides, herbicides, fertilizers, genetics, and mechanization. ⁵One reason, among several, why poor countries have lagged behind in food production is because their farmers have not had access to appropriate technologies, such as sufficient fertilizers, irrigation, improved seeds, pesticides, storage facilities, and transportation. ⁶The world's poor are thus driven to world food markets to supplement their needs. ⁷However, they must compete there with richer nations whose own increased demands have forced the price of grain upward. ⁸With food prices rising beyond their purchasing power, the poor countries can buy less and less with their precious dollars.

¹近年アメリカの穀物の収穫高が大いに高くなっているのは我々にとって，また世界にとっても，都合のよいことである。²穀物倉庫がいっぱいで，穀物の値段が安いのは，このように生産性が高いことの証拠である。³しかし，食糧生産の大幅な増加は，人口が最も急速に増えているところでは起きていない。⁴生産高を増やすには，灌漑，殺虫剤，除草剤，肥料，遺伝学，そして機械化を組み合わせた近代的なエネルギー集約型の方法が必要である。⁵貧しい国々が食糧生産において遅れをとってしまった理由としていくつかあるうちの１つは，その国の農業従事者が十分な肥料，灌漑，品種改良された種子，殺虫剤，貯蔵設備，輸送などの適切な技術を利用する機会がなかった，ということである。⁶したがって，世界の貧しい国々は，必要なものを補うために，世界の食糧市場へと駆り立てられるのである。⁷ところが，貧しい国々は，国内需要が増えたせいで穀物の価格が跳ね上がってしまっているより豊かな国々と世界の食糧市場で競争をしなければならない。⁸食糧価格が購買力を超えるレベルまで高騰するにつれ，貧しい国々がその貴重なドルで買うことのできる量がどんどん減ることになる。

1 the world's＝the world's advantage

　□ It is to A's advantage that 節「…はAにとって都合のよいことである」

　□ X and Y as well「XだけでなくYも」　　　□ harvest「収穫(高)」

　□ result in A「Aという結果になる」　　　□ enormous「莫大な，巨大な」

　□ yield「収穫(量)」

2 □ overflow「氾濫する，いっぱいになってあふれる」　　　□ mark「印，特徴」

　□ productivity「生産性」

3 □ where S V ...「…するところで」

4 □ gain in A「Aの増加」　　　□ energy-intensive「エネルギー集約型の」　　　□ irrigation「灌漑」

　□ pesticide「殺虫剤，害虫駆除剤」　　　□ herbicide「除草剤」　　　□ fertilizer「肥料」

　□ genetics「遺伝学」　　　□ mechanization「機械化」

5 One reason why ... is because 節「…の１つの理由は～である」because 節の代わりに that 節を用いるのが普通。

　among several＝among several reasons

　□ have access to A「Aを利用できる」　　　□ appropriate「適切な」　　　□ sufficient「十分な」

　□ improve「を改良する」　　　□ storage facilities「貯蔵設備」　　　□ transportation「輸送」

6 □ drive A to B「AをBに追いやる，駆り立てる」　　　□ thus「したがって」

　□ supplement「を補う，補完する」

8 □ precious「貴重な」

[1]According to some estimates, world agriculture could produce enough to feed up to 30 billion people. [2]What appears to be a food shortage may, in fact, be an uneven worldwide distribution of economic power; we have the producer nations with surpluses to sell, the affluent consumer nations who have money to buy, and the low income consumer countries that cannot effectively compete in the world food markets. [3]These differentials represent an ever-growing number of hungry people. [4]Thus there is famine in some parts of the world, most notably on the Indian subcontinent and some countries of Africa and Latin America, and an overabundance of food in a number of others.

[1]いくつかの推定によれば，世界の農業は最大300億人を養うのに十分な量を生産できるということである。[2]一見すると食糧不足に見えるものは，実際は，経済力の世界全体における不均衡な分布なのかもしれない。売ることのできる余剰を持った生産国があり，買う金を持った裕福な消費国があり，そして世界の食糧市場でうまく競争することができない低収入の消費国があるのである。[3]このような格差は飢餓で苦しむ人々が常に増えていることを表している。[4]したがって，世界の一部の地域，最も顕著にはインド亜大陸，アフリカやラテンアメリカの国々において飢饉が起き，他の多くの国々では食糧の余剰が起きるのである。

1 □ estimate「推定，見積もり」　　□ up to A「A まで，最大で A」

2 □ food shortage「食糧不足」　　□ uneven「不均衡な」　　□ distribution「分布」
　　□ producer nation「生産国」　　□ surplus「余剰」　　□ affluent「豊かな，裕福な」
　　□ consumer nation「消費国」　　□ effectively「効果的に」

3 □ represent「を表す」　　□ ever-growing「絶えず増え続ける」

4 □ notably「目立って，特に」
　　□ subcontinent「亜大陸」大陸の一部で，大陸としての諸条件を比較的満たしている一区画のこと。　　□ Latin America「ラテンアメリカ，中南米」　　□ overabundance「過剰，過多」
　　□ a number of A「たくさんの A ／いくつかの A」

　現在，穀物等の国際的な需給調整機関がないために，食糧調達は基本的に各国に任されており，国の豊かさや政治戦略とも絡み，地域的に過剰と不足，飽食と飢餓が併存している。また，発展途上国における爆発的な人口増加(population　explosion)や，肉類の需要に伴う飼料穀物の需要の増加，地球温暖化 ➡ **Topic ⑫** をはじめとする地球環境問題から生じる生産制約，耕地拡大の困難のため，これまでと同様の食糧生産の増加は極めて難しいと予想される。食糧の安定供給は人類にとって大きな問題であり，貧富の差に関わらず世界のすべての人々が必要な食糧を手にすることができるように，国家という枠組みを越えて人類はこの問題に取り組む必要がある。

自宅教育

解答

問1 (1a) イ．advantages and disadvantages

(1b) ア．who does not believe home schooling is always the best system

(1c) ウ．don't want to intervene too much

(1d) エ．seem to lack confidence in developing their children's social skills

(1e) エ．quit teaching her children at home

問2 ア．about 70,000 children

問3 親がこれまでになく子育てに関わるようになっているから。(27字)

問4 学校は安全でない場所であるという認識に突き動かされて，多くの親はいじめが解決するまでのたとえ6ヶ月間だけだとしても，自宅で教育すべきであるという結論に達する。

問5 (5a) イ．individual (5b) エ．right (5c) ア．difficult

(5d) ウ．likely

問6 ウ

▶▶▶ 設問解説 ◀◀◀

問1 (1a) the pros and cons は「賛否両論」という意味。第2段落以降で自宅教育の良い面と悪い面が論じられていることから推測する。

ア．「理論と実践」 イ．「長所と短所」 ウ．「理想と現実」 エ．「質と量」

(1b) be committed to A は「Aに肩入れしている，傾倒している」，on principle は「主義としては」という意味。

ア．「自宅教育が常に最もよいやり方であるとは考えていない」

イ．「道徳的なしつけを家庭で教えることに反対している」

ウ．「家庭での初等教育には関わっていない」

エ．「自宅教育という考えを実践している」

(1c) hands-off は「干渉しない，無干渉の」という意味。後ろの文の「自宅教育の支援団体の代表は，自宅教育を行っている家庭は年に1回30分の面接のために訪問を受ける，と述べている」という内容から推測する。

ア.「自宅教育を行っている家庭を全面的に支持している」

イ.「連絡をとることは決してない」

ウ.「あまり干渉したくないと思っている」

エ.「否定的な見解を持っている」

(1d)defensive は「弁解がましい，自己防衛的な」という意味。this subject は前の文の引用文の内容を指し，「家庭で教育を受けた子供は同年代の集団や外の世界とうまく付き合っていくのに必要な社会生活上の技能を身につけるのかどうか」という問題のこと。

ア.「この問題の専門家であるという印象を与える」

イ.「自宅教育に対する謝罪を聞き入れる」

ウ.「数学と科学は必ず学ばなくてはならない科目であると言う」

エ.「子供の社会生活上の技能を伸ばすのには自信がないようである」

(1e)pack A in は「Aをやめる」という意味の熟語。後ろの文の「彼女はちょうど一年が過ぎたところで自宅教育をあきらめた」という内容から推測する。ア.「自分の実験室を片づけた」イ.「学校で教えることをあきらめた」ウ.「集団活動を終えた」エ.「子供を自宅で教育することをやめた」

問2 下線部の the rest とは「学校を中途で退学した these children のおよそ半数」の「残り」のことである。この these children とは第2段落第2文の140,000 children を指しているので，the rest は「およそ7万人の子供」になる。

問3 下線部(3)は「なぜこの選択肢を選ぶ親が増えているのであろうか」という意味。this option とは前の段落で述べられている「子供を自宅で教育すること」である。この問いに対する理由として，第3段落では「教師の能力など従来の学校に対する不安」，第4段落では「いじめや学級崩壊の問題」，第5段落では「官僚的な学校制度に対する不安」について述べられているが，いずれも学校制度自体に起因する理由である。第6段落第2文には「自宅教育の増加は，現代の親が以前にもまして子育てという仕事に関わっている，という事実の反映でもある」とあるので，この内容を制限字数内でまとめればよい。

□ option「選択肢」

問4 that schools are unsafe places は The perception と同格の名詞節。drive A to B は「AをBに追いやる」という意味なので，The perception … the conclusion を直訳すれば「学校は安全でない場所であるという認識が多くの親を…の結論に追いやる」であるが，「学校は安全でない場所であるという認識に突き動かされて，多くの親は…の結論に達する」と訳すと自然な日本語になる。that they … is resolved は the conclusion と同格の名詞節であり，if only ＋期間・目的・理由を表す表現は「…だけでも」という意味。よって，the conclusion ... is resolved は「いじめが解決するまでのたとえ 6 ヶ月間だけだとしても，自宅で教育すべきであるという結論」となる。

　例　You must attend the meeting, if only for an hour.

　　「たとえ 1 時間だけでも，その会議に出席しなければならない」

□ perception「認識」　　□ conclusion「結論」　　□ bullying「いじめ」

□ resolve「を解決する」

問5　(5a)空所を含む第 5 段落は「特殊な問題を抱えた子供にとって，官僚的な学校制度では十分対応できない」という親の不安について述べられている。したがって，空所を含む部分が「学校は子供一人一人の要求に応えられないことが多い」となるように，イ. individual を入れる。

(5b)on the right track で「正しい方向に進んで」という意味の熟語。

(5c)後ろの文に「基礎レベル以上の数学や科学を教えられる素養がある親はほとんどいない」とあることから，空所を含む部分が「もっとも子供が大きくなるにつれて家庭での教育は難しくはなっていく」となるように，ア. difficult を入れる。

(5d)空所を含む第11段落は「自宅教育は時間がかかる」という問題点について述べられている。したがって，空所を含む文が「時間というのはたいていの現代の大人が欠いている唯一のものなので，自宅教育は増加しているとはいえ，利用するのはほんの少数の親に限られることになりそうである」となるように，ウ. likely を入れる。

問6　ア.「最近まで親が自宅で子供を教育するために学校をやめさせるのは一風変わったことであった」第 1 段落第 3 文の内容に一致。

イ.「校内暴力について心配しているある母親は，教師はもはやクラスを掌握していないと主張している」第 4 段落第 3 ・ 4 文の内容に一致。

ウ.「過保護な育児により，子供が自由に 1 人で世界を探求するようになっている」第 6 段落第 3 文の内容に不一致。

エ.「本や出版物に加えて，自宅教育を行う者に役に立つ多くの教材がインターネット上にある」第 8 段落第 5 文の内容に一致。

オ.「親が子供を適切に自宅で教育しようとするとき，親が仕事を続けたり，他の子供の面倒を見たり，家事を行ったりする時間はほとんど残らない」第11段落第 1 文の内容に一致。

要　約

　英国では自宅で子供の教育を行う人が増えている。いじめや学級崩壊，教育の水準など従来の学校に対する不満に加えて，以前より親が子育てに関わるようになっているという背景があ

る。自宅教育を始めることは容易ではあるが，基礎レベル以上の教育や社会生活上の技能の養成，時間がかかるといった問題点もある。(144字)

▶▶ 構文・語句解説 ◀◀

— 第1段落 —

[1]Primary education in Britain begins at the age of five. [2]Parents have a responsibility to educate their children but not always in schools. [3]And yet, until recently, home schooling was associated with zealous parents having eccentric ideas. [4]Today, however, dinner-table conversations among middle-class parents who are conscious of their children's education often lead to debate about the pros and cons of educating children at home.

[1]英国では初等教育は5歳から始まる。[2]親は子供を教育する責任があるが，必ずしも学校で教育が行われるわけではない。[3]それでも最近までは，自宅教育は一風変わった考えを持つ熱心な親を連想させた。[4]ところが今日では，子供の教育に対する意識の高い中産階級の親が夕食の席で交わす会話は，子供を自宅で教育することの賛否をめぐる討論へと発展することが多い。

1 □ primary education「初等教育」secondary education「中等教育」, higher education「高等教育」に対して小学校での教育のことをいう。

2 but not always in schools＝but they do not always educate their children in schools

3 □ home schooling「自宅教育，自宅学習」
　□ associate A with B「AをBと結びつけて考える，AでBを連想する」
　□ zealous「熱心な」　　□ eccentric「一風変わった，普通でない」

4 □ middle-class「中産階級の」　　□ be conscious of A「Aを意識している」
　□ lead to A「Aにつながる」　　□ debate about A「Aに関する討論」

— 第2段落 —

[1]A depressing catalogue of complaints — large classes, bullying and school violence, teaching standards, and despair with the incessant pressure of examinations — has led many parents to think the unthinkable. [2]It is estimated that 140,000 children, about 1.5% of the school population, are home-schooled in Britain, a growth of about 10% during the past year. [3]About half of these children have been withdrawn from school; the rest were home-schooled from the start.

¹気の滅入るような不平の数々，大人数授業，いじめや校内暴力，授業の水準，試験の絶え間ない圧力に対する失望によって，多くの親が思いもよらぬことを考えるようになった。²英国では学齢人口のおよそ1.5パーセントにあたる14万人の子供が自宅で教育を受けており，ここ１年でおよそ10パーセント増加したと推定されている。³こうした子供のおよそ半数は学校を中途で退学し，残りは最初から自宅で教育を受けていた。

1 □ depressing「気の滅入るような」　　□ catalogue「一覧，カタログ」

　□ complaint「不平，不満」　　□ incessant「絶え間ない」

　□ lead O to *do*「Oに…するように仕向ける」　　□ the unthinkable「思いもよらぬこと」

2 a growth of about 10% during the past year は直前の that 節の内容を補足説明している。

　□ estimate「だと見積もる」　　□ school population「学齢人口」

　□ home-school「を自宅で教育する」

3 □ withdraw A from B「AをBから退かせる」

第3段落

¹So why are more parents choosing this option?　²The new generation of home teachers tends to be motivated more by fears that their children are not thriving in conventional schools.　³A mother of a seven-year-old daughter in an industrial town, for example, is pragmatic about her decision to take her daughter out of her local primary school.　⁴"Her teachers lacked the ability to stimulate and encourage her," claims she, who is not committed to home schooling on principle.　⁵"I would put her back in the system if there was a decent school in this area."

---

¹それではなぜこの選択肢を選ぶ親が増えているのであろうか？²自宅で教育を行う新たな層は，子供が従来の学校ではうまくいっていないのではないかという不安が動機となっていることが多い。³たとえば，ある工業都市で暮らす７歳になる娘の母親は，娘に地元の学校をやめさせる決断に関して現実的であった。⁴「娘の先生たちは，この子を刺激し励ます能力がないんです」と彼女は主張するが，主義として自宅教育に肩入れしているわけではない。⁵「もしこの地域にまともな学校があれば，娘を学校に戻します」

2 that 以下は fears と同格の名詞節。

　□ motivate「に動機を与える」　　□ thrive「うまくいく」　　□ conventional「従来の」

3 □ pragmatic「現実的な，実用的な」　　□ take A out of B「AをBから連れ出す，取り出す」

4 stimulate と encourage が and で結ばれていて，共通する目的語が her。

□ lack「を欠く」　　　□ stimulate「を刺激する」　　　□ claim「と主張する」

5 □ put A back in B「AをBに戻す」

□ the system「その体制」ここでは従来の学校のこと。　　　□ decent「まともな」

---

[1]The fear of bullying is also often raised. [2]The perception that schools are unsafe places drives many parents to the conclusion that they should educate at home, even if only for six months until the bullying is resolved. [3]Another mother, who is also representative of a home schooling support group, says that the erosion of classroom discipline means that many schools resemble a "war zone." [4]She believes that it is now group pressure rather than teachers that dominates the classroom.

[1]いじめに対する不安が持ち出されることも多い。[2]学校は安全でない場所であるという認識に突き動かされて，多くの親はいじめが解決するまでのたとえ6ヶ月間だけだとしても，自宅で教育すべきであるという結論に達する。[3]自宅教育支援団体の代表も務める別の母親は，教室での規律が崩壊したことで，多くの学校が「交戦地帯」のようになっていると言う。[4]教室を支配しているのは今では教師というよりは集団の圧力である，と彼女は考えている。

1 □ raise「を持ち出す，提起する」

3 □ be representative of A「Aの代表である」

□ erosion「〈力・権力などが〉衰えること／侵食」　　　□ discipline「規律」

□ war zone「交戦地帯」

4 it is now group pressure rather than teachers that ... は強調構文。

□ X rather than Y「YというよりむしろX」　　　□ dominate「を支配する」

---

[1]Some parents worry that children who are either specially gifted or have learning difficulties are often overlooked within a highly bureaucratic school system. [2]A mother, who is as well an author of a book on a woman's role at home, has decided to school her daughters at home throughout the primary years. [3]She argues that schools often "fail to respond to the individual needs of children."

¹特別な才能に恵まれているか，あるいは学習障害を抱えた子供が，極めて官僚的な学校制度の中では，ないがしろにされることが多いのではないかと心配する親もいる。²家庭における女性の役割に関する本の著者でもある母親は，初等教育の間ずっと娘たちを自宅で教えることに決めた。³学校は「子供一人一人の要求に応えられない」ことが多いと彼女は主張する。

1 □ worry that 節「…ではないかと心配する」　　□ gifted「才能のある」
　 □ overlook「を見落とす」　　□ bureaucratic「官僚的な」
2 □ as well「…も」　　□ school「を教育する」　　□ the primary years「初等教育の年月」
3 □ argues that 節「…だと論ずる，主張する」　　□ fail to *do*「…できない」
　 □ respond to A「Aに応ずる，反応する」

--- 第6段落 ---

¹The growth of home education is not simply a reflection of the unhappy state of the British education system. ²It can also reflect the fact that modern-day parents are more concerned with the task of child-raising than ever before. ³Our overprotective parenting has led to a steady expansion of the amount of time mothers and fathers spend looking after their children and a corresponding reduction in the freedom children are given to explore their world with one another. ⁴Home schooling takes this one step further.

¹自宅教育の増加は英国の教育制度の不幸な状態を反映しているだけではない。²現代の親が以前にもまして子育てという仕事に関わっている，という事実の反映でもある。³過保護な育児により，母親と父親が子供の面倒を見るのに費やす時間が着実に増加し，それに伴い，子供たちが与えられている自分たちの世界を子供どうしで探求する自由が減少することになった。⁴自宅教育はこれをさらに一段階推し進めるのである。

1 not simply は第2文の also と呼応し，「…だけではない。～もまた」という意味。
　 □ reflection「反映」　　□ state「状態／国家」
2 that 以下は the fact と同格の名詞節。
　 □ reflect「を反映する」　　□ be concerned with A「A に関係している，関心を持っている」
　 □ child-raising「子育て」　　□ than ever before「以前にもまして，これまでないほど」
3 a steady ... their children と a corresponding ... one another の2つの名詞句が and で結ばれている。また，mothers and ... their children は the amount of time を修飾する関係代名詞節。children are given は the freedom を修飾する関係代名詞節で，to explore ... one another は

the freedom を修飾する形容詞用法の不定詞句。

☐ overprotective「過保護な」　　☐ parenting「育児，子育て」　　☐ steady「着実な」

☐ expansion「拡大」　　☐ look after A「Aの面倒を見る」　　☐ corresponding「対応する」

☐ reduction「減少」　　☐ explore「を探求する」

4 ☐ take O one step further「Oをさらに一段階推し進める」

─── 第7段落 ───

[1]In addition, it is surprisingly easy to begin home schooling.　[2]Parents do not even need permission from the local education authority to educate their families at home.　[3]However, those who withdraw their child from school in England and Wales need to inform the head of their education authority.　[4]After this, parents can expect education officers to inquire about the arrangements they are making.

[1]そのうえ，自宅教育を始めることは驚くほど簡単である。[2]親は子供を家庭で教育する許可を地元の教育当局から得る必要すらない。[3]ただし，イングランドとウェールズで子供を退学させる親は教育当局の長に通知する必要がある。[4]この後，親は，準備している計画について教育担当官に尋ねられることになる。

1 ☐ in addition「そのうえ，さらに」

2 ☐ permission to *do*「…する許可」　　☐ authority「当局／権威」

　☐ family「子供／家族」ここでは一家の子供という意味。

3 those who ... の those は the parents の代用。　　☐ inform「に通知する，報告する」

　☐ head「長，長官」

4 they are making は the arrangements を修飾する関係代名詞節。

　☐ inquire about A「Aについて尋ねる」　　☐ arrangement「手はず，計画」

─── 第8段落 ───

[1]Most authorities take a fairly hands-off attitude.　[2]The representative of a home schooling support group notes that home-educating families are visited once a year for a half-hour session.　[3]She found these visits useful, since they affirmed that what she was teaching was on the right track.　[4]There is also an elaborate network of support available to those opting to home-educate.　[5]Materials and advice for different levels of teaching are readily available on the Internet as well as in books and other publications.　[6]Many parents join local support groups.

¹たいていの当局はあまり干渉しないという姿勢をとっている。²自宅教育の支援団体の代表は，自宅教育を行っている家庭は年に1回30分の面接のために訪問を受ける，と述べている。³こうした訪問によって，自分の行っていることがうまくいっていることが確認できるので，有益であると彼女は思ったのである。⁴自宅教育を選択する者に利用できる行き届いた支援ネットワークもある。⁵様々な教育レベルに応じた教材や助言が本やその他の出版物だけでなくインターネット上でも容易に入手できる。⁶地元の支援団体に加入する親も多い。

2 □ note that 節「…と述べる」　　□ session「会合／〈特定の目的のための〉活動」

3 □ affirm that 節「…を確認する」

4 those opting to home-educate の opting 以下は those を修飾する現在分詞句で，those は「（…する）人々」という意味。

　　□ elaborate「周到な，念入りな」　　□ available to A「Aに利用できる」

　　□ opt to *do*「…することを選択する」

5 □ material「教材，資料」　　□ different A「様々なA」

　　□ X as well as Y「XもYも／YだけでなくXも」　　□ publication「出版物」

6 □ join「に加わる」

───── 第9段落 ─────

¹In principle, there is no reason children cannot be successfully educated at home, although it is more difficult as they get older. ²While there are some successful cases, few parents are equipped to teach mathematics and science beyond a basic level. ³Others might ask, "Do children educated at home gain the social skills necessary to relate to their age group and the outside world?" ⁴Most supporters of home schooling say yes but sound a little defensive on this subject. ⁵One supporter says: "We spend a considerable amount of time scheduling group activities for the children!"

¹原則として，自宅でうまく教育できないという理由はないが，もっとも子供が大きくなるにつれて難しくはなっていく。²うまくいっている事例もあるが，基礎レベル以上の数学や科学を教えられる素養がある親はほとんどいない。³「家庭で教育を受けた子供は同年代の集団や外の世界とうまく付き合っていくのに必要な社会生活上の技能を身につけるのだろうか」と問う者もいるかもしれない。⁴自宅教育を支持する者はたいていイエスと答えるが，この件についてはいささか弁解がましく聞こえる。⁵ある支持者は言っている。「私たちは子供のために集団活動の予定を立てるのにかなりの時間を費やしているんです」

1 children cannot ... at home の直前に関係副詞 why が省略されている。

  □ in principle「原則として」

2 □ be equipped to *do*「…する素養がある」

3 necessary 以下は the social skills を修飾する形容詞句。

  □ social「社会生活上の／社会の」   □ relate to A「Aとうまく付き合う」

5 □ considerable「かなりの，相当な」

- -

┌─ 第10段落 ─

  ¹So what's the downside of home education? ²It is the loss of free time for the home teacher. ³That was why a mother, who lives in south London, packed in her experiment. ⁴She removed her twelve-year-old and thirteen-year-old from their state schools because of concern about their education, but gave up home schooling after just over a year. ⁵"One year of home teaching finished me off," she recalls. ⁶Her solution was to move near a "good school."

┌──────────────────────────────────────┐

  ¹それでは自宅教育の問題点とは何であろうか？²自宅で教える者の自由時間が失われることである。³そんなわけで，ロンドン南部で暮らすある母親は実験をやめてしまった。⁴彼女は12歳と13歳の子供を2人の教育に関する懸念から公立学校をやめさせたが，ちょうど1年が過ぎたところで自宅教育をあきらめた。⁵「1年間の自宅教育でくたくたになってしまいました」と彼女は振り返って言う。⁶彼女の解決策は「良い学校」の近くに引っ越すことだった。

1 □ downside「否定的側面」

3 □ that is why ...「そんなわけで…，だから…」

4 □ remove A from B「AをBからやめさせる」   □ concern about A「Aに関する心配」

5 □ finish A off「Aを参らせる，くたくたに疲れさせる」   □ recall「と振り返って言う」

6 □ solution「解決策」

- -

┌─ 第11段落 ─

  ¹Home schooling is time-consuming if it is done properly, and leaves little space to run a career, look after other children, or run a home. ²Since time is the one thing most modern-day adults lack, it seems likely that despite its growth home teaching will be used only by a small minority of parents. ³Indeed, many children are taken out of schools for only short periods of time before their parents resume their careers.

¹自宅教育は，適切に行うと時間がかかり，仕事をしたり，他の子供の面倒を見たり，家庭を切り盛りする余地をほとんど残さない。²時間というのはたいていの現代の大人が欠いている唯一のものなので，自宅教育は増加しているとはいえ，利用するのはほんの少数の親に限られることになりそうである。³実際，多くの子供は，親が仕事を再開するまでのごく短い期間だけ学校に行かないのである。

1 □ time-consuming「時間のかかる」　　□ properly「適切に」
　　□ space to *do*「…するための余地」　　□ run「を行う，運営する」
2 most modern-day adults lack は the one thing を修飾する関係代名詞節。
　　□ the one A「唯一のA」　　□ minority「少数(派)」
3 □ resume「を再開する」

Topic ③　自宅教育

　本問は，様々な問題を抱える伝統的な学校に対する不満を背景に，教育の選択肢を拡大しようという運動の1つとして，1970年代以降イギリスやアメリカで盛んになってきた自宅教育(home schooling)の利点と欠点を論じたもの。特にアメリカでは，自宅教育以外にも，子供の自由と自主性を尊重するフリースクール(free school)，教師や親が設置し公費で運営されるチャーター・スクール(charter school)などオルタナティブ・スクール(alternative school)と呼ばれる多様なタイプの学校が生まれている。日本においても，義務教育(compulsory education)の見直し，学校選択の多様化等の教育改革が進む中で，こうした先駆的試みを紹介した文章は今後出題が増加すると予想される。

高齢化社会

問1　ウ. the aging of populations

問2　今日，先進国に生まれた女子は80歳を優に越えて生きることが見込めるし，男子は80代のはじめまでは生きることが見込める。

問3　エ. an increased burden on workers

問4　合衆国やいくつかのヨーロッパ諸国の失業率がほぼ過去最低となり，いくつかの分野においては熟練労働者が相当に不足しているため，高齢の労働者を抱えておこうという強力な動きが進んでいる。

問5　1. 上級管理職には30代の社員が好ましいということ。(23字)
　　　2. 50歳を越えた社員がまず退職すべきだということ。(23字)

問6　我々が65歳になったとき，職場がまだ我々を必要としているだけでなく，我々も職場を必要としていることだろう。

問7　エ

▶▶▶ 設問解説 ◀◀◀

問1　空所(1)を含む文の前には「早期退職という状況が変わろうとしている」ことが述べられている。その理由として，続く第2段落以降に「人口の高齢化と出生率の低下，これに伴って生じる労働力の減少」が述べられている。したがって，正解はウ。
　　　ア.「雇用に関する法律の変化」
　　　イ.「低い失業率」
　　　ウ.「人口の高齢化」
　　　エ.「好況な経済」

問2　born in a developed country は a girl を修飾する過去分詞句。live into her 80s とは直訳すれば「80歳代に入るまで生きる」ということ。and 以下では反復を避けるための省略が行われている。これを補うと a boy born in a developed country can expect to live until his early 80s となる。
　　　□ developed country「先進国」　　□ expect to do「…することを予想する」
　　　□ well「〈時・場所の副詞・前置詞の前で〉優に，相当」

問3　空所(3)を含む文の前には「先進国の人口の減少と高齢化」が述べられているの

で，「その主な結果」がどのようなものになるのかを考える。空所の後ろには「年金受給者を支える現役労働者の数の減少」について言及されているので，正解はエ。

ア．「人口の減少」

イ．「経済の衰退」

ウ．「年金受給者に対する負担の増加」

エ．「労働者に対する負担の増加」

問4　文頭の付帯状況を表す前置詞句 With unemployment ... some areas の構造理解がポイント。with A *doing* and A′＋副詞句という形になっており「A が…している状態で，そして A′ が…にある状態で」が直訳。A に当たるのが unemployment in the USA and some European countries, A′ に当たるのが significant skills shortages である。なお，to retain older workers は主語である a strong push を修飾する形容詞用法の不定詞句。

□ unemployment「失業率」　　□ hit「に達する，着く」　　□ record「記録的な，空前の」

□ low「最低値」　　□ significant「相当な，かなりの」

□ skills「職務能力」ここでは「熟練労働者」という意味で用いられている。

□ shortage「不足」　　□ push「動き／努力」　　□ retain「を保持する」

問5　these prejudices「こうした偏見」の具体的内容は同一の第3段落第3文の調査結果に示されている。したがって，when looking ... their 30s と 65% of ... to go の内容をそれぞれ制限字数内でまとめる。

□ prejudice「偏見」

問6　主節では not only X but also Y「X だけでなく Y も」の not only が SV の前に置かれたことで倒置（疑問文の語順）が起きている。なお，they と them はともに直前の文にある our places of work を指している。

例　Not only did we lose our money, but we were also in danger of losing our lives.

「お金を失っただけでなく命まで落とすところだった」

□ not only X but also Y「X だけでなく Y も」　　□ still「まだ，依然として」

問7　ア．「20世紀になって初めて定年の制度が導入された」第1段落第2文の内容に不一致。

イ．「先進国において高齢の労働者を抱え続けるのは大変不利なことである」第4段落第1・2文の内容に不一致。

ウ．「イギリスでは高齢の労働者を雇う企業に政府が財政面で便宜を図っている」第3段落第5・6文の内容に不一致。

エ．「アメリカの大多数のベビーブーマー世代は65歳以降も働き続けたいと思っ

ている」第5段落第2文の内容に一致。

オ.「定年に対してヨーロッパとアメリカの考え方には大きな違いがある」本文には述べられていないので不一致。

要 約

　少子高齢化に伴い定年についての考え方に変化が起きている。高齢者の雇用が新規採用に比べて経費の面でも経済的であり，65歳以降も働くことを望む高齢者も増えているからだ。(81字)

▶▶ 構文・語句解説 ◀◀◀

─ 第1段落 ─

¹The concept of retirement is a modern one. ²In the 1870s, the German statesman Bismarck introduced 65 as the age at which citizens could stop working and receive a pension. ³This was a humane initiative at a time when work usually meant heavy manual labor and life expectancy was much lower than it is now. ⁴The typical retirement age for men has been set at around 65 in most developed countries since the Second World War. (⁵Though women live longer, their retirement age has generally been set rather lower.) ⁶But in recent years, people have been retiring, willingly or unwillingly, much earlier ─ as young as 50 in some cases ─ mainly because many companies have been trying to reduce the size of their workforce. ⁷Some workers have thus been able to look forward to many years of retirement. ⁸This, however, is about to change. ⁹The reason is the aging of populations.

　¹定年制という考え方は近代的なものである。²1870年代にドイツの政治家ビスマルクが，市民が仕事をやめて年金を受け取れる年齢として65歳を導入した。³これは労働が通常つらい手仕事であり平均余命が現在よりもずっと短かった時代には，配慮に満ちた決定であった。⁴男性の典型的な定年は第二次世界大戦以降ほとんどの先進国でだいたい65歳に設定されている。(⁵女性のほうが長生きだが女性の定年は一般にもっと低い。) ⁶しかし近年，自ら望んでであろうと嫌々ながらであろうと，ずっと早く，場合によっては50歳という若さで退職するようになっている。その主な理由は多くの企業が被雇用者の数を減らそうとしているということである。⁷したがって，一部の労働者は退職後の長い年月を楽しみに待つことができるようになった。⁸しかし，この状況がまさに変わろうとしている。⁹理由は人口の高齢化である。

1 one は concept の代用。

　□ retirement「退職，引退」

38

2 the German statesman と Bismarck は同格の関係。

   □ introduce「〈制度など〉を導入する，〈議案〉を提出する」

   □ receive a pension「年金を受け取る」

3 □ humane「思いやりのある」　　□ initiative「決定／首唱」　　□ manual labor「手仕事」

   □ life expectancy「平均余命」　　□ much＋比較級「はるかに…，ずっと…」

4 □ typical「典型的な」　　□ around A「Aのあたりに，近くに」

5 □ live long「長生きする」

6 willingly or unwillingly は，X or Y「XでもYでも」という譲歩の意味。

   as young as 50 in some cases は，much earlier を具体的に説明し have been retiring を修飾する副詞句。

   □ retire「退職する」　　□ as young as A「Aという若さで」

   □ workforce「被雇用者集団，労働力」

7 □ thus「したがって」　　□ look forward to A「Aを楽しみに待つ」

8 □ be about to *do*「今にも…しようとしている」

───── 第 2 段落 ─────

¹During the twentieth century life expectancies around the world increased by one third. ²Today, a girl born in a developed country can expect to live well into her 80s, and a boy until his early 80s. ³Meanwhile, since the beginning of the 1950s global birth rates have halved. ⁴The populations of developing countries will keep growing for several more decades because of the numbers of young people still to reach childbearing age, but the populations of Europe and the rich countries of Asia will shrink and age. ⁵The main consequence will be an increased burden on workers. ⁶At present in developed countries there are about three workers for every pensioner. ⁷As the babyboomer generation begins to hit retirement age, this ratio will fall dramatically. ⁸By 2030 it is expected to average 1.5 to one, and in Germany and Italy it will be one to one or lower. ⁹A distinguished economist has recently written that "we are confronting such great changes in terms of population that they could redefine economic and political systems in the developed countries over the next generation."

¹20世紀の間に世界全体で平均余命は３分の１延びた。²今日，先進国に生まれた女子は80歳を優に越えて生きることが見込めるし，男子は80代のはじめまでは生きることが見込める。³一方，1950年代初頭以降，世界全体で出生率は２分の１になっている。⁴発展途上国の人口はこれから子供を生み育てる年齢に達する若者の数がまだ多いため，今後さらに数十年増え続けるだ

ろうが，ヨーロッパやアジアの先進国の人口は減少し高齢化するだろう。[5]その主な結果は労働者にかかる負担が増すということだ。[6]現在，先進国では年金受給者 1 人に対して労働者はおよそ 3 人である。[7]ベビーブーマー世代が定年に達し始めるとこの割合は劇的に下がる。[8]2030年までには 1 人の年金生活者に対して労働者は平均1.5人と見込まれている。ドイツやイタリアでは 1 人かそれ以下になるだろう。[9]ある著名な経済学者は最近次のように書いている。「人口という点で我々は現在非常に大きな変化に直面しているので，次世代には先進国の経済や政治の体制が見直されることになる可能性がある」

1 □ increase by A「Aだけ増える」

3 □ meanwhile「一方」　　□ global「全世界の，世界的な」　　□ birth rate「出生率」
　　□ halve「2分の1になる」

4 still to reach childbearing age は young people を修飾する形容詞用法の不定詞句。
　　□ developing country「発展途上国」　　□ keep *doing*「…し続ける」　　□ decade「10年間」
　　□ childbearing「出産」　　□ shrink「減少する」　　□ age「高齢化する」

5 □ consequence「結果」

6 □ at present「現在」　　□ pensioner「年金受給者」

7 □ babyboomer「ベビーブーマー」第 2 次大戦後のベビーブームに生まれた人のこと。
　　□ ratio「割合」　　□ dramatically「劇的に」

8 □ average「平均が…となる」

9 □ distinguished「著名な」　　□ economist「経済学者」　　□ confront「に直面する」
　　□ such ... that～「とても…なので～」　　□ in terms of A「Aの観点から」
　　□ redefine「を再検討する」

- -

---- 第 3 段落 ----

[1]With unemployment in the USA and some European countries hitting near record lows and significant skills shortages in some areas, a strong push to retain older workers is developing. [2]However, this will require big shifts in attitudes among both employees and employers. [3]A recent Australian survey found that, when looking to fill senior management jobs, 60% of companies still preferred people in their 30s, and 65% of companies said employees over 50 would be the first to go. [4]Governments are just beginning to take positive action to counter these prejudices. [5]In Japan, the government is providing financial help to companies to encourage them to retain older workers. [6]In Britain, where early retirement is estimated to cost around $27 billion a year, a major effort is being made to help older unemployed people get back into jobs. [7]The British government minister in charge of employment has declared that age discrimination is "bad for the economy and

unfair to the individual."

---

¹合衆国やいくつかのヨーロッパ諸国の失業率がほぼ過去最低となり，いくつかの分野においては熟練労働者が相当に不足しているため，高齢の労働者を抱えておこうという強力な動きが進んでいる。²しかし，これには被雇用者，雇用者双方の態度に大きな変化を求めることになるだろう。³最近のオーストラリアの調査では，上級管理職に登用しようと努めるとき，今でも企業の60％が30代の人を好んでいること，また企業の65％は50歳を越えた社員がまず退職すべきだと言っていることが明らかになった。⁴こうした偏見を打ち砕く積極的な取り組みを政府はやっと始めたばかりである。⁵日本では，高齢の労働者を抱えておくのを促進するように政府が企業に財政援助をしている。⁶イギリスでは，早期退職が年間270億ドルほどのコストになると推定され，高齢で仕事に就いていない人々が職場に戻れるよう大きな努力が払われている。⁷イギリスの雇用担当の大臣は，年齢差別は「経済にとって悪いものであり，個人にとっては不公正なものだ」と公言している。

2 □ shift「変化」　　□ attitude「態度」

3 When looking＝When they are looking

　□ survey「調査」　　□ be looking to *do*「…しようと努める」

　□ senior management job「上級管理職」ここでの senior は「上位の，首席の」という意味。

　□ in A's 30s「30代の」

4 □ positive「積極的な」　　□ counter「を打ち砕く，に対抗する」

5 □ provide A to B「AをBに与える」　　□ financial「財政上の」

　□ encourage O to *do*「Oに…するように促す」

6 □ estimate O to *do*「Oを…だと推定する」　　□ billion「10億」

　□ help O *do*「Oが…するのを助ける」

7 □ minister「大臣」　　□ in charge of A「Aを担当している」

　□ declare that 節「…だと断言する」　　□ discrimination「差別」

—— 第4段落 ——

¹Some companies are now realizing that getting rid of their older workers was, in fact, a false economy. ²Older workers have lower rates of absenteeism and stay in a job longer, which saves money on recruitment and training. ³Also some companies have discovered that older workers have more respect for their firms' values and traditions. ⁴British Telecom recently became the first company in Britain to raise the retirement age for its workers to 70. ⁵In the Netherlands, where unemployment is at a 20-year low, a job

agency specializing in recruiting workers over the age of 65 is finding that demand for its services is booming.

　　¹企業の中には，高齢の労働者を職場から追い出すのは実際に経費面で間違っている，と実感し始めたところもある。²高齢の労働者は仕事を休む率が低いし，１つの仕事を長く続けるが，これは新しい社員を雇い訓練する費用を削減してくれることになる。³また，高齢の労働者のほうが会社の価値観や伝統を尊重すると気づいた企業もある。⁴ブリティッシュ・テレコムは最近イギリスではじめて社員の定年を70歳に引き上げた。⁵失業率が過去20年間で最低のオランダでは，65歳以上の労働者を専門に就職の斡旋をする会社が，そうしたサービスに対する需要がにわかに増えてきていることを実感している。

1 □ get rid of A「Aを取り除く」　　□ false「誤った」　　□ economy「節約，倹約（の事例）」
2 which は前文の内容全体を補足説明する非制限用法の関係代名詞。
　　□ recruitment「〈社員などの〉新規採用，募集」
3 □ firm「会社」　　□ values「価値観」
4 to raise 以下は the first company を修飾する形容詞用法の不定詞句。
　　□ raise「を引き上げる」
5 □ the Netherlands「オランダ」　　□ be at a 20-year low「過去20年間で最低である」
　　□ job agency「就職斡旋をする会社」　　□ specialize in A「Aを専門にする」
　　□ recruit「を新規採用する」　　□ demand for A「Aに対する需要」
　　□ boom「〈景気・人気などが〉急に沸く，好況になる」

── 第 5 段落 ──

　　¹Not all older people want to be in the workforce, of course. ²But in a survey in the USA, 80% of babyboomers reported that they intended to continue working after they are 65, at least part time. ³Only 13% said they did not ever want to lift a finger again. ⁴The issue is thus not only one of economic efficiency, but also of the health and well-being of the fastest-growing sector of the population. ⁵Though we often complain about them, for most of us, our places of work are where we find conversation, stimulation, friendship — and a reason to get up in the morning. ⁶When we are 65, not only will they still need us, but we will also need them.

¹もちろん高齢者のすべてが働きたいと思っているわけではない。²しかし，合衆国のある調査では，ベビーブーマーの80％は65歳を越えても少なくともパートタイムでも働き続けるつもりだと言っている。³もう何もしたくないという人は13％しかなかった。⁴したがって，問題は経済効率だけの問題ではなく，人口の中で最も急速に数を増している人たちの健康と幸福の問題でもある。⁵しばしば文句を言いはするが，我々のほとんどにとっては，職場は会話や刺激，友情そして朝起きる理由が見つかる場なのだ。⁶我々が65歳になったとき，職場がまだ我々を必要としているだけでなく，我々も職場を必要としていることだろう。

1 Not all ... は部分否定で「すべてが…とは限らない」という意味。

2 at least part time は working を修飾する副詞句。
   □ intend to *do*「…するつもりである」

3 □ not ... lift a finger「何もしない，縦のものを横にもしない」ここでは退職後はたとえパートタイムの仕事であれ二度と仕事をしたくない，ということ。

4 not only one of ... は not only X but also Y の not only が one の前に出た形。Xに当たるのが of economic efficiency, Y に当たるのが of the health ... the population である。
   one は issue の代用。
   □ issue「問題」   □ efficiency「効率」   □ well-being「幸福」   □ sector「部門」

5 where we ... the morning は are の補語となる名詞節。
   □ complain about A「Aについて不平を言う」   □ stimulation「刺激」
   □ reason to *do*「…する理由」

Topic ④　少子高齢化社会

　21世紀に入り，日本や西欧諸国では少子化(decline in the number of birth)が急速に進行し，人口の高齢化(population aging)の最大の要因となっている。総人口に占める65歳以上の人口が7％に達した社会は高齢化社会(aging society)，14％に達した社会は高齢社会(aged society)，21％に達した社会は超高齢社会(super-aged society)と区別される。少子高齢化の進行によって，年金(pension)など社会保障(social security)制度の維持が問題化する中で，高齢労働力の活用は今後の経済社会にとって必須の条件である。定年年齢(retirement age)に達した者の再雇用や，定年年齢の延長などを含めて多様な雇用・勤務形態の開発とともに，大半は健康で自由に使える時間も十分に持っている高齢者に対して価値観の多様化や経済社会の変化に対応した能力開発や再訓練などの実施を推進していくことが緊急の課題である。

AI は人間を凌駕するか

問1　近い将来多くの人々が職を失うという見方と，自動化により新たな仕事が
生まれ誰もが今以上に繁栄し続けるという見方。(55字)

問2　産業革命が始まって以来，機械のせいで1つの職が失われるごとに，少な
くとも1つの新たな職が生み出され，平均生活水準は劇的に高まってきた。

問3　ウ

問4　食品から結婚相手に至るまであらゆることについての私たちの選択は，謎
めいた自由意思ではなく，むしろ一瞬のうちに確率を計算する何十億もの
ニューロンに起因することがわかった。

問5　(5a)　イ. far from　　(5b)　エ. no more than

問6　An AI equipped with the right sensors could do

問7　ウ

▶▶▶　設問解説　◀◀◀

問1　直前の第1段落第2文に「機械学習とロボット工学がほとんどすべての職業を
変えるという点では，だいたい意見が一致している」と述べられ，下線部(1)を
含む第3文では，「しかし」と逆接の副詞で始まり，「相反する見解」があるこ
とが述べられている。続く第4文には「わずか10年か20年のうちに，何十億も
の人々が経済的に余剰人員となると考える人もいる」ことが，また第5文には
「長期的に見ても，自動化が万人に新たな職を生み出し，一層の繁栄をもたらし
続けると主張する人もいる」と，相反する見解が具体的に述べられている。し
たがって，この内容を制限字数内でまとめる。

　　□ conflicting「相反する」　　□ view「見解」

問2　for every ... was created と the average ... increased dramatically という2
つの節が and で結ばれている。前半の for は「～に対して，～につき」とい
う意味。lost to a machine は every job を修飾する過去分詞句。

　　□ the Industrial Revolution「産業革命」　　□ at least「少なくとも」

　　□ create「を生み出す」　　□ average「平均的な」　　□ standard of living「生活水準」

　　□ increase「高まる」　　□ dramatically「劇的に」

問3　下線部(3)は「身体活動の分野と認知活動の分野以外に，人間が常に確実な優位

を保つ第3の活動分野があるのかについてはわからない」という意味。下線部を含む第3段落の最初から文脈をたどると「人間には身体能力と認知能力の2つの能力があり，かつては身体能力の面で機械が人間と競い合っていたが，認知能力では人間が優位を保っていた。だが，自動化が進み，認知技能においても，AIが人間の感情の理解を含めて，人間を凌駕し始めている」と述べられている。したがって，下線部は「人間がAIをしのぐ別の分野があるのか今のところわかっていない」ということになるので，正解はウ。

ア.「AIが身体的および認知能力において人間に勝る能力を持つ，ということを我々は確信できない」

イ.「人間は身体能力と認知能力の両方を使うことで安全な立場にとどまることができる」

ウ.「人間は今のところAIをしのぐことのできる活動分野を見つけていない」

エ.「AIが人間に勝つことのできる活動分野を我々が見つけるのはとても難しい」

□ field of activity「活動分野」　　□ beyond A「Aを超えて」　　□ physical「身体的な」
□ cognitive「認知の」　　□ retain「を保持する」　　□ secure edge「確実な優位」

問4　It turns out that 節は「…だとわかる，判明する」という意味。節内は S result from A「SはAから結果として起こる，Aに起因する」が用いられ，from A の部分に not X but Y「XではなくY」が用いられている。なお，from food to mates は everything を修飾する前置詞句で，that calculate probabilities within a split second は billions of neurons を修飾する関係代名詞節。

□ choice「選択」　　□ mate「結婚相手」　　□ mysterious「謎めいた，不可解な」
□ free will「自由意思」　　□ rather「むしろ」　　□ billions of A「何十億ものA」
□ neuron「ニューロン，神経単位」　　□ calculate「を計算する」　　□ probability「確率」
□ split second「ほんの少しの間」

問5　空所(5a)を含む文は「人間の脳の生化学的アルゴリズムは完璧には（　5a　）こともわかった」という意味。直後の第6・7文には「それは都会のジャングルではなくアフリカのサバンナに適した経験則，近道，時代遅れの回路に頼っている。優秀な運転手，銀行家，弁護士でさえ，ときには愚かな過ちを犯すことがあるのも不思議ではない」と述べられている。したがって，「人間の脳の生化学的アルゴリズムは完璧には程遠い」ことがわかる。正解はイ。

空所(5b)を含む第7段落第2文以降の文脈をたどると，「神が創造した人間の精神がつかさどる感情や欲求をコンピュータが理解できるはずがないのだから，コンピュータが人間の運転手や銀行家に取って代わることはできないと考えら

れていた」と述べられている。空所(5b)を含む文は逆接の Yet で始まり，主節には「コンピュータがこれらのアルゴリズムを解読できず，ましてどんなホモサピエンスよりもはるかにうまくやることができない理由はない」と述べられていることから，「こうした感情と欲求は生化学的アルゴリズム<u>にすぎない</u>」となる。したがって，正解はエ。

ア.「それだけいっそう」　イ.「決して…ない，…には程遠い」　ウ.「いつも」
エ.「…にすぎない」

問6 下線部(6)を含む第8段落第1，2文には「有能な運転手や銀行家は魔法に頼らず，表情，声の調子など様々なものを分析している」ことが述べられている。したがって，「<u>適切なセンサーを備えた AI なら</u>，そのすべてを人間よりはるかに正確かつ確実に<u>行うことができるだろう</u>」という意味の文を作ればよいとわかる。なお，equipped with the right sensors は An AI を修飾する過去分詞句。

□ equip A with B「AにBを備え付ける」　　□ sensor「センサー」

問7 本文では，AI が人間の労働に取って代わる可能性に関して，人間の身体能力に取って代わったこれまでの機械化と同様に，人間の認知能力に取って代わる可能性を指摘している。したがって，正解はウ。

ア.「AI は様々な感情を持ち人間に似たものになるだろう」
イ.「AI は50年したら人間の意思決定のほとんどを管理するだろう」
ウ.「人間は将来，認知面で AI と競うことはできないかもしれない」
エ.「人間は征服されるのを避けるために AI と競う必要がある」

要　約

　これまでの機械化では，機械が人間の身体能力を上回り肉体労働が自動化されたが，認知能力では人間が優位を保ち，認知技能を必要とする新たな職を生み出してきた。しかし，今やAI が認知技能でも人間を凌駕し始めており，神経科学や行動経済学の分野の進歩に伴い，AI は人間の直観に取って代わる可能性がある。(145字)

▶▶ **構文・語句解説** ◀◀

── 第1段落 ──

¹We have no idea what the job market will look like in fifty years. ²It is generally agreed that machine learning and robotics will change almost every line of work — from producing yoghurt to teaching yoga. ³However, there are conflicting views about the nature of the change and its imminence. ⁴Some believe that within a mere decade or two, billions of people will become economically redundant. ⁵Others maintain that even in

the long run, automation will keep generating new jobs and greater prosperity for all.

¹50年後に求人市場がどうなっているのか私たちにはまったくわからない。²機械学習とロボット工学がヨーグルトの生産からヨガのレッスンまでほとんどすべての職業を変えるという点では，だいたい意見が一致している。³しかし，その変化の性質とその切迫の度合については相反する見解がある。⁴わずか10年か20年のうちに，何十億もの人々が経済的に余剰人員となると考える人もいる。⁵長期的に見ても，自動化が万人に新たな職を生み出し，一層の繁栄をもたらし続けると主張する人もいる。

1 □ have no idea「見当もつかない」　　□ job market「求人市場」
　 □ look like A「Aのように見える」
2 It は形式主語で that 以下が真主語。
　 □ generally「一般に」　　□ agree「で意見が一致する」　　□ machine learning「機械学習」
　 □ robotics「ロボット工学」　　□ line of work「仕事，業種」　　□ yoghurt「ヨーグルト」
3 □ the nature of A「Aの性質」
4 □ mere「ほんの，単なる」　　□ decade「10年」　　□ economically「経済的に」
　 □ redundant「余剰な」
5 and は new jobs と greater prosperity を結び，generating の目的語になっている。
　 □ maintain that 節「…と主張する」　　□ in the long run「長期的には」
　 □ automation「自動化」　　□ generate「を生み出す」　　□ prosperity「繁栄」

─── 第2段落 ───

¹So are we on the verge of a terrifying upheaval, or are such forecasts yet another example of ill-founded Luddite hysteria? ²It is hard to say. ³Fears that automation will create massive unemployment go back to the nineteenth century, and so far they have never materialized. ⁴Since the beginning of the Industrial Revolution, for every job lost to a machine, at least one new job was created, and the average standard of living has increased dramatically. ⁵Yet there are good reasons to think that this time it is different, and that machine learning will be a real game changer.

¹それでは我々は恐ろしい大混乱の瀬戸際にいるのだろうか，それともそのような予想は確かな根拠のないラッダイト・ヒステリーのさらにもう１つの例なのだろうか。²それは答えるのが難しい。³自動化が大量の失業者を生み出すという恐怖は19世紀にさかのぼるが，これまでのと

ころ実際に起こってはいない。4産業革命が始まって以来，機械のせいで１つの職が失われるごとに，少なくとも１つの新たな職が生み出され，平均生活水準は劇的に高まってきた。5しかし，今回はこれまでとは違い，機械学習は本当に大変革をもたらすだろうと考えるだけの十分な理由がある。

1 □ on the verge of A「Aの瀬戸際で」　　□ terrifying「恐ろしい」　　□ forecast「予測」
　□ yet another A「さらにもう１つのA」　　□ ill-founded「事実の裏付けのない」
　□ hysteria「ヒステリー」

3 Fears that ... の that 節は Fears と同格の名詞節。
　□ massive「大量の」　　□ unemployment「失業」　　□ go back to A「Aにさかのぼる」
　□ so far「これまでのところ」　　□ materialize「実現する」

5 and は２つの that 節を結び，think の目的語となっている。
　□ game changer「大きな影響を与える革新的な物」

── 第３段落 ──

¹Humans have two types of abilities — physical and cognitive. ²In the past, machines competed with humans mainly in raw physical abilities, while humans retained an immense edge over machines in cognition. ³Hence, as manual jobs in agriculture and industry were automated, new service jobs emerged that required the kind of cognitive skills only humans possessed: learning, analyzing, communicating and, above all, understanding human emotions. ⁴However, AI is now beginning to outperform humans in more and more of these skills, including the understanding of human emotions. ⁵We don't know of any third field of activity — beyond the physical and the cognitive — where humans will always retain a secure edge.

¹人間には身体能力と認知能力の２種類の能力がある。²昔は，機械は主に生身の身体能力で人間と競っていた一方，人間は認知においては機械に対して大きな優位を保っていた。³このため農業や工業における肉体労働が自動化されるにつれて，人間しか持たないような認知技能，すなわち学習，分析，コミュニケーション，そして何より人間の感情の理解を必要とする新しいサービス業が登場した。⁴しかし，今や AI が人間の感情の理解を含め，これらの技能のますます多くにおいて人間を凌駕し始めている。⁵身体活動の分野と認知活動の分野以外に，人間が常に確実な優位を保つ第３の活動分野があるのかについてはわからない。

1 □ humans「人間」

2 □ compete with A「Aと競う」 □ mainly「主に」 □ raw「ありのままの」
□ immense「膨大な，計り知れない」 □ edge over A「Aに対する優位」
□ cognition「認知」

3 that required ... humans possessed は new service jobs を修飾する関係代名詞節。only humans possessed は the kind of cognitive skills を修飾する関係代名詞節。：（コロン）以下は cognitive skills の具体的内容。
□ hence「これゆえに」 □ manual job「肉体労働」 □ agriculture「農業」
□ industry「工業」 □ automate「を自動化する」 □ emerge「現れる」
□ analyze「を分析する」 □ above all「何よりも」 □ emotion「感情」

4 □ AI「人工知能」（＝artificial intelligence） □ outperform「をしのぐ，上回る」
□ including A「Aを含めて」

— 第4段落 —

¹It is crucial to realize that the AI revolution is not just about computers getting faster and smarter. ²It is fueled by breakthroughs in the life sciences and the social sciences as well. ³The better we understand the biochemical mechanisms that form the base for human emotions, desires and choices, the better computers can become at analyzing human behavior, predicting human decisions, and replacing human drivers, bankers and lawyers.

---

¹AI 革命とはコンピュータがより速く賢くなっているということだけではない，と認識することが非常に重要である。²それは生命科学と社会科学の飛躍的進歩によっても加速される。³人間の感情，願望，選択の基礎を形成する生化学的な仕組みについて理解が進めば進むほど，コンピュータは人間の行動を分析し，人間の決定を予測し，人間の運転手，銀行家，弁護士の代わりになるのがうまくなるだろう。

1 It は形式主語で to realize 以下が真主語。computers は動名詞 getting の意味上の主語。
□ crucial「極めて重大な」 □ realize that 節「…だと認識する」 □ smart「賢い」

2 and は the life sciences と the social sciences を結んでいる。as well は前文の not just と呼応して「…だけでなく～もまた」の表現。
□ fuel「に勢いを与える／に給油する」 □ breakthrough「大発見，飛躍的進歩」

3 the＋比較級 ...， the＋比較級～「…すればするほど，ますます～」の表現。that form ... and choices は the biochemical mechanisms を修飾する関係代名詞節。and は analyzing human behavior と predicting human decisions と replacing human drivers, bankers and lawyers の

3つの動名詞句を結んでいる。

□ biochemical「生化学の」　　□ mechanism「仕組み，メカニズム」　　□ form「を形成する」
□ base「基礎」　　□ desire「願望」　　□ behavior「行動」　　□ predict「を予測する」
□ replace「に取って代わる」　　□ banker「銀行家」

第5段落

[1]In the last few decades, research in areas such as neuroscience and behavioral economics have allowed scientists to analyze humans, and in particular to gain a much better understanding of how humans make decisions. [2]It turned out that our choices of everything from food to mates result not from some mysterious free will, but rather from billions of neurons that calculate probabilities within a split second. [3]What we boast about as 'human intuition' is in reality 'pattern recognition'. [4]Good drivers, bankers and lawyers don't have magical intuitions about traffic, investment or negotiation — rather, by recognizing recurring patterns, they spot and try to avoid careless pedestrians, untrustworthy borrowers and dishonest clients. [5]It also turned out that the biochemical algorithms of the human brain are far from perfect. [6]They rely on heuristics, shortcuts and outdated circuits adapted to the African savannah rather than to the urban jungle. [7]No wonder that even good drivers, bankers and lawyers sometimes make stupid mistakes.

---

[1]過去数十年間に，神経科学や行動経済学といった分野の研究のおかげで，科学者は人間を分析し，特に人間がどのように決定を行うのかについて大いに理解が進んだ。[2]食品から結婚相手に至るまであらゆることについての私たちの選択は，謎めいた自由意思ではなく，むしろ一瞬のうちに確率を計算する何十億ものニューロンに起因することがわかった。[3]我々が「人間の直観」として誇りに思うものは，実は「パターン認識」である。[4]優秀な運転手，銀行家，弁護士は，交通，投資，交渉について魔法のような直観が働くのではなく，繰り返し起こるパターンを認識することによって，不注意な歩行者，信用できない借り手，不正直な依頼人を見抜いて避けようとする。[5]人間の脳の生化学的アルゴリズムは完璧には程遠いこともわかった。[6]それは都会のジャングルではなくアフリカのサバンナに適した経験則，近道，時代遅れの回路に頼っている。[7]優秀な運転手，銀行家，弁護士でさえ，ときには愚かな過ちを犯すことがあるのも不思議ではない。

1 2つめの and は to analyze humans と to gain ... make decisions の2つの不定詞句を結んでいる。

□ research「研究」　　□ area「分野」　　□ A such as B「たとえばBのようなA」

□ neuroscience「神経科学」　　　□ behavioral economics「行動経済学」

□ allow O to *do*「Oが…するのを可能にする」　　　□ in particular「特に」

□ gain「を手に入れる」

3 what we boast about as 'human intuition' は is の主語となる名詞節。

　□ boast about A「Aを自慢する」　　　□ intuition「直観」　　　□ in reality「実際は」

　□ pattern recognition「パターン認識」

4 □ magical「魔法のような」　　　□ traffic「交通(量)」　　　□ investment「投資」

　□ negotiation「交渉」　　　□ recognize「を認識する」　　　□ recurring「繰り返し起こる」

　□ spot「を見抜く」　　　□ avoid「を避ける」　　　□ pedestrian「歩行者」

　□ untrustworthy「信用できない」　　　□ client「依頼人」

5 □ biochemical「生化学的な」

　□ algorithm「アルゴリズム／計算や問題を解決するための手順，方式」

6 adapted to ... urban jungle は heuristics, shortcuts and outdated circuits を修飾する過去分詞句。

　□ rely on A「Aに頼る」　　　□ shortcut「近道，手っ取り早い方法」

　□ outdated「時代遅れの」　　　□ circuit「回路」

　□ adapt A to B「AをBに適合させる，合わせる」　　　□ savannah「サバンナ」

　□ X rather than Y「YよりむしろX」　　　□ urban「都会の」　　　□ jungle「ジャングル」

7 □ No wonder that 節「…は不思議ではない」

── 第6段落 ──

　¹This means that AI can outperform humans in tasks that supposedly demand 'intuition'. ²If you think AI needs to compete against the human soul in terms of mystical hunches — that sounds impossible. ³But if AI really needs to compete against neural networks in calculating probabilities and recognizing patterns — that sounds far less difficult.

---

　¹つまり AI は「直観」をおそらく必要とする課題においても人間を凌駕できるということである。²AI が神秘的な勘に関して人間の魂と競う必要があると考えるなら，それは不可能に思われる。³しかし，もし AI が実際に確率の計算とパターンの認識において神経回路と競う必要があるなら，それははるかに簡単なことに思われる。

1 that supposedly demand 'intuition' は tasks を修飾する関係代名詞節。

　□ task「課題，仕事」　　　□ supposedly「おそらく，たぶん」　　　□ demand「を要求する」

2 □ compete against A「Aと競う」　　　□ in terms of A「Aの観点から，Aに関しては」

3 and は calculating probabilities と recognizing patterns の2つの動名詞句を結んでいる。

□ neural network「神経回路」　　□ calculate「を計算する」

□ sound C「Cに思われる」　　□ far＋比較級「はるかに…，ずっと…」

── 第7段落 ──

[1]In particular, AI can be better at jobs that demand intuitions about other people. [2]Many lines of work — such as driving a vehicle in a street full of pedestrians, lending money to strangers, and negotiating a business deal — require the ability to correctly assess the emotions and desires of other people. [3]Is that kid about to jump onto the road? [4]Does the man in the suit intend to take my money and disappear? [5]Will that lawyer act on his threats, or is he just bluffing? [6]As long as it was thought that such emotions and desires were generated by an immaterial spirit, it seemed obvious that computers would never be able to replace human drivers, bankers and lawyers. [7]For how can a computer understand the divinely created human spirit? [8]Yet if these emotions and desires are in fact no more than biochemical algorithms, there is no reason why computers cannot decipher these algorithms — and do so far better than any Homo sapiens.

---

[1]特に，AI のほうが他者についての直観を要求する仕事がうまくできる。[2]多くの仕事──歩行者でいっぱいの通りで車両を運転する，見ず知らずの人にお金を貸す，商取引の交渉をするなど──は他者の感情と欲求を正しく評価する力を必要とする。[3]あの子どもは道路に飛び出そうとしているのか。[4]スーツを着たあの男は私の金を奪って姿をくらますつもりなのか。[5]あの弁護士は脅しをかけるつもりなのか，それともただはったりをかましているだけなのか。[6]そのような感情と欲求は実体のない精神によって生み出されると考えられていた間は，コンピュータが人間の運転手，銀行家，弁護士に取って代わることが決してできないのは明白に思われた。[7]というのも，神が創造した人間の精神をコンピュータが理解できるはずがないのだから。[8]だが，こうした感情と欲求が実は生化学的アルゴリズムにすぎないなら，コンピュータがこれらのアルゴリズムを解読できず，ましてどんなホモサピエンスよりもはるかにうまくやることができない理由はない。

1 that 以下は jobs を修飾する関係代名詞節。

□ be good at A「Aが得意だ」

2 □ vehicle「乗り物」　　□ stranger「見知らぬ人」　　□ negotiate「を交渉する」

□ deal「取引」　　□ assess「を評価する」

3 □ be about to *do*「今にも…しようとしている」

4 □ intend to *do*「…するつもりだ」

5 □ act on A「Aに基づいて行動する」　　□ threat「脅迫」　　□ bluff「はったりをかける」

6 □ as long as S V「…する限り」　　□ immaterial「実体のない」　　□ spirit「精神」

　□ obvious「明らかな」

7 □ divinely「神の力で」

8 why 以下は reason を修飾する関係副詞節。

　□ in fact「実際」　　□ decipher「を解読する，判読する」

　□ Homo sapiens「ホモサピエンス，人類」

── 第8段落 ──

[1]A driver predicting the intentions of a pedestrian, a banker assessing the credibility of a potential borrower, and a lawyer judging the mood at the negotiation table don't rely on witchcraft. [2]Rather, their brains are recognizing biochemical patterns by analyzing facial expressions, tones, hand movements, and even body odors. [3]An AI equipped with the right sensors could do all that far more accurately and reliably than a human.

---

[1]歩行者の意図を予測する運転手，お金を借りるかもしれない人の信頼性を見極める銀行家，交渉の場の雰囲気を判断する弁護士は魔法に頼ったりしない。[2]むしろ，彼らの脳は表情，声の調子，手の動き，さらには体臭さえも分析することによって，生化学的パターンを認識している。[3]適切なセンサーを備えた AI なら，そのすべてを人間よりはるかに正確かつ確実に行うことができるだろう。

---

1 predicting the intentions of a pedestrian は A driver を，assessing the credibility of a potential borrower は a banker を，judging the mood at the negotiation table は a lawyer を修飾する現在分詞句。

　□ credibility「信頼性」　　□ potential「潜在的な」　　□ witchcraft「魔法」

2 □ facial expression「表情」　　□ tone「声の調子」　　□ odor「におい」

3 □ accurately「正確に」　　□ reliably「確実に」

　人工知能(Artificial Intelligence: AI)は，近年急速に発展し，小売り，流通，医療，金融，農業，教育など，様々な分野で活用されている。AI は，人間の労働を支援・代替することで，生産性の向上につながるだけでなく，新たなコンテンツの創造や，既存のコンテンツの改良・拡充にも活用できる可能性がある。他方で，AI が人間の仕事を奪う可能性があることや，AIの判断に偏りや差別が含まれる可能性があること，AI の利用によって個人情報が漏洩するリスク，AI は複雑なシステムであるため，想定外の動作や不具合が発生する問題などが指摘されている。また，AI が人間の知能を凌駕するほどの能力を獲得し，人類のコントロールを逸脱する可能性についても議論されている。AI のメリットを最大限に活かし，デメリットを最小限に抑えるためには，AI の倫理や安全性に関する議論を深め，適切なルールやガイドラインを策定していくことが重要である。

言語の遍在性

問1　ウ. New Guinea had been explored.

問2　ウ

問3　夕暮れになるまでに，彼の驚嘆は警戒へと変わった。なぜなら，遠方に点々と光が見えたからであり，それはその渓谷に人が住んでいる明らかな証拠であった。

問4　1960年代までにニューギニアの高地で発見された800の異なる言語の１つで，抽象的な概念，目に見えないもの，複雑な推論の流れを表現することのできる手段。(73字)

問5　those nearest to me backed away

問6　それ以前に言葉を持たなかった集団に言葉が広まっていくような，言葉の「発祥地」としての役割をある地域が果たしたという記録はない。

問7　The universality of complex language is a discovery that fills linguists

問8　文化によって産み出されたものの洗練度は社会によって異なるが，言語の洗練度は社会の違いに関わらず，ほぼ同じである。(56字)

▶▶▶　設問解説　◀◀◀

問1　下線部(1)は「世界で２番目に大きな島であるニューギニアも例外ではなかった」という意味。前の文に「1920年代まで，人間が住むのに適した場所で踏査されていないところが地球上には一つもない，と考えられていた」と述べられていることから，下線部(1)は「ニューギニアも踏査の例外ではなかった」つまり「ニューギニアも踏査されていた」ということになるので，正解はウ。なお，New Guinea と the world's second largest island は同格の関係。

　　ア.「ニューギニアには居住に適した場所があった」

　　イ.「ニューギニアは踏査されないままになっていた」

　　ウ.「ニューギニアは踏査されていた」

　　エ.「ニューギニアは人間の居住に適していなかった」

　　□ New Guinea「ニューギニア」オーストラリア北方にある大島。

　　□ the second＋最上級「２番目に…な」　　□ exception「例外」

問2　not ... until ～は「～してはじめて…する」という意味の表現なので，下線部(2)

は「大きな川の1つの支流で金が発見されてはじめて，そのベールが剥がされた」という意味になる。「ベールが剥がされる」とは「隠されていたことが明らかになる」ことの比喩である。前の文に「石器時代には数多くの人々がそうした高原に暮らし，4万年もの間，世界から孤立していた」と述べられていることから，ここでの「ベールが剥がされる」は「多数の人が高原で暮らしていたことが一般に知られるようになる」ことである。したがって，正解はウ。

□ veil「ベール」　　□ lift「を上げる」

問3 obvious 以下は points of light in the distance と同格の関係。なお，that 以下は signs と同格の名詞節。

□ by nightfall「夕暮れまでに」　　□ turn to A「Aに変わる」　　□ alarm「警戒（心）」

□ in the distance「遠方に，遠くに」　　□ obvious「明らかな，明白な」

□ sign「証拠，しるし」　　□ valley「渓谷，谷」　　□ be populated「人が住んでいる」

問4 the highlanders は「高地人」という意味で，レイヒーの一行が出会ったニューギニアの高地人のことである。この人たちが話していた言葉は，第1段落②第8文に jabbering「わけのわからないことをまくし立てている」という表現で表されており，さらに第2段落第1文と第3段落第1文でその概要が説明されている。したがって，この2文の内容を制限字数内でまとめる。

問5 下線部(5)の前に When I took off my hat という副詞節があることから，下線部がその主節となると考えられる。選択肢の中で主語となりえるのは those のみであり，述語動詞となりえるのは backed のみである。次に，those はしばしば修飾語を後ろに伴うことに着目し，near to A「Aの近くに」が最上級となった nearest to me「私に最も近い」を those の後ろに置いて those nearest to me「私の最も近くにいる人たち」とすることができる。また文末の in terror「恐怖から」という副詞句に着目すると，前の文で「現地の人がレイヒーたちの外見を恐れていた」と述べられていることから，「レイヒーが帽子をとったときに，レイヒーの最も近くにいた人たちは，恐怖からどんな反応を示したか」を考えればよい。述語動詞を backed away とすると，下線部全体で「私の最も近くにいた人たちが後ずさりした」という意味になり，文脈に適した表現となる。

□ back away「後ずさりする」

問6 that 以下は record と同格の名詞節であり，there is no record that S V ... で「…という記録はない」という意味になる。from which 以下は a "cradle" of language を修飾する関係代名詞節。

□ region「地域」　　□ serve as A「Aの役割を果たす，Aとして機能する」

□ cradle「発祥の地／ゆりかご」　　□ spread to A「Aに広まる」

56

□ previously「以前に」　　□ languageless「言葉を持たない」

問7 下線部(7)を含む文の後半に and is the first reason to suspect that ... という表現があることから，整序部分の主語は and の後ろの is 以下の主語でもあることがわかる。したがって，「言語が文化によって産み出されるものであるだけでなく，人間特有の本能の産物であると考える第1の理由」となるものは何であるのかを考えて，the universality of complex language「複雑な言語が普遍的に存在すること」を主語にする。また，空所の直後に with awe があることから fills linguists with awe の形が確定する。さらに，that を関係代名詞と考えて is a discovery that fills linguists という述部を作れば，and による並列関係も成立する形になる。

□ universality「普遍性」　　□ fill A with B「AをBで満たす」

問8 下線部(8)の ruins this correlation は「この相関関係を破綻させる」という意味。「この相関関係」とは，前の2文で述べられた「文化によって産み出されるものの洗練度と社会との相関関係」を指す。また，下線部の後ろの2文では「言語の洗練度に関しては，社会によって差がない」こと，すなわち前述の「相関関係が破綻している」ことが述べられている。したがって，これらの内容を制限字数内でまとめる。

□ ruin「を崩す，台無しにする」　　□ correlation「相関関係」

要　約

言語はあらゆる社会に存在し，どの言語も抽象的な概念や目に見えないものや複雑な論理を表現することができる。また，言語の洗練度は，文化によって産み出されるその他のものとは異なり，社会の洗練度に影響されることがない。(105字)

▶▶▶ 構文・語句解説 ◀◀◀

— 第1段落① —

¹By the 1920s it was thought that no corner of the earth fit for human habitation had remained unexplored. ²New Guinea, the world's second largest island, was no exception. ³The European missionaries, planters, and administrators clung to its coastal lowlands, convinced that no one could live in the treacherous mountain range that ran in a solid line down the middle of the island. ⁴But the mountains visible from each coast in fact belonged to two ranges, not one, and between them was a mildly warm plateau crossed by many fertile valleys. ⁵A million Stone Age people lived in those highlands, isolated from the rest of the world for forty thousand years. ⁶The veil would not be lifted until gold was discovered in a tributary of one of the main rivers. ⁷The gold rush that followed

attracted many prospectors, including Michael Leahy, an Australian who on May 26, 1930 set out to look for gold in the mountains with a fellow prospector and a group of native lowland people hired as carriers. [8]After climbing the heights, Leahy was amazed to see grassy open country on the other side. [9]By nightfall his amazement turned to alarm, because there were points of light in the distance, obvious signs that the valley was populated. [10]After a sleepless night in which Leahy and his party loaded their weapons and assembled a crude bomb, they made their first contact with the highlanders. [11]The astonishment was mutual. [12]Leahy wrote in his diary:

---

[1]1920年代まで，人間が住むのに適した場所で踏査されていないところが地球上には１つもない，と考えられていた。[2]世界で２番目に大きな島であるニューギニアも例外ではなかった。[3]ヨーロッパの宣教師，大農園主，そして統治者たちは，島の真ん中を切れ目なく走る危険な山脈には誰も住むことができないと確信して，海岸沿いの低地から離れようとしなかった。[4]しかし，それぞれの海岸から見える山々は，実際は１つではなく２つの山脈に属し，その間には温暖な高原があり，たくさんの肥沃な渓谷があった。[5]石器時代には数多くの人々がそうした高原に暮らし，４万年もの間，世界から孤立していた。[6]そのベールが剥がされたのは，大きな川の１つの支流で金が発見されてからだった。[7]その後に起きたゴールドラッシュが多くの探鉱者を引きつけたが，その１人にマイケル・レイヒーがいた。彼はオーストラリア人で，1930年５月26日に，仲間の探鉱者と，運搬人として雇った現地の低地住民の一団とともに，金を探すために山中へと出発した。[8]高地を登りきると，レイヒーは向こう側にある，草の生い茂る広々とした土地を見て驚嘆した。[9]夕暮れになるまでに，彼の驚嘆は警戒へと変わった。なぜなら，遠方に点々と光が見えたからであり，それはその渓谷に人が住んでいる明らかな証拠であった。[10]レイヒーとその一行は，武器に弾を込め粗製の爆弾を組み立てて眠れぬ夜を過ごした後，高地人たちと最初の接触を持った。[11]驚きは双方にあった。[12]レイヒーは日記にこう書いた。

---

1 fit for human habitation は no corner of the earth を修飾する形容詞句。

☐ corner「片隅，辺鄙なところ」　　☐ fit for A「Aに適した」

☐ human habitation「人間による居住」　　☐ remain C「Cのままである」

☐ unexplored「踏査されていない，未踏の」

3 convinced 以下は分詞構文。

☐ missionary「(キリスト教の)宣教師」　　☐ planter「大農園主」

☐ administrator「統治者」　　☐ cling to A「Aにこだわる，しがみつく」

☐ coastal「海岸の，海岸沿いの」　　☐ lowland「低地」

☐ convince O that 節「Oに…ということを確信させる」

58

4 visible from each coast は the mountains を修飾する形容詞句。

and の後ろは between them（副詞句）was(V) a mildly warm plateau(S) という語順になっている。crossed by many fertile valleys は plateau を修飾する過去分詞句。

5 isolated 以下は連続・結果を表す分詞構文。

7 an Australian 以下は Michael Leahy に対する同格的な説明となっている。

第 1 段落②

¹It was a relief when the natives came in sight, the men in front armed with bows and arrows, the women behind bringing stalks of sugarcane. ²When he saw the women, one of the native carriers told me at once that there would be no fight. ³We waved to them to come on, which they did cautiously, stopping every few yards to look us over. ⁴When a few of them finally got up courage to approach, we could see that they were utterly thunderstruck by our appearance. ⁵When I took off my hat, those nearest to me backed away in terror. ⁶One old man came forward with open mouth, and touched me to see if I was real. ⁷Then he knelt down, and rubbed his hands over my bare legs, possibly to find if they were painted, and grabbed me around the knees and hugged them, rubbing his bushy head against me. ⁸The women and children gradually got up courage to approach also, and presently the camp was swarming with the lot of them, all running about and jabbering at once, pointing to everything that was new to them.

¹現地人が見えたときはほっとした。男性は前にいて弓矢で武装し、女性は後ろでサトウキビの茎を運んでいた。²現地の運搬人の1人は、その女性たちを見るとすぐに、戦いにはならないだろう、と私に言った。³私たちが手を振ってこちらに来るよう合図すると、数ヤードごとに立ち止まっては私たちをじろじろ見ながら、彼らは用心深く近づいてきた。⁴その中の数人がついに勇気を振り絞って近寄ってきたとき、私たちの外見にすっかり驚愕していることがわかった。⁵私が帽子を脱ぐと、最も近くにいた人たちが恐怖のために後ずさりした。⁶1人の老人が口をぽかんとあけたまま前に進み、私が本物の人間かどうかを確かめるために私に触れた。⁷そしてひざまずいて、色が塗ってあるのかどうかをおそらくは確かめるためか、私のむき出しの脚に両手をこすりつけ、そして私の膝のあたりをつかんで抱きかかえると、毛がもじゃもじゃした頭をこすりつけてきた。⁸女性と子供もまた、次第に勇気を振り絞って私たちに近づき、まもなく野営地は現地人であふれんばかりになり、走り回ると同時にわけのわからないことをまくし立て、自分たちにとって目新しいものをすべて指した。

1 the men ... and arrows と the women ... of sugarcane は分詞構文。
- □ relief「ほっとさせるもの、安堵感」　□ come in sight「見えてくる、視界に入る」
- □ armed with A「Aで武装して」　□ bow「弓」　□ arrow「矢」　□ stalk「茎、幹」
- □ sugarcane「サトウキビ」

2 □ at once「すぐに／同時に、一斉に」

3 which they did cautiously = and they came on cautiously

stopping 以下は分詞構文。
- □ wave to A to *do*「Aに…するよう手を振る」　□ cautiously「用心深く、慎重に」
- □ look A over「Aをじろじろ見る、調べる」

4 □ get up courage to *do*「勇気を奮い起こして…する」　□ utterly「すっかり、完全に」
- □ thunderstruck「驚愕した／雷に打たれた」　□ appearance「外見、見かけ」

5 □ take A off「A〈身につけているもの〉を脱ぐ、とる」

6 □ with open mouth「口をぽかんと開けて」　□ see if S V ...「…かどうか確かめる」

7 □ kneel down「ひざまずく」　□ rub「をこすりつける」　□ bare「むき出しの、裸の」
- □ possibly「ひょっとすると」　□ find if S V ...「…かどうか確かめる」
- □ grab「をつかむ」　□ hug「を抱く、抱きかかえる」
- □ bushy「毛がもじゃもじゃした、毛むくじゃらの」

8 all running ... to them は分詞構文。
- □ presently「やがて、まもなく」　□ swarm with A「Aでいっぱいになる」
- □ lot「連中、群れ」　□ run about「走り回る」
- □ jabber「早口でわけのわからない言葉をしゃべる」　□ point to A「Aを指さす」

¹That "jabbering" was language — an unfamiliar language, one of eight hundred different ones that would be discovered among the isolated highlanders right up through the 1960s. ²Leahy's first contact repeated a scene that must have taken place hundreds of times in human history, whenever one people first encountered another. ³All of them, as far as we know, already had language. ⁴No mute tribe has ever been discovered, and there is no record that a region has served as a "cradle" of language from which it spread to previously languageless groups.

¹そのように「まくし立てていた」のは言語であった―孤立していた高地人の間で1960年代までに発見されることになる800の異なる言語のうちの１つの，未知の言語だったのだ。²レイヒーの高地人との初めての接触は，人間の歴史の中で，ある民族が別の民族と初めて出会うたびに何百回も起きてきたに違いない場面の繰り返しだった。³私たちの知る限り，そのすべての民族が言葉を持っていた。⁴言葉を持たない部族は今までに一度も発見されたことがなく，それ以前に言葉を持たなかった集団に言葉が広まっていくような，言葉の「発祥地」としての役割をある地域が果たしたという記録はない。

1 an unfamiliar language 以下はダッシュの前の language に関する補足説明となっている。
　□ unfamiliar「耳慣れない，なじみのない」　　□ right up through A「Aまでずっと」
2 □ must have *done*「…したに違いない」
　□ take place「起きる，生じる」　　□ people「〈可算名詞で〉民族」
　□ encounter「と出会う，遭遇する」
3 □ as far as A know「Aが知っている限り」
4 □ mute「無言の，しゃべらない」　　□ tribe「部族」

¹As in every other case, the language spoken by Leahy's hosts turned out to be no mere jabber but a medium that could express abstract concepts, invisible entities, and complex trains of reasoning. ²The highlanders consulted each other intensively, trying to agree upon the nature of the light-skinned beings. ³The leading opinion was that they were ancestors that came back to this world with renewed bodies or other spirits in human form, perhaps one that turned back into skeletons at night. ⁴They agreed upon an empirical test that would settle the matter. ⁵"One of our people hid," recalls one of the

61

highlanders, "and watched them going to excrete. ⁶He came back and said, 'Those men from heaven went to excrete over there.' ⁷Once they had left many men went to take a look. ⁸When they saw that it smelt bad, they said, 'Their skin might be different, but their shit smells bad like ours.'"

¹他のすべての場合と同様に，レイヒーを迎えた人たちが話していた言葉は，単なるわけのわからない言葉などではなく，抽象的な概念，目に見えないもの，複雑な推論の流れを表現することのできる手段であった。²高地人は互いに徹底的に相談し，白い肌の人間の本性について意見をまとめようとしていた。³有力な見解は，新しい肉体でこの世に戻ってきた先祖たちか，または人間の形をした他の霊で，おそらくは夜になると骸骨の姿に戻るものか，というものであった。⁴彼らは問題を解決する実験を行おうという意見で一致した。⁵高地人の1人は次のように回想する。「私たちの部族の1人が身を隠し，彼らが排泄に行くのを見ていた。⁶その男は戻ってきて言った。『天から来た人たちはあそこに排泄しに行った』⁷彼らがその場を離れるやいなや，たくさんの男たちが見に行った。⁸それがひどい臭いがすることがわかると，男たちはこう言った。『彼らの肌の色は私たちと違うかもしれないが，彼らの大便は私たちのと同様にひどい臭いがする』」

1 Leahy's hosts は「レイヒーを迎えてくれた現地人たち」のこと。
　□ as in A「Aにおけるのと同様に」
　□ turn out to be C「（結果として）Cになる，Cだとわかる」
　□ no＋名詞「決して…でない，…どころではない」　　□ medium「手段，媒体」
　□ abstract「抽象的な」　　□ concept「概念」　　□ invisible「目に見えない」
　□ entity「実体，存在物」　　□ complex「複雑な」
　□ a train of A「一連のA，Aのつながり」　　□ reasoning「推論，論証」

2 trying 以下は分詞構文。
　□ consult「に意見を求める」　　□ intensively「徹底的に，激しく」
　□ agree upon A「Aに関して意見が一致する」　　□ the nature of A「Aの本性，本質」
　□ light-skinned「肌の色が白い」　　□ being「存在物，生物」

3 ancestors that ... renewed bodies と other spirits ... at night が or で結ばれている。
perhaps 以下は other spirits の補足説明で，one は a spirit のこと。
　□ leading「主要な，主な」　　□ ancestor「先祖，祖先」
　□ renewed「新しくなった，復活した」　　□ spirit「霊」
　□ in human form「人間の形をした」　　□ turn back into A「Aに戻る」
　□ skeleton「骸骨，骨格」

4 □ empirical「経験的な，実証的な，実験と観察に基づいた」　　□ test「検査，実験」

　□ settle「を解決する」

5 □ recall「を回想する」　　□ watch O *doing*「Oが…しているのを見る」

6 Those men from heaven はレイヒーの一行のことを指す。

　□ heaven「天，天国」

7 □ once S V ...「…するやいなや，いったん…すると」

8 it smelt bad の it はレイヒー一行の排泄物を指す。

　□ shit「大便」

── 第4段落 ──

¹The universality of complex language is a discovery that fills linguists with awe, and is the first reason to suspect that language is not just any cultural invention but the product of a special human instinct. ²Cultural inventions vary widely in their sophistication from society to society; within a society, the inventions are generally at the same level of sophistication. ³Some groups count by carving lines on bone and cook on fires lit by spinning sticks in logs; others use computers and microwave ovens. ⁴Language, however, ruins this correlation. ⁵There are Stone Age societies, but there is no such thing as a Stone Age language. ⁶Early in the last century the anthropological linguist Edward Sapir wrote, "When it comes to linguistic form, Plato walks with the Macedonian swineherd, Confucius with the headhunting savage of Assam."

---

¹複雑な言語が普遍的に存在することは，言語学者を畏敬の念で満たす発見であり，言語が文化によって産み出されるものであるだけでなく，人間特有の本能の産物であると考える第1の理由である。²文化によって産み出されるものは，社会によってその洗練度が大いに異なるが，1つの社会の内部では，一般にその洗練度は同じ水準にある。³骨の表面に線を彫って数を数え，丸木に突き立てた棒切れを回転させて起こした火で料理をする集団もあれば，コンピュータや電子レンジを使う集団もある。⁴ところが，言語はこの相関関係を破綻させている。⁵石器時代の社会は存在するが，石器時代の言語などというものは存在しない。⁶前世紀の初めに人類言語学者のエドワード・サピアはこう書いた。「言語の形態ということになると，プラトンはマケドニアの豚飼いと歩みを共にし，孔子はアッサムの首狩り族と歩みを共にしている」

1 □ awe「畏敬」　　□ suspect that 節「…だと思う」

　□ not just X but Y「XだけでなくYも」　　□ invention「発明（品）」

　□ product「産物／製品」　　□ instinct「本能」

2 □ vary in A from B to B「AはBによって異なる」　　□ sophistication「洗練の度合い」

3 □ carve「を彫る，彫りつける」　　□ lit＜light「〈火〉をつける」　　□ spin「を回転させる」

□ log「丸木，丸太」　　□ microwave oven「電子レンジ」

5 □ there is no such thing as A「Aなどというものはない」

6 When it ... of Assam. は，プラトンや孔子のような思想家が使う言語も，マケドニアの豚飼いやアッサムの首狩り族が使う言語も，洗練度においては違いがないことが walk with A「Aと共に歩む」という比喩を用いて述べたもの。

Confucius with ... ＝ and Confucius walks with ...

□ anthropological linguist「人類言語学者」人類言語学(anthropological linguistics)は言語と文化の関連を研究する言語学の一分野。

□ when it comes to A「Aということになると，Aに関しては」

□ Plato「プラトン」古代ギリシャの哲学者。

□ Macedonian「マケドニアの」マケドニア(Macedonia)はアレクサンダー大王の統治の下に栄えたギリシャ北部の王国。　　□ swineherd「豚飼い」　　□ headhunting savage「首狩り族」

Topic ⑥　言語論

　言語について論じた長文は入試では頻出であり，様々な観点からの言語論が出題されてきたが，代表的なものとしては次のような論考がある。①そもそも人間の言語とは何か，ミツバチのダンスなど人間以外の生物が持つ交信手段と人間の言語とはどのように違うのか，を扱うもの。②どの社会で使われている言語も他のどの社会で使われている言語と比べて優劣がない，という言語の相対性を論じるもの。③最近の認知科学の知見を取り入れながら，思考の手段としての言語を論じるもの。④現実世界の認識のあり方が言語の語彙や文法構造によって決定される，すなわち言語によって現実世界の認識のあり方が基本的に異なる，というサピア・ウォーフの仮説を紹介するもの。⑤人間の子供がどのように母語(mother tongue[language])を習得するのか，という言語習得(language acquisition)について論じるもの。⑥コミュニケーションの手段としての言語という視点から，言語によるコミュニケーション(verbal communication)がジェスチャーなど言語を介在しないコミュニケーション(nonverbal communication)とどのように異なるのかを扱うものなどがある。本問は「言語は世界のあらゆる社会に存在し，そのどれもが抽象的な概念，目に見えないもの，複雑な推論の流れなどを表現することができる，という点で優劣がない」という言語の遍在性および相対性を扱った論考であり，②の論点が基本にある。

英語の将来

解答

問1　イ．A regional language will replace English as an international language.

問2　イ．too limited to produce

問3　エ．the local language

問4　それは，グローバル化に抵抗するだけでなく，グローバル化がこうした歴史的価値体系に対してもたらすと思われる「脅威」によって実際に強められる文化的信念や解釈の核心に相当する。

問5　have there been as many standardized languages as there are

問6　ア．subjective — practical

問7　ほとんど，あるいはまったく正式の教育を受けていない膨大な数の農民に，収穫高を上げるための作物の種のまき方や輪作の方法を教える最善の方法が，こうした地域言語で行うことである

問8　民主主義や国際貿易，経済は何語であっても繁栄するから。（27字）

▶▶▶ 設問解説 ◀◀◀

問1　下線部(1)は「英語がやがて影響力の点で衰えるであろう」という意味。その理由に関しては，第2段落第2文に「言語を支える力の衰退」が，第4文には「英語を使用する者が社会の一部に限られていること」が，第5文には「広域言語の拡大」が，第6文には「地域言語の復興」が挙げられている。したがって，述べられていないものはイである。なお，regional language「広域言語」とは，地理的・社会的・文化的特徴を有する広範囲にわたる地域で使用される言語のことであり，local language「地域言語」とは特定の地域に限られて使用される言語のことである。

ア.「英語の拡大による圧力が地域言語の復興を促す」

イ.「広域言語が国際語として英語に取って代わるであろう」

ウ.「実際に英語を使用しているのは社会の中のほんの一部の人々にすぎない」

エ.「言語はそれを支える力が衰退するにつれて影響力を失うことがある」

オ.「グローバル化によって生まれる交流が広域言語の拡大を促進する」

□ eventually「やがて，結局は」　　□ wane「衰える」

問2　第3段落第1文では「英語の拡大は社会階層，年齢，性差，職業と密接に結び

ついている」ことを述べ，第２文でその具体例として「マドンナの新曲が世界中で歌われても，英語の会話力や理解力の向上には結びついていない」ことが挙げられている。この２つの文内容に矛盾しないように，「たいていの学習者が英語と接する短期間の公教育は，永続的な読み書き能力や会話能力，理解力を生むのに<u>不十分である</u>」という意味になるものを選ぶ。正解イの too limited to produce は too ... to *do*「あまりに…なので〜できない」の構文である。

ア.「を習得するのに充分で」

イ.「を生むにはあまりに限られて」

ウ.「を失うことがないほど集中的で」

エ.「を彼らにもたらすので奨励されて」

問3　空所(3)に入るものは，「正統性の印として強力な象徴的機能」を果たすものである。次の文には「正統性が文化的に理想化された過去から現在へと至る認識された道筋を表すもの」であり，それは「その地域社会の起源と結びついた言語によって伝えられる」とある。したがって，エが正解。

　　ア.「英語」イ.「世界的な言語」ウ.「広域言語」エ.「地域言語」

問4　主語の It は前の文の Authenticity を指し，amount to A は「Aに相当する，等しい」という意味。that are ... historical values は cultural beliefs and interpretations を修飾する関係代名詞節で，節内では not only X but Y「XだけでなくYも」が用いられている。また，that globalization 以下は the "threat" を修飾する関係代名詞節。

　　□ core「核，芯」　　　　□ interpretation「解釈」　　　□ be resistant to A「Aに抵抗する」

　　□ reinforce「を強化する」　　　□ threat「脅威」

　　□ present A to B「AをBにもたらす，引き起こす」　　　□ values「価値体系，価値観」

問5　下線部の直前に never before in history という否定を表す副詞表現があることから，倒置が生じる。また，下線部(5)を含む文が As a result から始まっているので，その前で述べられた「地域住民はグローバル化の脅威に対しては正統性と地域の母語を守る」という内容を原因として，その結果生じることを表す文にしなければならない。したがって，「今日ほど多くの標準化した言語が存在したことは歴史上かつてなかった」という意味の文を作ればよい。

　　□ standardize「を標準化する」

問6　第５・６段落では「local languages が果たす地域ごとの文化的結びつきを確認する機能」について論じられていたのに対し，第７段落では「local languages が果たす実用的な役割」について論じられている。したがって，空所(　6a　)に subjective「主観的な」，(　6b　)に practical「実用的な」を入れると，空所を含む文が「地域的な一体感の主観的な重要性を呼び覚ますことに加えて，地

域言語を奨励する人々は実用的な理由からそれらを使い続けることを擁護する」となり，文脈が自然につながる。

問7 主語の the best way を修飾する形容詞用法の不定詞句内の構造の把握がポイント。teach O_1 O_2「O_1〈人〉に O_2〈こと〉を教える」の O_1 が the vast ... formal education，O_2 が how to ... higher yields である。with little or no formal education は the vast number of farmers を修飾する形容詞句であることに注意。また，sow と rotate が and で結ばれていて，共通する目的語が crops である。したがって，「ほとんど，あるいはまったく正式の教育を受けていない膨大な数の農民に，収穫高を上げるための作物の種のまき方や輪作の方法を教える最善の方法が，こうした地域言語で行うことである」となる。

    □ vast「膨大な」   □ sow「の種をまく」   □ rotate「を輪作する／を回転させる」

    □ crop「作物，農産物」   □ yield「収穫高，産出」

問8 下線部(8)の sink into the sea の文字通りの意味は「海へ沈む」であるが，ここでは「衰退する」という内容の比喩として用いられている。また，if and when S V ... は「もし…する時は」という意味で，that は前の文の its regional ... growth spurts を指しており，下線部は全体として「もし英語と競い合うことになる広域言語がそれぞれ急成長を遂げる時でも，文明が衰退することはないだろう」という意味になる。その理由としては，第8段落第5文に「民主主義や国際貿易，経済発展は何語であっても隆盛を極めるであろう」と述べられている。

要 約

　グローバル化に伴い英語が世界中に広まっている。しかし，英語を実際に使うのは社会の中の恵まれた層にすぎず，広い範囲での相互交流が増大することで広域言語が今後さらに拡大し，グローバル化に抵抗する中で地域言語が復興するであろう。したがって，英語が将来にわたって今日のように必要とされるとは考えにくい。(147字)

▶▶ 構文・語句解説 ◀◀

— 第1段落 —

[1]As you read this sentence, you are one of approximately 1.6 billion people who will use English in some form today. [2]Although English is the mother tongue of only 380 million people, it is the language of the lion's share of the world's books, academic papers, newspapers, and magazines. [3]American radio, television, and blockbuster films export English-language pop culture worldwide. [4]Whether we regard the spread of English as benign globalization or linguistic imperialism, its expansive reach is undeniable.

¹この文を読んでいる以上は，今日何らかの形で英語を使っている概算で16億人の１人だということになる。²英語はわずか３億８千万人の母語であるにもかかわらず，世界的な本や学術論文，新聞，雑誌では最も大きな部分を占める言語である。³アメリカのラジオや，テレビ，そして大ヒット作の映画が，英語による大衆文化を世界中に輸出する。⁴英語の拡大を恵み深いグローバル化と見なそうと，言語による帝国主義と見なそうと，英語が広範囲に及んでいることは否定しようがない。

1 □ approximately「およそ，約」

2 □ mother tongue「母語」　　□ academic papers「学術論文」

3 □ pop culture「大衆文化」

4 □ regard O as C「OをCと見なす」　　□ spread「拡大」　　□ globalization「グローバル化」
　□ linguistic「言語の」　　□ imperialism「帝国主義」　　□ expansive「広範囲の」
　□ reach「範囲，勢力範囲」　　□ undeniable「否定できない」

第2段落

¹Yet professional linguists hesitate to predict far into the future the further globalization of English. ²Historically, languages have risen and fallen with the military, economic, cultural, or religious powers that supported them. ³Beyond the ebb and flow of history, there are other reasons to suppose that the English language will eventually wane in influence. ⁴For one, English actually reaches, and is then utilized by, only a small and atypically fortunate minority. ⁵Furthermore, the kinds of interactions identified with globalization, from trade to communication, have also encouraged regionalization and with it the spread of regional languages. ⁶Finally, the spread of English and regional languages collectively have created pressure on small communities, producing pockets of local-language revival resistant to global change.

---

¹しかしながら，言語の専門家は遠い将来にわたって英語のさらなるグローバル化を予測するのをためらう。²歴史的に見れば，言語はそれを支える軍事的，経済的，文化的，あるいは宗教的力とともに盛衰してきた。³歴史的な盛衰以外に，英語がやがて影響力の点で衰えるであろうと推測する理由が他にもある。⁴１つには，実際に英語に触れ，そして利用するのは，わずかな数の例外的に恵まれた少数の人にすぎない。⁵さらに，貿易から通信に至るまで，グローバル化と同一視されるような相互交流はまた，広域化，そして同時に広域言語の拡大を促してきた。⁶最後に，英語と広域言語の拡大が一緒になって，小規模な地域社会に対する圧力を加え，世界

規模の変化に抵抗する地域言語の復興地域を生み出したのである。

1 the further globalization of English は predict の目的語。

  □ linguist「言語学者」　　□ hesitate to *do*「…するのをためらう」

  □ predict「を予測する」

2 □ rise and fall「盛衰する」　　□ military「軍事の」　　□ religious「宗教的な」

3 □ beyond A「A以外に」　　□ ebb and flow「盛衰」

4 reaches と is then utilized by が and で結ばれていて，only 以下が共通して続いている。

  □ for one「1つには」　　□ utilize「を利用する」　　□ atypically「例外的に，異常に」

  □ minority「少数(派)」

5 □ furthermore「さらに，そのうえ」　　□ interaction「相互交流」

  □ identify A with B「AをBと同一視する」　　□ regionalization「広域化，地域主義」

6 producing 以下は，連続・結果を表す分詞構文。resistant to global change は local-language revival を修飾する形容詞句。

  □ collectively「一緒になって，集合的に」　　□ pocket「〈周囲と異なる〉地域，集団」

  □ revival「復興，復活」

- -

─── 第3段落 ───

[1]Globalization has done little to change the reality that, regardless of location, the spread of English is closely linked to social class, age, gender, and profession. [2]Just because a wide array of young people around the world may be able to sing along to a new Madonna song does not mean that they can hold a simple conversation in English, or even understand what Madonna is saying. [3]The brief formal educational contact that most learners have with English is too limited to produce lasting literacy, fluency, or even comprehension.

[1]グローバル化が進んでも，場所に関係なく，英語の拡大は社会階層，年齢，性差，職業と密接に結びついているという現実が変わることはほとんどなかった。[2]世界中で多くの若者がマドンナの新曲を歌うことができるからといって，簡単な英会話ができるわけでも，ましてマドンナの言っていることを理解することすらできるわけでもない。[3]たいていの学習者が英語と接する短期間の公教育はあまりに限られているため，永続的な読み書き能力や会話能力，理解力さえ生むことはない。

1 that 以下は the reality と同格の名詞節。

□ regardless of A「Aに関係なく」　　□ location「場所，位置」

□ be linked to A「Aと結びついている」　　□ social class「社会階級」

□ gender「性差」社会的，文化的意味づけをされた男女の差異のこと。

2 □ Just because S V ... does not mean that 節「…だからといって～というわけではない」because 節が主語になる口語的表現。同じ意味を Just because S V ..., it does not mean that 節で表すこともできる。

例　Just because I don't complain doesn't mean that I'm satisfied.

「私が不平を言わないからといって，満足しているわけではない」

□ an array of A「多くのA」　　□ Madonna「マドンナ」米国のポップシンガー。

3 □ lasting「永続的な」　　□ literacy「読み書きの能力」　　□ fluency「流暢さ」

□ comprehension「理解力」

第4段落

[1]Indeed, for all the enthusiasm generated by grand-scale globalization, it is the growth in regional interactions — trade, travel, the spread of religions, interethnic marriages — that touches the widest array of local populations. [2]These interactions promote the spread of regional languages. [3]Mandarin Chinese is spreading throughout China and in some of its southern neighbors. [4]Spanish is spreading in the Americas. [5]And Arabic is spreading in North Africa and Southeast Asia both as the language of Islam and as an important language of regional trade. [6]The importance of regional languages should increase steadily in the near future.

[1]実際のところ，大規模なグローバル化によって生まれた熱狂にもかかわらず，地域住民の大多数に影響を及ぼすのは，貿易，移動，宗教の拡大，異民族間の結婚といった，広域内での相互交流の増大なのである。[2]こうした交流が広域言語の拡大を促進する。[3]標準中国語は中国全土と中国南部で国境を接する隣国で広まっている。[4]スペイン語は南北アメリカで広まっている。[5]また，アラビア語は北アフリカと東南アジアで，イスラム教の言語として，また域内貿易のための重要な言語として広まっている。[6]広域言語の重要性は近い将来着実に増加するだろう。

1 it is the growth in regional interactions ... that ～は強調構文。

□ for all A「Aにもかかわらず」　　□ enthusiasm「熱狂」　　□ generate「を生む」

□ grand-scale「大規模な」　　□ interethnic「異民族間の」　　□ touch「に影響を与える」

□ local population「地域住民」（＝locals）

2 □ promote「を促進する」

3 □ Mandarin Chinese「標準中国語」　□ neighbor「隣国」

4 □ the Americas「南北アメリカ」

5 □ Arabic「アラビア語」　□ Islam「イスラム教」

6 □ steadily「着実に」

── 第5段落 ──

¹Even if the end result of globalization is to make the world smaller, its scope seems to foster the need for more intimate local connections among many individuals. ²In most communities, the local language serves a strong symbolic function as a clear mark of "authenticity." ³Authenticity reflects a perceived line from a culturally idealized past to the present, carried by the language and traditions associated with the community's origins. ⁴It amounts to a central core of cultural beliefs and interpretations that are not only resistant to globalization but are actually reinforced by the "threat" that globalization seems to present to these historical values. ⁵Scholars may argue that cultural identities change over time in response to specific reward systems. ⁶But locals often resist such explanations and defend authenticity and local mother tongues against the perceived threat of globalization with near religious ardor.

---

¹たとえグローバル化の最終的な結果が世界をより狭くすることであるとしても，それが及ぶ範囲では，多くの個人の間で地域でのより親密な結びつきに対する必要性が促されると思われる。²たいていの地域社会では，地域言語が「正統性」の明らかな印として強力な象徴的機能を果たしている。³正統性とは，その地域社会の起源と結びついた言語と伝統によって伝えられる，文化的に理想化された過去から現在へと至る認識された道筋を表す。⁴それは，グローバル化に抵抗するだけでなく，グローバル化がこうした歴史的価値体系に対してもたらすと思われる「脅威」によって実際に強められる文化的信念や解釈の核心に相当する。⁵文化的アイデンティティは，特定の報酬体系に応じて時がたてば変化すると学者は主張するかもしれない。⁶しかし，地域住民はしばしばそのような説明には抵抗し，グローバル化の認識された脅威に対しては宗教的ともいえる情熱を持って正統性と地域の母語を守るのである。

1 □ scope「範囲」　□ foster「を促す」　□ intimate「親密な」
　□ connection「結びつき，つながり」

2 □ serve「を果たす」　□ symbolic「象徴的な」　□ mark「印」
　□ authenticity「正統性」

3 carried by the language and traditions associated with the community's origins は a perceived ... the present を修飾し，associated 以下は the language and traditions を修飾する過去分詞句。

☐ reflect「を表す，反映する」　　☐ perceive「を認識する，知覚する」

☐ line「道筋，経路」　　☐ idealize「を理想化する」

☐ associate A with B「AをBと結びつけて考える，AでBを連想する」

5 ☐ scholar「学者」　　☐ in response to A「Aに応じて」　　☐ specific「特定の」

☐ reward system「報酬体系」

6 ☐ resist「に抵抗する」　　☐ defend「を守る」

第6段落

¹As a result, never before in history have there been as many standardized languages as there are today: roughly 1,200. ²Many smaller languages, even those with far fewer than one million speakers, have benefited from state-sponsored or voluntary preservation movements. ³In the Basque, Catalan, and Galician regions of Spain, such movements are fiercely political and frequently involve staunch resistance to the Spanish government over political and linguistic rights.

---

¹その結果，今日ほど多くの標準化した言語が存在したことは歴史上かつてなかった。今ではおよそ1,200も存在するのである。²多くの少数言語は，話し手が100万人を大幅に下回るものでさえ，国家の支援による，あるいは自発的な保存運動から恩恵を受けている。³スペインのバスク，カタロニア，ガリシア地方では，そうした運動は極めて政治的で，しばしば政治や言語の権利をめぐってスペイン政府に対する頑強な抵抗を伴う。

1 ☐ roughly「およそ，概算で」

2 those は languages のこと。

☐ far fewer than + 数詞「…を大幅に下回る」

☐ benefit from A「Aから恩恵を受ける，利益を得る」

☐ state-sponsored「国家の支援による」　　☐ voluntary「自発的な」

☐ preservation「保存，保護」

3 ☐ Basque「バスク語[人]の」バスクはピレネー山脈西部，フランス・スペイン国境にまたがる地方。1960年頃から独立運動が活発化している。バスク語は系統不明の言語。

☐ Catalan「カタロニア語[人]の」カタロニアはスペイン北東部の地方。カタロニア語はスペイン語とともにロマンス諸語の1つ。

72

第7段落

[1]In addition to invoking the subjective importance of local roots, people who encourage local languages defend continuing to use them on practical grounds. [2]Local tongues foster higher levels of school success, higher degrees of participation in local government, more informed citizenship, and better knowledge of one's own culture, history, and faith. [3]Navajo children who were schooled initially in Navajo were found to have higher reading competency in English than those who were first schooled in English. [4]Governments and relief agencies can also use local languages to spread information about industrial and agricultural techniques as well as modern health care to diverse audiences. [5]Development workers in West Africa, for example, have found that the best way to teach the vast number of farmers with little or no formal education how to sow and rotate crops for higher yields is in these local tongues. [6]The world's practical reliance on local languages today is every bit as great as the identity roles these languages fulfill.

[1]地域的な一体感の主観的な重要性を呼び覚ますことに加えて，地域言語を奨励する人々は実用的な理由からそれらを使い続けることを擁護する。[2]地域言語を用いることで，学業がうまくいき，地方自治への参加が高まり，市民として多くの情報が得られ，自らの文化や，歴史，信仰についてよりよく知ることができる。[3]最初にナバホ語で教育を受けたナバホ族の子供は，最初から英語で教育を受けた子供よりも英語の読解力が高いことがわかった。[4]政府や救援機関はまた地域言語を用いて，多様な対象者に対して，最新の健康管理の他に産業や農業技術に関する情報を広めることができる。[5]たとえば，西アフリカの開発事業者は，ほとんど，あるいはまったく正式の教育を受けていない膨大な数の農民に，収穫高を上げるための作物の種のまき方や輪作の方法を教える最善の方法が，こうした地域言語で行うことであることがわかった。[6]今日世界中で実用的に地域言語に頼っていることは，こうした言語が果たすアイデンティティを確認する役割とまったく同じように大きなものである。

3 those who ... の those は Navajo children のこと。

　□ school「を教育する」　　　□ initially「最初に」

　□ reading competency in A「Aでの読解力」

4 □ relief agency「救援機関」　　□ spread A to B「AをBに広める，流布させる」

　□ X as well as Y「XもYも／YだけでなくXも」　　□ health care「健康管理」

　□ diverse「多様な」　　□ audience「(伝達の)対象者」

6 these languages fulfill は the identity roles を修飾する関係代名詞節。

　□ reliance on A「Aに頼ること」　　□ every bit as ... as ～「～とまったく同じくらい…」

　□ fulfill「を果たす」

- -

第8段落

¹What is to become of English?　²There is no reason to assume that English will always be as necessary as it is today, particularly after its regional rivals experience their own growth spurts.　³Civilization will not sink into the sea if and when that happens.　⁴The decline of the use of English around the world does not mean the values associated today with its spread must decline.　⁵Ultimately, democracy, international trade, and economic development can flourish in any tongue.

¹英語はどうなるのであろうか？²特に英語と競い合うことになる広域言語がそれぞれ急成長を遂げた後に，今日と同じくらい英語が常に必要とされると想定する理由はない。³もしそのようなことが起きる時でも，文明が海の藻屑と消えてしまうようなことはないだろう。⁴世界中で英語の使用が衰退したからといって，今日英語の拡大と結びついている価値観も衰退することになるわけではない。⁵究極的には，民主主義や国際貿易，経済発展は何語であっても隆盛を極めるであろう。

1 □ What is to become of A?「Aはどうなるのであろうか」
2 □ rival「競争相手」its regional rivals とは「英語の競争相手となる広域言語」のこと。
4 □ decline「衰退／衰退する」
5 □ ultimately「究極的には，結局のところ」　　□ flourish「繁栄する」

74

　英語について論じた文章はこれまでも数多く出題されてきたが，本問のような主要な国際語 (international　language) としての英語を主題とした文章が近年目立っている。グローバル化 (globalization) の進行と共に，地域主義 (regionalism) が及ぼす影響➡　Topic ①　によって，異なる言語共同体間の共通語として用いられる言語が今後ますます拡大する過程は，同時に地域の文化や伝統を伝える媒体としての言語の保持を促す過程でもある。その一方で，現在世界に存在する言語の9割以上が今世紀中に消滅すると予想されている。言語的多様性の保全は，人類全体の責任として今後ますます重視されることになるであろう。

8 イランでの旅

解 答

問1 ちょうど私たちが一斉に深く息をしようとすると，彼はさらに90度向きを変えてまた通路を歩き始め，私たちを驚かす。今度はいろいろな乗客の肩を軽くたたく。

問2 ア．I hope I will be allowed to remain seated

問3 警備兵がバスを降りると，私はほっとし，彼がもし何かを探しているなら，何を探しているのだろうと思う。

問4 イランでは外国人がわずらわしい思いをすること。(23字)

問5 similar being required for all

問6 ウ. warning me to put a cover on my passport before

問7 イ. I wonder if I've done the right thing

問8 エ. shakes

問9 エ

問10 ウ

▶▶▶ 設問解説 ◀◀◀

問1 surprise O by *doing*「…することによってOを驚かす」の *doing* の位置に，and で結ばれた completing his turn と starting down the aisle again がきている。completing his turn は直訳すれば「回転を完成させる」ということだが，ここでは前の文の makes a half-turn toward the door「ドアの方へと90度向きを変える」を受けて，さらに半分，つまり90度回転して180度の回転をし終えたことを表している。this time to tap 以下の不定詞句は，completing his ... aisle again を修飾する目的を表す副詞用法の不定詞句だが，結果を表すように訳してもよい。

□ just as S V ...「ちょうど…するとき」　　□ collective「集団の，共同の」

□ aisle「〈バス・列車・飛行機などの中の〉通路」

□ tap A on the shoulder「Aの肩を軽くたたく」　　□ passenger「乗客」

問2 would just as soon *do* は「むしろ…したい」という意味の表現で，下線部は「私としてはむしろ自分の席に座っていたい」という意味になる。したがって，正解はア。

□ remain「とどまる」

ア.「座ったままでいることを許してもらえるといいなと思う」

イ.「すぐに私は席に着いて，そこにとどまる」

ウ.「あまり長く席を離れないでいられるといいと思う」

エ.「私は席に着いたままでいようとすぐに決心する」

問3　wondering 以下は付帯状況を表す分詞構文であるが，結果を表すように訳して もよい。if anything は省略を補うと if he is looking for anything であり，「どちらかと言えば」という慣用的な意味ではないことに注意。

　　　□climb out of A「A〈乗り物〉から降りる，Aの外に出る」

問4　下線部(4)は「私が予想していたこと」という意味であり，直前の contrary to A は「Aに反して，Aとは逆で」という意味。下線部(4)の後ろの foreigners are seldom bothered here は contrary to what I had expected の言い換えと考えられるので，下線部は foreigners are seldom bothered here と反対の内容となる。なお，here は，After two months in Iran から，イランを指していることがわかる。

問5　下線部の前の it は my long black raincoat を指している。選択肢の required に着目すると，it 以下は「イランではすべての女性は人前でそれかそれに類似するものが必要とされる」という意味になることが推測できる。something は修飾する形容詞が後ろに置かれることから，it or something similar で「それかそれに類似するもの」という意味をつくることができ，正解は it or something <u>similar being required for all</u> women となる。なお，it or ... in Iran は意味上の主語を伴った分詞構文である。

問6　前の文で「アメリカ合衆国と表紙に印刷されたパスポートを渡す」という内容が述べられており，後ろの文で「遅すぎる」と述べられていることから，ウが正解。

　　　ア.「(イランに入った)後は警備員には反抗しないようにと警告してくれたこと」

　　　イ.「(イランに入る)前に基本的なペルシャ語を少し覚えるようにと助言してくれたこと」

　　　ウ.「(イランに入る)前にパスポートにカバーをつけておくようにと警告してくれたこと」

　　　エ.「(イランに入った)後はパスポートを携帯するのを忘れないようにと助言してくれたこと」

問7　筆者のビザにはジャーナリストと書かれているにもかかわらず，警備兵の「観光客か」という質問に筆者はうなずいている。自らのそのような行為を筆者がどのように思ったかを考える。

ア.「自分がジャーナリストならいいのにと思う」

イ.「自分は正しいことをしたのだろうかと思う」

ウ.「自分があまりにも観光客のように見えるということに気づく」

エ.「英語で tourist と言うべきだったということに気づく」

問8 空所(8)を含む文の前で筆者はスーツケースを開けようとしているが，これに対して警備兵が首をどうするのが自然かを考える。この場面の後で，「スーツケースを開ける」という記述がないことから，筆者がスーツケースを開けようとするのをやめさせるために警備兵は「首を横に振る」と考えるのが自然。なお，通例 shake *one's* head は拒絶・否定などを表す身振り。

問9 下線部(9)は「すると，最初の警備兵が姿勢を正して深呼吸をし，顔を赤らめる」という意味。これは最初の警備兵が緊張して恥ずかしがっている様子を描写したものである。第34段落の内容から，その警備兵がアメリカ人と英語で話すのが初めてであることがその理由である。したがって，正解はエ。

ア.「暑すぎて外には立っていられない」

イ.「彼は以前に女性と話をしたことがない」

ウ.「彼は自分のペルシャ語に強い訛りがあるのを恥ずかしく思っている」

エ.「彼がアメリカ人と英語で話すのはこれが初めてだ」

　□ straighten *one's* shoulder「姿勢を正す」　　　□ blush「顔を赤らめる，赤面する」

問10 ア.「警備兵が筆者のバスに乗り込むと，乗客は驚いて警備兵を見る」第2段落第2文の内容に不一致。

イ.「警備兵が筆者をとても長く引き留めるので，バスは筆者を乗せずに出発する」第31段落第1・2文の内容に関連するが，バスが出発するという記述はないので不一致。

ウ.「筆者以外に，バスに外国人は乗っていない」第5～9段落第8文の内容に一致。

エ.「2番目の警備兵は筆者に流ちょうな英語で話しかける」第33・34段落第4～6文に関連するが，「流ちょうな英語で」とは述べられていないので不一致。

オ.「警備兵は筆者にバスの荷物入れからカバンを出すようにと命令する」第5～9段落第12文の内容に不一致。

要　約

　イランの砂漠を通るバスが検問所で止められ，筆者は2人の警備兵から質問を受ける。警備兵は最初は権威を振りかざす態度だったが，最後に2人とも顔を赤らめて筆者に丁重にあいさつをする。彼らにとって筆者は初めて会うアメリカ人だったのだ。(113字)

▶▶ 構文・語句解説 ◀◀

— 第1段落 —

[1]I am on a bus traveling through the desert between Kerman and Yazd when we pull over to a checkpoint. [2]Checkpoints are common along Iranian highways and I've grown accustomed to stopping every hundred miles or so to watch the driver climb out, papers in hand. [3]Sometimes a guard in a dark green uniform enters the bus and walks up and down the aisle, eyes flicking from side to side, pistol gleaming in the shadowed interior light.

[1]私がケルマンとヤズドの間の砂漠を通って走るバスに乗っていると、検問所で停止する。[2]検問所はイランの幹線道路にはよくあり、百マイルかそこら走るごとに停車して、運転手が書類を手に車を降りていくのを見ることに私は慣れてきた。[3]ときには濃いグリーンの制服を着た警備兵がバスに入り、左右に目をやり、ピストルを暗い室内灯の中でかすかに光らせながら、通路を行ったり来たりする。

1 □ desert「砂漠」　　□ pull over to A「(車を)Aの脇に寄せて止める」
　 □ checkpoint「検問所」

2 papers in hand は「書類を手にして」という意味の付帯状況を表す表現。
　 to watch 以下は結果を表す副詞用法の不定詞句。
　 □ highway「幹線道路」　　□ grow accustomed to *doing*「…することに慣れる」
　 □ every + 数詞 + 複数名詞「…毎に」　　□ 数詞 + or so「…かそこら」
　 □ watch O *do*「Oが…するのを見る」　　□ papers「書類」

3 eyes flicking ... to side と pistol gleaming ... interior light は分詞構文。
　 □ guard「警備兵」　　□ up and down A「Aを行ったり来たりして」
　 □ flick「ぐいと動く、急に動く」　　□ from side to side「左右に、横に」
　 □ gleam「かすかに光る」　　□ shadowed「〈明かりなどが〉暗い」　　□ interior light「室内灯」

— 第2段落 —

[1]This is one of those times. [2]The bus falls silent as a young guard enters, and we all determinedly stare straight ahead, as if by our pretending to ignore the guard, he will ignore us. [3]We listen to his footfalls sound down the Persian carpet that lines the aisle, turn, and come back again. [4]He reaches the front of the bus and makes a half-turn toward the door. [5]But then, just as we begin a collective deep breath, he surprises us by completing his turn and starting down the aisle again, this time to tap various passengers

on the shoulder. ⁶They gather their belongings together and move slowly out of the bus and up the steps of a cement block building.

¹今回もそういったときの１つである。²若い警備兵が入ってくると，バスの中は静まり返り，私たちが彼を無視するふりをすることであたかも彼が私たちを無視してくれるかのように，みな断固としてまっすぐ前を見つめる。³私たちは足音が通路に敷かれたペルシャじゅうたんに沿って行き，向きを変え，また戻ってくるのに耳を傾ける。⁴彼はバスの一番前に着くと，ドアの方へと90度向きを変える。⁵しかしそのとき，ちょうど私たちが一斉に深く息をしようとすると，彼はさらに90度向きを変えてまた通路を歩き始め，私たちを驚かす。今度はいろいろな乗客の肩を軽くたたく。⁶彼らは荷物をまとめてゆっくりとバスから出て，コンクリートブロックの建物の階段を上る。

2 as if S V ... は「まるで…のように」という意味。by our pretending to ignore the guard は he will ignore us を修飾する副詞句。our は動名詞 pretending の意味上の主語。
　□ fall silent「黙り込む」　　□ determinedly「断固として，決然として」
　□ stare (at A)「（Aを）見つめる」　　□ pretend to *do*「…するふりをする」

3 sound down ... the aisle と turn と come back again が and で結ばれている。
　□ listen to O *do*「Oが…するのに耳を傾ける」　　□ footfall「足音／足どり」
　□ line「に沿って敷く，並べる」

4 □ make a half-turn「90度向きを変える」

6 out of the bus と up the steps of a cement block building が and で結ばれている。
　□ gather A together「Aをまとめる」　　□ belongings「持ち物，荷物」
　□ steps「階段」　　□ cement block「コンクリートブロック」

───── 第3・4段落 ─────

¹I sit frozen, hoping that the guard will not notice me and the blond hair sticking out of my *rusari*, or head scarf. ²I've seen guards pull passengers off buses before, and although it never seems to be anything serious — the passengers always return within five or ten minutes — I'd just as soon remain in my seat.

³The guard climbs out of the bus and I relax, wondering what, if anything, he is looking for. ⁴I've been told that these searches are usually about drugs and smuggling, but to me, they seem to be more about the display of power.

¹私は凍りついたように座って，警備兵が私のことと，ルサリ，つまり頭にかぶるスカーフから飛び出しているブロンドの髪には気づかないようにと願っている。²以前に私は警備兵が乗客をバスから引っ張り出すのを見たことがあるが，それはちっともたいしたことには見えないけれども—乗客はいつも5分か10分以内に戻ってくる—私としてはむしろ自分の席に座っていたい。

³警備兵がバスを降りると，私はほっとし，彼がもし何かを探しているなら，何を探しているのだろうと思う。⁴こういった捜索はたいてい麻薬と密輸に関するものだと聞いているが，私にとっては，むしろ権力の誇示に関するもののように思える。

1 hoping 以下は分詞構文。

me と the blond ... head scarf が and で結ばれている。

□ sit frozen「凍りついたように座っている」　　□ stick out of A「Aから突き出ている」

2 □ pull A off B「AをBから離す」

4 □ search「捜索」　　□ drug「麻薬」　　□ smuggling「密輸」

□ display「誇示，見せびらかし」　　□ power「権力」

— 第5〜9段落 —

¹The guard is back, and instinctively, I know why.　²He points to me.

³Me?　⁴I gesture, still not completely convinced that he wants me.　⁵After two months in Iran, I've learned that — contrary to what I had expected — foreigners are seldom bothered here.

⁶You, he nods.

⁷Copying my fellow passengers, I gather my belongings together and stand up.
⁸Everyone is staring at me — as usual, I am the only foreigner on the bus.

⁹I climb out, nearly falling over my long black raincoat — it or something similar being required for all women in public in Iran.　¹⁰My heart is knocking against my chest.
¹¹The guard and one of his colleagues are waiting for me on the steps of the guardhouse.
¹²At their feet is my bag, which they've dragged out of the belly of the bus.　¹³It looks like a fat green watermelon.

---

¹警備兵が戻ってくると，私は本能的にその理由がわかる。²彼は私を指す。
³私？⁴私は身振りでそう伝えるが，彼が私に用があるということをまだ完全には確信できていない。⁵イランに2カ月いて，私は—自分が予想していたのとは裏腹に—外国人はここではめ

ったにわずらわしい思いをしないことを知った。

⁶お前だ，と彼がうなずく。

⁷仲間の乗客にならって，私は身の回りのものをまとめて立ち上がる。⁸みんなが私を見ている。いつものように，私はバスに乗っているただ１人の外国人だ。

⁹私は外に出て，危うく黒の長いレインコートにつまずきかける。イランではすべての女性は人前でそれかそれに類似するものが必要とされる。¹⁰心臓がどきどきしている。¹¹警備兵とその同僚の１人が詰め所の階段のところで私を待っている。¹²彼らの足もとには私のカバンがあり，それはバスの荷物入れから彼らが引っ張り出したものだ。¹³それは丸々とした緑色のスイカのように見える。

1 □ instinctively「本能的に」

2 □ point to A「Aを指さす」

4 still 以下は分詞構文。

　□ convince O that 節「Oに…ということを確信させる」

5 □ bother「をわずらわせる，に迷惑をかける」

6 □ nod「うなずく，首を縦に振る」

7 Copying my fellow passengers は分詞構文。

　□ copy「をまねる」　　□ fellow「仲間の」

8 □ as usual「いつものように」

9 nearly falling ... black raincoat と it or ... in Iran は分詞構文。

　□ fall over A「Aにつまずく」　　□ in public「人前で，公の場で」

10 □ chest「胸」

11 □ colleague「同僚」　　□ guardhouse「警備兵の詰め所」

12 At their feet is my bag は副詞句＋V＋S の語順。

　□ drag A out of B「BからAを引っ張り出す」

　□ belly「〈バスの胴体部分の下にある〉荷物入れ／腹，脇腹」

13 □ watermelon「スイカ」

── 第10〜19段落 ──

¹'Passport,' the young guard barks in Persian.

²I hand him my crisp, dark blue document, suddenly feeling that *United States of America* is printed across the front much too boldly. ³I remember someone back home warning me to put a cover on my passport before entering Iran. ⁴Too late now.

⁵'Visa?'

⁶I show him the appropriate page in my passport.

⁷'Where are you coming from?' ⁸His Persian has a strange accent that I haven't heard before.

⁹'Kerman,' I say.

¹⁰'Where are you going to?'

¹¹'Yazd.'

¹²'Tourist?'

¹³I nod, thinking there's no need to complicate matters by telling him that I'm here in Iran to write a *safarnameh*, the Persian word for travelogue or, literally, 'travel letter.' ¹⁴But then immediately I wonder if I've done the right thing. ¹⁵My visa says *Journalist*.

---

¹「パスポート」とその若い警備兵はペルシャ語でどなる。

²私は彼にピシッとした濃紺の書類を手渡すと，突然「アメリカ合衆国」の文字があまりにもくっきりと大きく表紙に印刷されていると思う。³私は本国で誰かがイランに入る前にパスポートにカバーをつけるようにと注意してくれたのを思い出す。⁴もう遅い。

⁵「ビザは？」

⁶私はパスポートの該当ページを彼に見せる。

⁷「どこから来たんだ？」⁸彼のペルシャ語には私が以前に聞いたことのない強い訛りがある。

⁹「ケルマンです」と私は言う。

¹⁰「どこへ行くんだ」

¹¹「ヤズドです」

¹²「観光客か？」

¹³ペルシャ語で旅行記という意味の safarnameh，文字通りには「旅行の手紙」を書くためにこのイランにいる，などと言って事態を複雑にする必要はないと考え，私はうなずく。¹⁴しかしそのとき急に，自分は正しいことをしたのだろうかと思う。¹⁵私のビザには「ジャーナリスト」と書かれているのだ。

---

1 □ bark「とどなって言う」　　□ Persian「ペルシャ語」

2 suddenly feeling 以下は分詞構文。

　□ hand O₁ O₂「O₁にO₂を手渡す」　　□ crisp「〈紙が〉ピシッとした，手の切れるような」

　□ document「書類」　　□ much too ...「あまりにも…」　　□ boldly「くっきりと」

3 □ remember A *doing*「Aが…したのを覚えている」　　□ back home「故郷にいる，祖国の」

　□ warn O to *do*「Oに…するよう警告する」

4 Too late now. = It is too late now.

5 □ visa「ビザ，査証」

6 □ appropriate「適切な，ふさわしい」

8 □ accent「訛り」

13 thinking 以下は分詞構文。

the Persian ... 'travel letter'は *safarnameh* と同格の関係。

□ there is no need to *do*「…する必要はない」　　□ complicate「を複雑にする」

□ travelogue「旅行記，紀行文」　　□ literally「文字通りには」

14 □ immediately「すぐに，急に」

- -

―― 第20～30段落 ――

[1]Slowly, the young guard flips through the pages of my passport, examining the immigration stamps and the rules and regulations listed in the back. [2]He studies my picture long and hard, and then passes my passport to his unsmiling colleague, who asks me the same questions I've just been asked.

[3]'Where are you coming from?'

[4]'Kerman.'

[5]'Where are you going to?'

[6]'Yazd.'

[7]'Tourist?'

[8]I nod again.　[9]I can't change my answer now.

[10]The second guard hands my passport back to the first, who reluctantly hands it back to me.　[11]I look at his smooth boyish face and wonder if he's old enough to shave.

[12]'Is this your suitcase?' he says, looking at my bag.

[13]'Yes,' I say, and move to open it.

[14]He shakes his head.

[1]ゆっくりと若い警備兵は私のパスポートのページをめくり，入国管理局のスタンプと裏面に載っている規則や規制をチェックする。[2]彼は私の写真を長い間じっくりと見つめ，それから私のパスポートをにこりともしない同僚に渡すと，その同僚は私に今されたばかりのと同じ質問をする。

[3]「どこから来たんだ？」

[4]「ケルマンです」

[5]「どこへ行くんだ？」

[6]「ヤズドです」

[7]「観光客か？」

84

⁸私はまたうなずく。⁹もう答えは変えられない。

¹⁰2番目の警備兵は私のパスポートを最初の警備兵に返すと，彼はしぶしぶそれを私に返す。¹¹私は彼のひげのない少年のような顔を見て，ひげを剃るような年頃なんだろうかと思う。

¹²「これはお前のスーツケースか？」と彼は私のバッグを見ながら言う。

¹³「はい」と私は答え，それを開けようと身体を動かす。

¹⁴彼は首を振る。

1 examining 以下は分詞構文。
　□ flip through A「Aをパラパラとめくる」　　□ immigration「入国管理局」
　□ regulation「規制」
2 □ study「をじろじろと見る」
8 □ nod「うなずく」
10 □ reluctantly「しぶしぶ，いやいやながら」
11 □ smooth「ひげの生えていない，つるりとした」
12 looking 以下は分詞構文。

- 第31段落 -

¹All of the other passengers are now back on the bus, and I wonder how much longer the guards will keep me. ²What will happen, I worry, if the bus leaves without me? ³We're out in the middle of the desert; there are no other buildings in sight. ⁴Hardened dust-white plains, broken only by thin grass, stretch in all directions. ⁵The sky is a pale metallic dome sucking the color and moisture out of the landscape.

¹他の乗客はみな，もうバスに戻っていて，あとどのくらい警備兵は私を引き留めておくのかと思う。²もしバスが私を乗せずに出てしまったらどうなるのだろう，と私は心配する。³私たちは砂漠の真っ只中にいて，他に建物はまったく見えない。⁴地面が固くなった，砂埃で真っ白の平原は，まばらな草地によってところどころ途切れているだけで，四方八方に広がっている。⁵空は，風景から色と水分を吸いとっていく，淡い色をした金属質のドームだ。

2 What will ... without me? ＝I worry, 'What will happen if the bus leaves without me?'
3 □ in sight「視界の中に，目に見えて」
4 broken only by thin grass は分詞構文。
　□ hardened「固い」　　□ dust-white「砂埃で真っ白になった」　　□ plain「平原，平野」

85

□ thin「まばらな」　　□ grass「草原，草地」　　□ stretch「広がる，伸びる」

□ in all directions「四方八方に」

5 □ pale「色の薄い，淡い色の」　　□ metallic「金属質の」　　□ dome「ドーム」

□ suck A out of B「BからAを吸いとる」　　□ moisture「水分」

□ landscape「風景，景色」

― 第32段落 ―

¹Clearing his throat, the first guard stares at me intently. ²His eyes are an unusual smoke blue, framed by long lashes. ³They're the same eyes I've noticed before on more than a few Iranians. ⁴He looks at his colleague and they whisper together. ⁵Sweat is slipping down their foreheads, and down mine.

---

¹咳払いをして，最初の警備兵は私をじっと見る。²彼の目は珍しいスモークブルーで，長いまつ毛で縁取られている。³それは私が以前に何人ものイラン人が持っているのに気づいたのと同じ目だ。⁴彼は同僚に目を向け，2人は小声で話し合う。⁵汗が彼らの額からすべり落ちているし，私の額からもすべり落ちている。

1 clearing his throat は分詞構文。

□ clear *one's* throat「咳払いをする」　　□ intently「熱心に，夢中で」

2 □ smoke blue「スモークブルー，くすんだ青色」　　□ frame「に枠を付ける」

□ lash「まつ毛」

4 □ whisper「ささやく，小声で話す」

5 □ sweat「汗」　　□ slip down A「Aをすべり落ちる」　　□ forehead「額」

― 第33・34段落 ―

¹Then the first guard straightens his shoulders, takes a deep breath, and blushes. ²'Thank you,' he says carefully in stiff, self-conscious English. ³'Nice to meet you.'
⁴'Hello.' ⁵The second guard is now blushing as furiously as the first. ⁶'How are you?' ⁷He falls back into Persian, only some of which I understand. ⁸'We will never forget this day. ⁹You are the first American we have met. ¹⁰Welcome to the Islamic Republic of Iran. ¹¹Go with Allah.'

---

¹すると，最初の警備兵が姿勢を正して深呼吸をし，顔を赤らめる。²「ありがとう」と彼はぎ

こちない，しゃちこばった英語で慎重に言う。³「お会いできてうれしいです」

⁴「こんにちは」⁵ 2番目の警備兵も今は最初の警備兵と同じくらいひどく赤面している。⁶「ご きげんはいかがですか？」⁷彼はペルシャ語に戻り，私にはほんの少ししかわからない。⁸「私た ちはこの日を決して忘れないでしょう。⁹あなたは私たちが出会った初めてのアメリカ人なので す。¹⁰イラン・イスラム共和国へようこそ。¹¹アラーと共にあらんことを」

2 □ stiff「ぎこちない」　　□ self-conscious「内気な，恥ずかしげな」

5 □ furiously「猛烈に」

7 □ fall back into A「Aに戻る／Aまで後退する」

Topic⑧　文化論

　　日本文化論，アメリカ文化論，イギリス文化論，及びこれらの比較文化論は，従来から入試 では最もよく出題されるトピックであったが，これらに加え，近年アジアの文化やアジア諸国 の問題を論じた文章の出題が増加している。本問もアメリカ人によるイランへの旅行記の抜粋 である。この背景としては，アジアがユーラシア大陸の面積の約80％を占め，世界人口の約60 ％を抱えているために，非常に広範で多様な文化を持っていること，またアジアにおけるグ ローバル化(globalization)や地域主義(regionalism) ➤ Topic ① のさらなる進行に伴い，ア ジアの地域間の協力や対立が深まっていること，さらには，中国とインドが今や世界でトップ レベルの経済大国になったことによってアジアからの情報の発信が増加していること，などが 挙げられる。日本というアジアの一国に生きるものとして，多様な文化と複雑な問題を抱えた アジアという地域に対する理解は，今後ますます必要となるであろう。

9　文化と社会

問1　文化は，社会の成員が互いの行動を正しく解釈することを可能にし，彼らの生活に意味を与える共通の要素である。

問2　survival

問3　人間の場合，文化のない社会と社会のない文化はどちらもありえないものだが，他の動物の場合は，文化のない社会が存在できる。(59字)

問4　ウ. not everything

問5　ア. biological differences between the sexes

問6　したがって，生殖に直接関連する違いを除けば，かつて存在していたジェンダーによる役割の違いのどのような生物学的な根拠も，大部分が消えてしまった。

問7　それぞれの文化が独自のやり方で男女の生物学的な差異に意味を与え，男女がお互いと，また世の中全般とどう関わるべきかを決定するから。(64字)

問8　言い換えれば，今日の西洋社会における男性と女性の行動の違いは，人間の生物学的特徴に根ざすものと多くの人が考えているが，実はそのようなものにはまったく根ざしていないのである。

問9　ウ. cultures

問10　大人になる時期は，年齢というよりはむしろ，ある種の確立された儀式を通過することと結びついている。

▶▶▶　設問解説　◀◀◀

問1　主語の it はこの文の冒頭にある Culture を指す代名詞。強調構文の it ではないことに注意。that 以下は the common element を修飾する関係代名詞節。that 節の中では，allows the ... other's actions と gives meaning to their lives が and で結ばれている。

　　□ common「共通の」　　　□ element「要素」

　　□ allow O to *do*「Oが…するのを可能にする」　　　□ interpret「を解釈する」

問2　空所(2)を含む第1段落第4文は「彼らは(　2　)という共通の利害を持ち，共に暮らし働くための技術を開発するであろう」という意味。この文の主語 They は前の文で述べられている「無人島に一定の期間取り残された様々な文

化の人々からなる集団」のことであり，そのような人々が持つ「共通の利害」
とは何かを考える。同じ段落の第５・６文で「この集団は救出されるとすぐに
ばらばらになるが，それは各自がそれぞれの文化を保持していて共通の文化を
持たないから」という内容が述べられ，さらに第７文で「社会とは，生存のた
めに互いに依存するばかりでなく，共通の文化を共有する人々の集団である」
という内容が述べられる。つまり，無人島に残された人々の集団は，社会とし
て成立するための要件である①「生存のために依存し合うこと」と②「共通の
文化を持つこと」の２点のうち，①しか満たしていないことがわかる。したが
って，彼らの共通の利害として考えられるのは「生存(survival)」である。

問3 人間については第２段落第２・３文に述べられており，他の動物については第
２段落第４〜６文に述べられているので，それぞれの内容を制限字数に留意し
てまとめる。

問4 空所(4)を含む文の後ろの文で「まったく同じ型の文化を持つ人はいない」とい
う内容が述べられ，さらに第３文で「文化の内部にさらなる違いが存在する」
という内容が述べられていることから，空所を含む段落全体が「文化を共有し
てはいても，差異がないわけではない」という内容を述べていることがわか
る。したがって，空所に not everything を入れると「すべてが同じというわけ
ではない」という部分否定の意味を表すことになり，文意が通じる。

問5 下線部(5)の them は，同じ文中にある explaining them の them と同様に，
その前にある these differences を指している。この these differences は前の
文の obvious differences between male and female bodies のことなので，正
解はア。
ア.「男女間の生物学的な違い」イ.「男性と女性」ウ.「文化の内部における歴史
的変化」エ.「文化的差異」

問6 文全体は whatever biological ... role differences(S) has disappeared(V) とい
う構造。whatever A (S) V が名詞節になる場合は「…するどんなAも」とい
う意味になり，副詞節になる場合は「たとえどんなAが[を]…しても」という
意味になる。また，directly related to reproduction は differences を修飾する
過去分詞句である。
□ thus「したがって」　　□ apart from A「Aを除けば，A以外に」
□ directly「直接に」　　□ related to A「Aと関連している」
□ reproduction「生殖，繁殖」　□ biological「生物学的な」
□ basis for A「Aの根拠」　□ gender「〈社会的・文化的〉性差」
□ largely「大部分は」

問7 下線部(7)の these は some distinctions of gender roles を指し，下線部全体

は「これら（＝ジェンダーによる役割の違い）は一部の社会においては他の社会よりはるかに大きい」という意味。第3段落第8文にも同じ内容があり，そこではその理由として each culture does this in its own way と述べられている。この does this は第3段落第6・7文の「男女の差異に意味を与え，男女が互いにどう関わり，また世の中全般とどう関わるべきかを決定する」という内容を指しているので，この2文の内容を含めて制限字数に留意してまとめる。

問8 文全体は differences between ... societies today(S), ... , are not so rooted(V) という構造。which are ... human biology は differences between ... societies today を補足説明する非制限用法の関係代名詞節。not so rooted の so は in human biology の代用だが，訳出は「そのように」で構わない。なお，human biology は「人間の生物学的特徴」と意訳するとよい。また，by many の many は名詞で「多くの人々」という意味。
　　□ in other words「言い換えれば」　　□ be thought to *do*「…すると考えられている」
　　□ be rooted in A「Aに根ざしている，Aを起源とする」

問9 空所(9)を含む文は「ここでもまた，年齢の違いは自然なものだが，（　9　）が人間のライフサイクルに独自の意味を与えている」という意味。後ろの2文の「多くの場合，大人になる時期は，年齢というよりはある種の確立された儀式を通過することと結びついている」という内容から，空所には「ある種の確立された儀式を通過すること」を含意する表現が入ると考えられる。また，Again と give their own meaning に着目すれば，第3段落第6文に What every culture does is to give meaning ... とあることから，「ある種の確立された儀式を通過すること」を含意するものが「文化」であることがわかる。したがって，正解はウ。
　　ア.「ジェンダーによる役割」イ.「個人」ウ.「文化」エ.「生物学的な差異」

問10 it は前の文の adulthood を指す。not so much X as Y は「XというよりはむしろY」という意味。一般的には X と Y には同じ働きをするものが入るが，as 以下でも文の SV が明示されることがある。
　　例　What he said was not so much an excuse as it was an apology.
　　　　「彼の発言は弁明というよりはむしろ謝罪だった」
　　□ be tied to A「Aと結びついている」　　□ passage「通過」
　　□ established「確立された」　　□ ritual「儀式」

──── 要　約 ────
　文化とは，社会の成員が共有する一連の理想や価値観，行動基準であり，社会と不可分である。それぞれの文化は独自のやり方で男女間の生物学的な差異に意味を与え，また年齢による

差異にも意味を与えている。（96字）

▶▶ 構文・語句解説 ◀◀

─ 第1段落 ─

¹Culture is a set of shared ideals, values, and standards of behavior; it is the common element that allows the members of a society to correctly interpret each other's actions and gives meaning to their lives. ²Because they share a common culture, people can predict how others are most likely to behave in a certain circumstance and react accordingly. ³A group of people from different cultures, deserted on an uninhabited island for a period of time, might appear to become a sort of society. ⁴They would have a common interest — survival — and would develop techniques for living and working together. ⁵Each of the members of this group, however, would retain his or her own identity and cultural background, and the group would break up easily as soon as its members were rescued from the island. ⁶The group would have been merely a collection of individuals without a unified cultural identity. ⁷Society may be defined as a group of people who not only are dependent on each other for survival but also share a common culture. ⁸How these people depend on each other can be seen in such things as their economic systems and their family relationships; moreover, members of society are held together by a sense of common identity. ⁹The rule-governed relationships that hold a society together, with all their rights, duties, and obligations, are known as its social structure.

¹文化とは一連の共有された理想，価値観，行動基準のことである。それは，社会の成員が互いの行動を正しく解釈することを可能にし，彼らの生活に意味を与える共通の要素である。²人々は共通の文化を持っているので，他人がある状況においてどのように行動する可能性が最も高いかを予測することができ，それに応じて対応することができる。³様々な文化に属する人々の集団が一定の期間無人島に取り残されると，一種の社会となるように見えるかもしれない。⁴彼らは生存という共通の利害を持ち，共に暮らし働くための技術を開発するであろう。⁵しかし，この集団の成員は，それぞれが自分のアイデンティティーと文化的背景を保持しており，その島から救出されるとすぐに集団はばらばらになってしまうだろう。⁶その集団は，統一された文化的アイデンティティーを持たない個人の集まりにすぎなかったのであろう。⁷社会とは，生存のために互いに依存するばかりでなく，共通の文化を共有する人々の集団と定義できるかもしれない。⁸こうした人々がどのように互いに依存しているかは，経済のシステムや家族関係といったものに見ることができる。さらに，社会の成員は共通のアイデンティティーという感覚で結ばれている。⁹ある社会を1つに結びつける，規則に支配された関係は，権利や義務

や責任を伴い，その社会構造として知られている。

1 □ share「を共有する」　　□ ideal「理想」　　□ values「価値観」

2 predict how ... certain circumstance と react accordingly が and で結ばれている。

　□ predict「を予測する」　　□ be likely to *do*「たぶん…するだろう，…する可能性がある」

　□ certain A「あるA」　　□ circumstance「状況」　　□ react「対応する，反応する」

　□ accordingly「それに応じて」

3 deserted on ... of time は分詞構文。

　□ different A「様々なA」　　□ desert「を置き去りにする，見捨てる」

　□ uninhabited island「無人島」

4 □ interest「利害」

5 □ retain「を保持する」　　□ identity「アイデンティティー，自分らしさ」

　□ background「背景」　　□ break up「〈群衆が〉ばらばらになる，解散する」

　□ rescue「を救出する」

6 would have *done* は過去に関する推測を表す。

　□ collection「集まり」　　□ unify「を統一する」

7 □ define O as C「OをCだと定義する」

　□ be dependent on A for B「Bの点でAに依存している」

8 □ moreover「さらに，そのうえ」　　□ hold A together「Aをまとめる，結びつける」

9 □ rule-governed「規則で支配された」　　□ right「権利」　　□ duty「義務」

　□ obligation「責任，責務」　　□ be known as A「Aとして知られている」

── 第2段落 ──

¹Culture and society are two closely related concepts, and anthropologists study both. ²Obviously, there can be no culture without a society, just as there can be no society without individuals. ³Conversely, there are no known human societies that do not exhibit culture. ⁴Some other species of animals, however, do lead a social existence. ⁵Ants and bees, for example, instinctively cooperate in a manner that clearly indicates a degree of social organization, yet this instinctive behavior is not a culture. ⁶One can, therefore, have a society (but not a human society) without a culture, even though one cannot have a culture without a society.

---

¹文化と社会は密接に関係している2つの概念であり，人類学者は両方を研究している。²個人のいない社会がありえないのと同様に，社会のない文化などありえないのは明らかである。

³逆に言えば，知られている人間社会のうちで，文化を持たないものはない。⁴ところが，他の動物種で社会生活を営んでいるものも確かにいる。⁵たとえばアリやミツバチは，明らかにある程度の社会的組織を示すようなやり方で本能的に協力するが，しかしこの本能的な行動は文化ではない。⁶したがって，社会のない文化はありえなくても，文化のない社会（ただし，人間の社会ではない）はありうるのである。

1 ☐ closely「密接に」　　☐ concept「概念」　　☐ anthropologist「人類学者」
2 ☐ obviously「〈文修飾で〉明らかに，言うまでもなく」
3 ☐ conversely「〈文修飾で〉逆に言えば」　　☐ exhibit「を示す，表す」
4 ☐ species「（生物の）種」　　☐ lead a ... existence「…な生活を送る」
5 ☐ instinctively「本能的に」　　☐ cooperate「協力する」　　☐ manner「方法，やり方」
　 ☐ indicate「を示す」　　☐ a degree of A「ある程度のA」　　☐ organization「組織」

── 第3段落 ──

¹While a culture is shared by members of a society, it is important to realize that not everything is uniform. ²For one thing, no one has exactly the same version of his or her culture. ³Beyond such individual variation, however, there is bound to be some further variation within a culture. ⁴At the very least, in any human society, there is some difference between the roles of men and women. ⁵This stems from the fact that women give birth but men do not, and that there are obvious differences between male and female bodies. ⁶What every culture does is to give meaning to these differences by explaining them and deciding what is to be done about them. ⁷Every culture also determines how these two different kinds of people should relate to one another and to the world at large. ⁸Since each culture does this in its own way, there is tremendous variation from one society to another. ⁹Anthropologists use the term "gender" to refer to the cultural systems and meanings assigned to the biological difference between the sexes. ¹⁰Thus, though one's "sex" is biologically determined, one's sexual identity or gender is culturally constructed.

¹文化は社会の成員によって共有されるけれども，すべての点で同じとは限らないということを認識することは大切なことである。²1つには，まったく同じ型の文化を持っている人は誰もいないからである。³ところが，そのような個人差の他に，文化の内部にさらなる違いが必ず存在する。⁴少なくとも，いかなる人間社会においても，男性と女性の役割の間に何らかの違いが存在する。⁵これは，女性は子供を産むが男性は産まないという事実や，男性と女性の身体には

明らかな違いがあるという事実から生じる。⁶すべての文化が行うのは，これらの違いを説明し，それらについて何をすべきかを決定することによって，そうした違いに意味を与えることである。⁷どの文化もまた，この2種類の異なる人々がどのようにお互いと，そして世の中全般と関わっていくべきかを決定する。⁸それぞれの文化が独自の方法でこれを行うので，社会によって大きな違いがある。⁹人類学者は生物学的な性差に割り当てられた文化的な仕組みや意味を表すのに，「ジェンダー」という用語を用いる。¹⁰したがって，人の「性」は生物学的に決定されるが，その人の性に基づくアイデンティティーすなわちジェンダーは，文化的に構築されるのである。

1 □ uniform「同じの／同形の」

2 □ for one thing「1つには」   □ version「型，版」

3 □ beyond A「A 以外に」   □ variation「違い，差」   □ be bound to *do*「必ず…する」

4 □ at the very least「少なくとも」（= at least）

5 that women ... do not と that there ... female bodies が and で結ばれている。これら2つの that 節は the fact と同格の名詞節。

men do not = men do not give birth

□ stem from A「Aから生じる」   □ give birth「子供を産む，出産する」

□ male「男性(の)」   □ female「女性(の)」

7 □ determine「を決定する」   □ relate to A「Aと関係する」   □ A at large「一般の A」

8 □ tremendous「とても大きな」

9 □ term「用語，言葉」   □ refer to A「Aを表す，Aに言及する」

□ assign A to B「AをBに割り当てる」   □ sex「〈生物学的な〉性差，性別」

10 □ construct「を構築する，築く」

────────────────────

第4段落

¹The distinction between sex, which is biological, and gender, which is cultural, is an important one. ²Presumably, gender differences are as old as human culture — about 2.5 million years — and arose from the biological differences between early human males and females. ³Early human males were about twice the size of females, just as males are today among such species as gorillas and orangutans, which are related to humans. ⁴In the course of human evolution, however, the biological differences between the two sexes were radically reduced. ⁵Thus, apart from differences directly related to reproduction, whatever biological basis there once was for gender role differences has largely disappeared. ⁶Nevertheless, cultures have maintained some distinctions of gender roles ever since, although these are far greater in some societies than in others. ⁷Strangely

enough, gender differences were more extreme in late 19th and early 20th century Western societies, where women were expected to submit completely to male authority, than they are among most historically known pre-agricultural peoples whose ways of life resemble those of the late Stone Age ancestors of Western peoples. [8]Among them, relations between men and women tend to be characterized by a spirit of equality, and although they may not typically carry out the same tasks, such arrangements tend to be flexible. [9]In other words, differences between the behavior of men and women in Western societies today, which are thought by many to be rooted in human biology, are not so rooted at all. [10]Rather, they appear to have been recently elaborated in the course of history.

[1]生物学的な性と文化的なジェンダーの間の違いは，重要なものである。[2]おそらく，ジェンダーの違いは人間の文化と同じくらい古くからあり―およそ250万年前から―大昔の男女の生物学的な違いから生じたものである。[3]ゴリラやオランウータンなど人間と同類の種では今日でもそうであるように，大昔の人間の男性は女性の約2倍の大きさであった。[4]ところが，人間の進化の過程で，2つの性の間の生物学的な違いは大幅に縮小した。[5]したがって，生殖に直接関連する違いを除けば，かつて存在していたジェンダーによる役割の違いのどのような生物学的な根拠も，大部分が消えてしまった。[6]にもかかわらず，文化はそれ以降もずっとジェンダーによる役割の違いをいくつか維持してきた。もっとも，一部の社会においては他の社会よりその差がはるかに大きいのであるが。[7]奇妙なことに，生活様式が西洋諸民族の石器時代後期の祖先のものに似ている，歴史上知られている農耕以前の民族のほとんどと比べると，ジェンダーの違いは19世紀後半や20世紀初頭の西洋社会においてより極端であり，そこでは女性が男性の権威に完全に服従することを求められていた。[8]農耕以前の民族の間では，男性と女性の関係は平等の精神で特徴づけられる傾向があり，男女がいつも同じ作業を行うわけではないにせよ，そのような取り決めは柔軟なものである傾向がある。[9]言い換えれば，今日の西洋社会における男性と女性の行動の違いは，人間の生物学的特徴に根ざすものと多くの人が考えているが，実はそのようなものにはまったく根ざしていないのである。[10]むしろ，それは歴史の過程の中で最近になって作り出されたもののようである。

1 □ distinction「違い，差」

2 □ presumably「〈文修飾で〉おそらく…だろう」　　□ arise from A「Aから生じる」

3 just as males are = just as males are about twice the size of females

　□ be twice the size of A「Aの2倍の大きさである」

4 □ in the course of A「Aの過程で，Aの間に」　　□evolution「〈生物学上の〉進化」

　□ radically「根本的に，過激に」

6 □ nevertheless「それにもかかわらず」　　□ ever since「それ以来ずっと」

　□ far + 比較級「はるかに…，ずっと…」

7 those は the ways of life の代用。

　□ strangely enough「〈文修飾で〉奇妙なことに」　　□ extreme「極端な」

　□ be expected to *do*「…することを求められている」　　□ submit to A「Aに従う，服従する」

　□ authority「権威」　　□ pre-agricultural「農耕以前の」　　□ people「〈可算名詞で〉民族」

　□ Stone Age「石器時代（の）」　　□ ancestor「祖先，先祖」

8 Among them の them は most historically known pre-agricultural peoples のこと。

　□ characterize「を特徴づける，の特徴となる」　　□ spirit「精神」

　□ typically「いつもは，通常は」　　□ carry A out「Aを実行する」　　□ task「作業，任務」

　□ arrangement「取り決め」　　□ flexible「柔軟な，融通性のある」

10 □ rather「〈前言を言い直して〉もっと正確に言えば，というよりはむしろ」

　□ elaborate「を念入りに作る，苦心して仕上げる」

・・

──── 第 5 段落 ────

[1]In addition to cultural variation associated with gender, there will also be some related to differences in age.　[2]In any society, children are not expected to behave as adults, and the reverse is equally true.　[3]But then, who is a child and who is an adult?　[4]Again, although the age differences are natural, cultures give their own meaning to the human life cycle.　[5]In the United States, for example, individuals are not regarded as adults until the age of 21; in many others, adulthood begins earlier.　[6]Often, it is not tied so much to age as it is to passage through certain established rituals.

　[1]ジェンダーに関連する文化的差異に加えて，年齢差に関わる違いもある。[2]どんな社会においても，子供は大人として振る舞うようには期待されていないし，その逆も同様に真である。[3]しかしそれなら，誰が子供で誰が大人なのか。[4]ここでもまた，年齢の違いは自然なものだが，文化が人間のライフサイクルに独自の意味を与えている。[5]たとえばアメリカでは，個人は21歳になるまで大人と見なされないが，他の多くの国々では，大人になる時期はもっと早く始まる。[6]多くの場合，大人になる時期は，年齢というよりはむしろ，ある種の確立された儀式を通過することと結びついている。

1 some = some variation

　□ in addition to A「Aに加えて」

　□ associate A with B「AをBと結びつけて考える，AでBを連想する」

2 □ reverse「逆，反対」

5 □ regard O as C「OをCと見なす」　　　□ adulthood「大人の期間」

Topic ⑨　ジェンダー論

　ジェンダー論は，入試でも頻出のトピックである。女性と男性は平等に扱われるべきであるとするフェミニズム(feminism)の立場に加えて，ジェンダー(gender)という概念の導入によって，生殖機能の相違という生物学的な性差(sex)を除いて，「男らしさ」「女らしさ」といった性別役割(sex　role)は社会や文化によって作られたものであり，変化するものであるという認識が広まった。また一方で，ジェンダーはバイナリー(二分法)ではなくスペクトラム(連続体)であるという考え方も浸透してきた。レズビアン(lesbian)，ゲイ(gay)，バイセクシュアル(bisexual)，トランスジェンダー(transgender)の各単語の頭文字を組み合わせた LGBT などが一般的に使われるようになり，自分の性自認や表現を多様な形で表現する人々が社会的に認められるようになってきている。

10　環境と経済

解答

問1　(1a)ア．in opposition to　　(1b)ウ．harmonize

問2　(2a)　イ．worthless　　(2b)　イ．enormous　　(2c)　ア．while
　　　(2d)　ウ．overlooked

問3　低下した自然のサービスと戦うために必要な活動や製品が GDP を増大
　　させるから。(38字)

問4　what if we did put a price tag on

問5　天然資源を除くすべての生態系の資産は，値段をつけるのが困難なので，
　　市場では取り引きをしない，ということ。(52字)

問6　イ．devastate — protect

問7　自然が提供するすべてのもの。(14字)

問8　イ

▶▶▶　**設問解説**　◀◀◀

問1　(1a)at odds with は「と食い違って」という意味の熟語。下線部を含む文の
　　主語 this notion は，前の 2 文の「自然の価値は金銭的には測れない，とい
　　う一般的な考え」を指し，下線部の後ろの the economic system we've
　　created は第 2 段落以降で述べられている「あらゆるものに金銭的価値をつ
　　ける経済システム」であることから，下線部を含む文は「自然の価値は金銭
　　的には測れないという考えは，あらゆるものに金銭的価値をつける経済シス
　　テムとは相容れない」という意味になると推測できる。
　　　ア．「に反対して」イ．「に賛成して」ウ．「と一致して」エ．「と同じくらい重要な」
　　(1b)reconcile A with B は「A と B を調和させる」という意味。第 1・2 段落
　　で「自然の価値は金銭的には測れないという考えは，あらゆるものに金銭的価
　　値をつける私たちの経済システムとは相容れない」と述べられており，それを
　　受けて下線部を含む文では「ではどのようにして私たちは経済と環境を
　　reconcile するのか」と述べている。第 5 段落以降で「自然が提供してくれる
　　サービスにも金銭的価値をつけることで，経済と自然の折り合いをつける」た
　　めの方策が述べられていることから，reconcile は「折り合いをつける，調和さ
　　せる」という意味だと推測できる。

ア.「に適応させる」 イ.「を慰める」 ウ.「を調和させる」 エ.「を扱う」

問2 (2a)空所を含む文は「もし定量化して売ることができないものがあるなら，それは(2a)と見なされる」という意味。前の文で「価値のあるものにはすべて値札が付いている」という内容が述べられていることから，「売ることができないものは価値がない」ことがわかる。したがって，正解はイ。

ア.「優れた」 イ.「価値がない」 ウ.「劣った」 エ.「理解可能な」

(2b)空所を含む文の主語 The group とは，前の文で述べられた「自然の資産に値段をつければ，自然を保護するようになる」と考える ecologists の団体である。この団体の主張として，「コストがどのようになるまで，人類は自然のシステムを傷つけ続けるか」を考えれば，空所には「(コストが)大きい」という意味の形容詞を入れるのが自然である。したがって，正解はイ。

ア.「妥当な」 イ.「莫大な」 ウ.「低い」 エ.「無視できる」

(2c)空所の前の「この会社はその土地の野生の動物や植物を買ったり復元したりしている」という内容は，空所の後ろの「観光事業や野生動物の販売から収益を上げる」という内容とは対比的なので，対比を表すアの while が正解。ここでは，while の後ろに it is が省略されている。

ア.「ところが，一方…」 イ.「…に向かって」 ウ.「…なしで」 エ.「…でない限り」

(2d)空所を含む文の this potential to use natural services は，前の文の buy land ... filter water の内容を指し，それが「最近になって行われるようになった」と述べられているので，最近までそのような可能性がどうされていたのかを考えれば，空所には「見過ごされていた」という意味になるものを入れるのが自然である。したがって，正解はウ。

ア.「実践される」 イ.「試みられる」 ウ.「見過ごされる」 エ.「議論される」

問3 下線部(3)は「環境が不健全になり，生活の質が低下していることが実は経済にとってよいことである」という意味。前の文の「環境改善のための活動や製品，たとえばエアフィルター，ボトル入りの水，目薬や，質が低下したサービスに対処するために私たちが必要とするその他のものはすべて GDP を増加させるが，それを経済学者は成長と呼ぶ」という内容がその理由だと考えられるが，制限字数から，エアフィルターなどの具体例は含めなくてよい。

問4 下線部を含む文の後ろの文の「もし自然のシステムや機能に金銭的な価値を割り振るとしたら，もっとそれらを保護したくなるのだろうか」という内容とのつながりから，「きれいな空気や水などに値札を付けるとしたら，どうなるだろうか」という意味の文を作る。what if S V ... ? は「…するとしたら，どうなるだろうか」という意味で，if 節内には仮定法が用いられることがある。ここでは，動詞強調の助動詞 do が did となって，仮定法過去の形となっている。

例　"What if we moved the sofa over here?"　"Good idea."
　　「ソファをここに移動したらどうだろう」「いい考えね」

問5　後ろの文の「最近，観光や動植物の販売から収入を得ているオーストラリアの環境保護団体が株式市場に上場された」という内容が，下線部を含む文の「しかし，これは変わりつつある」という内容の具体例となっていることから，this は前の文の「天然資源を除いて，こうした資産のほとんどを私たちはすでに利用しているが，値段をつけるのが困難なため市場で取り引きしてはいないこと」という内容を指していることがわかる。なお，「こうした資産(these assets)が指すのは，第5・6段落第5文の all ecosystem assets であることを押さえ，「すべての生態系の資産」と具体的に説明することが必要。

問6　空所を含む文は前の2文で述べられている「カナダでは，森林はそれが提供する木材で主に評価されるが，そのために矛盾が起きている」という内容の具体例となっている。どんなことがその矛盾の例となるのかを考えれば，「法律では守ることになっているはずの河川を，木材搬出用の道路が荒らしている」という内容になるものを選べばよい。したがって，正解はイ。なお，選択肢の devastate は「を荒らす，荒廃させる」expand は「を広げる」という意味。

問7　下線部(7)を含む文は「たぶんそのとき，私たちはそれを当然のものと見なすのをやめるのであろう」という意味。前の文で「少なくとも，生態系のサービスに金銭的価値を割り振れば，私たちは自然が提供するものすべてを厳しい目で見ざるをえなくなるだろう」と述べられているので，私たちは all that nature provides を「厳しい目で見ていない」すなわち「当然のものと思っている」ということである。したがって，it は all that nature provides を指す。

問8　ア．「地球規模の経済は環境にとって破壊的なので，私たちはどんな犠牲を払っても，その成長を妨げなければならない」本文中に該当する記述がないので不一致。
　　イ．「環境を保護するための1つの方法は，そうしなければならないのはとても残念なことではあるが，自然を経済的観点から見ることである」第5段落以降，特に最終段落の内容と一致。
　　ウ．「環境に関わる問題は，私たちの経済システムを犠牲にしてでも取り組まなければならない」本文中に該当する記述がないので不一致。
　　エ．「科学技術は，より低いコストで共同体によりよいサービスを提供することができるので，環境問題を解決してくれるものといつも期待されている」第8段落の内容に関連するが，「科学技術が環境問題を解決すると期待されている」とは述べられていないので不一致。

　自然の価値は金銭的に測ることはできない，と一般に考えられているが，自然を保護していくためには，自然が人間に提供してくれるサービスを正しく評価し，たとえ傲慢に見えても，それに金銭的な価値を割り振ることが重要である。（106字）

▶▶▶ 構文・語句解説 ◀◀◀

── 第1・2段落 ──

¹Many people believe that nature's value cannot be put into dollars and cents. ²That is, they value the natural world for its own sake, regardless of what services or benefits it provides for humans. ³Yet this notion is fundamentally at odds with the economic system we've created.

⁴We live in a world that is increasingly dominated by a global economy, where it is assumed that everything of value has a price tag attached. ⁵If something can't be quantified and sold, it is considered worthless. ⁶The president of a forest company once said to me, "A tree has no value until it's cut down. ⁷Then it adds value to the economy."

　¹多くの人々は自然の価値は金銭に換算することはできないと信じている。²つまり自然界は，人間にどんなサービスや利益を提供しているかに関係なく，それ自体として価値があると考えるのである。³しかし，この考え方は私たちが創り出した経済システムとは基本的に相容れないものである。

　⁴私たちは，地球規模の経済にますます支配されている世界に暮らしていて，そこでは価値のあるものにはすべて値札が付いていると思い込んでいる。⁵もし定量化して売ることができないものがあるなら，それは価値のないものと見なされる。⁶ある林業の会社の社長がかつて私にこう言った。「木は切り倒されるまでは価値がない。⁷切り倒されてから，経済に価値を加えるのだ」

1 □ value「価値／を評価する，尊重する」　　□ put A into B「AをBで表す」

2 □ that is「つまり，すなわち」　　□ for A's own sake「Aそのもののために，A自体として」

　□ regardless of A「Aには関係なく」　　□ benefit「恩恵，利益」

　□ provide A for[to] B「BにAを提供する」（＝provide B with A）

3 □ notion「考え方，概念」　　□ fundamentally「基本的に」

4 □ dominate「を支配する」　　□ global economy「地球規模の経済」

　□ assume「を思い込む，想定する」　　□ of value「価値のある」

101

□ have O *done*「Oを…される」   □ price tag「値札」   □ attach「をくっつける」

5 □ quantify「を量で表す，定量化する」

6 □ forest company「林業の会社」   □ cut A down「Aを切り倒す」

7 □ add A to B「AをBに加える」

- 第3・4段落 -

¹So how do we reconcile our economy with ecology? ²The Earth provides us with essential natural services like air and water purification and climate stability, but these aren't part of our economy because we've always assumed such things are free.

³But natural services are only free when the ecosystems that maintain them are healthy. ⁴Today, with our growing population and increasing demands on ecosystems, we're degrading them more and more. ⁵Unfortunately, remedial activities and products like air filters, bottled water, eye drops and other things we need to combat degraded services all add to the GDP, which economists call growth. ⁶Something is terribly wrong with our economic system when poor environmental health and reduced quality of life are actually good for the economy!

¹それでは，私たちはどのようにして経済と環境の折り合いをつけるのだろうか。²地球は空気や水の浄化，気候の安定性といった必要不可欠な自然のサービスを提供してくれるが，私たちはこれまでずっとそういうものは無料だと思い込んでいたので，それらは経済の一部とはなっていない。

³しかし，自然のサービスが無料なのは，それを維持する生態系が健全なときだけなのである。⁴今日，人口が増加し生態系への負担が高まるにつれ，私たちは生態系をますます傷つけている。⁵残念なことに，環境改善のための活動や製品，たとえばエアフィルター，ボトル入りの水，目薬や，質が低下したサービスに対処するために私たちが必要とするその他のものはすべて GDP を増加させるが，それを経済学者は成長と呼ぶ。⁶環境が不健全になり，生活の質が低下していることが実は経済にとってよいことなら，私たちの経済システムは何かがひどく間違っているのである。

1 □ ecology「環境，生態」

2 □ essential「必要不可欠な」   □ purification「浄化」   □ climate「気候」
   □ stability「安定性」   □ free「無料の」

3 □ ecosystem「生態系」

4 □ demand on A「Aへの要求，負担」   □ degrade「を悪化させる，の質を低下させる」

5 we need to combat degraded services は other things を修飾する関係代名詞節。

　□ unfortunately「残念ながら」　　□ remedial「矯正の，改善のための」

　□ air filter「エアフィルター，空気濾過器」　　□ bottled「ボトルに入った」

　□ eye drop「目薬」　　□ combat「に立ち向かう，と戦う」

　□ add to A「Aを増やす，増加させる」　　□ GDP「国内総生産」（＝gross domestic product）

6 □ something is wrong with A「Aはどこか調子が悪い」　　□ terribly「ひどく」

─ 第5・6段落 ─

[1]But what if we did put a price tag on things like clean air and water? [2]If we assigned a monetary value to natural systems and functions, would we be more inclined to conserve them? [3]Yes, according to an international group of ecologists writing in the latest edition of the journal *Science*.

[4]The group argues that humanity will continue to degrade natural systems until we realize that the costs to repair or replace them are enormous. [5]So we must find a way to place a dollar value on all ecosystem assets — natural resources such as fish or timber, life-support processes such as water purification and pollination, and life-enriching conditions like beauty and recreation.

---

　[1]しかし，もしきれいな空気や水のようなものにほんとうに値札を付けたとしたらどうなるのだろう。[2]もし自然のシステムや機能に金銭的な価値を割り振るとしたら，もっとそれらを保護したくなるのだろうか。[3]サイエンス誌の最新号に記事を書いているある国際的な生態学者のグループによれば，答えはイエスである。

　[4]そのグループは，人類は自然のシステムを修復したり取り替えたりするためのコストが膨大であることを認識するまで，自然のシステムを傷つけることを続けるだろう，と論じている。[5]したがって，私たちはすべての生態系の資産―魚や木材のような天然資源，浄水や授粉のような生命維持のプロセス，そして美しさやレクリエーションのような生活を豊かにする状況―に金銭的価値を置く方法を見つけなければならない。

2 □ assign A to B「AをBに割り当てる」（＝assign B A）　　□ monetary「金銭的な」

　□ be inclined to *do*「…したいと思う」　　□ conserve「を保護する」

3 □ ecologist「生態学者」　　□ latest edition「最新号」　　□ journal「雑誌，専門誌」

4 to repair or replace them は the costs を修飾する形容詞用法の不定詞句。repair と replace が or で結ばれている。　　□ argue that 節「…だと論じる，主張する」　　□ humanity「人類」

　□ replace「を置き換える」

5 ☐ asset「資産」　　☐ natural resources「天然資源」　　☐ timber「木材，材木」

　☐ life-support「生命維持の」　　☐ purification「浄化」　　☐ pollination「授粉」

　☐ life-enriching「生活を豊かにするような」

― 第7段落 ―

　[1]Most of these assets, with the exception of natural resources, we already exploit but do not trade in the marketplace because they are difficult to price. [2]But this is changing. [3]For example, this spring an Australian organization became the first conservation group to be listed on a stock exchange. [4]The company buys and restores native wildlife and vegetation, while earning income from tourism and wildlife sales.

　[1]天然資源を除いて，こうした資産のほとんどを私たちはすでに利用しているが，値段を付けるのが困難なため市場で取り引きしてはいない。[2]しかし，これは変わりつつある。[3]たとえば今年の春，あるオーストラリアの団体が株式市場に上場される最初の環境保護団体となった。[4]この会社は観光事業や野生動物の販売から収益を上げる一方，その土地の野生の動物や植物を買ったり，復元したりしている。

1 Most of these assets は，exploit と trade に共通する目的語が文頭に移動したもの。

　☐ with the exception of A「Aを除いて」　　☐ exploit「を利用する」

　☐ trade「を取り引きする」　　☐ marketplace「市場」　　☐ price「に値段を付ける」

3 ☐ organization「団体，組織」

　☐ conservation group「環境保護団体」　　☐ list「を上場する」

　☐ stock exchange「株式市場，証券取引所」

4 native wildlife and vegetation は buys と restores に共通する目的語。

　☐ restore「を復元する」　　☐ native「その土地の」　　☐ wildlife「野生動物」

　☐ vegetation「植物」　　☐ earn「を稼ぐ」　　☐ tourism「観光事業」

― 第8段落 ―

　[1]In New York City, officials recently decided to buy land around watersheds and let the forest and soil organisms filter water instead of building a massive new filtration plant. [2]Until recently, this potential to use natural services rather than technology to solve problems has been largely overlooked, even though natural approaches may provide greater benefits to communities such as lower costs, reduced flooding and soil erosion and aesthetic benefits.

¹ニューヨーク市では，最近，大規模な濾過工場を新設するかわりに，川の流域の土地を買って森林や土壌に生息する生物に水を濾過させることを決定した。²自然を利用する手段は共同体により低いコスト，洪水や土壌浸食の減少，そして美的な恩恵といったより大きな利益を提供するかもしれないのだが，最近まで，問題解決のために科学技術ではなく自然のサービスを利用するこのような可能性は大部分が見過ごされてきた。

1 buy land around watersheds と let the ... filtration plant が and で結ばれている。

□ official「〈役所の〉役人」　　□ watershed「河川の流域」

□ forest and soil organism「森林や土壌に生息する生物」　　□ filter「を濾過する」

□ instead of *doing*「…する代わりに」　　□ massive「巨大な，大規模な」

□ filtration plant「濾過工場」

2 □ potential to *do*「…する可能性」　　□ X rather than Y「YというよりむしろX」

□ largely「大部分は，ほとんど」　　□ flooding「洪水，河川の氾濫」

□ soil erosion「土壌浸食」　　□ aesthetic「美的な」

第9段落

¹In Canada, forests are primarily valued for the timber they provide. ²But this leads to conflicts. ³For instance, a recent report from the Department of Fisheries and Oceans found that logging roads in British Columbia continue to devastate fish-bearing streams, even though legislation is supposed to protect them. ⁴In fact, our forests provide many services that, if assigned a monetary value, could completely change the way we use them.

¹カナダでは，森林はそれが提供する木材で主に評価される。²しかし，このために矛盾が起きる。³たとえば，漁業海洋省からの最近の報告書によると，ブリティッシュ・コロンビア州の木材搬出用の道路は魚が生息する河川を，法律では保護することになっているにもかかわらず，引き続き荒らしている。⁴実際，私たちの森林は，もし金銭的価値が割り振られれば私たちの利用法がまったく変わるかもしれない様々なサービスを提供している。

1 □ primarily「主に」

2 □ lead to A「Aを引き起こす」　　□ conflict「矛盾，葛藤」

3 □ the Department of Fisheries and Oceans「漁業海洋省」

□ logging road「木材搬出用の道路」

□ fish-bearing stream「魚の生息する小川」名詞の後ろに -bearing を付けると「…を含んだ」とい

う意味の形容詞となる。例 oxygen-bearing water「酸素を含んだ水」　□ legislation「法律」

□ be supposed to *do*「…することになっている」

4 if assigned a monetary value＝if they were assigned a monetary value

□ the way S V ...「…する方法」

── 第10段落 ──

¹As just one species out of perhaps 15 million, the notion of assigning value to everything on Earth solely for its utility to humans may seem like an act of incredible arrogance. ²But the harsh reality of today's world is that money talks and economies are a central preoccupation. ³At the very least, assigning monetary value to ecosystem services may force us to take a hard look at all that nature provides. ⁴Maybe then we'll stop taking it for granted.

---

¹およそ1,500万の生物種のうちのたった１つにすぎないのに，人間にとっての有用性という点からのみ地球上のすべてのものに価値を割り振るという考え方は，信じられないほどの傲慢な行為のように思えるかもしれない。²しかし，今日の世界の厳しい現実としては，金がものを言い，経済性が主要な優先事項の１つとなっているのである。³少なくとも，生態系のサービスに金銭的価値を割り振れば，私たちは自然が提供するものすべてを厳しい目で見ざるをえなくなるだろう。⁴たぶんそのとき，私たちはそれを当然のものと見なすのをやめるのであろう。

1 □ species「(生物の)種」　　□ X out of Y「YのうちのX」　　□ solely「単に，もっぱら」

□ utility to A「Aにとっての有用性，実用性」　　□ incredible「信じられない」

□ arrogance「傲慢さ，尊大さ」

2 □ harsh「厳しい」　　□ reality「現実」

□ money talks「金がものを言う」金銭の威力が絶大であるということ。

□ economies「経済性」　　□ preoccupation「優先事項」

3 □ at the very least「少なくとも」（＝at least）

□ force O to *do*「Oに…することを強要する」

□ take a hard look at A「Aを厳しい目で見る」

4 □ take A for granted「Aを当然のものと思う」

廃棄物(waste)や汚染(pollution)のような地域的な問題から，地球温暖化(global warming)➡
Topic ⑫　　　やオゾン層(ozone layer)の破壊，森林の減少(deforestation)，生物多様性
(biodiversity)の破壊などの地球環境問題に至るまで，今日の環境問題は，人間の経済活動と深
い関連がある。経済成長に伴い，生態系(ecosystem)の一構成要素であるはずの人間の経済活
動の規模が増大し，環境の収容力(carrying capacity)や再生能力を超えることで，環境問題は
深刻化している。環境問題を解決し，環境や資源を保全し，現在と将来の世代の必要をともに
満たすような持続可能な開発(sustainable development)のためには，経済と環境をいかに整合
させるのかが課題である。市場経済の中で環境を金銭的に評価することには困難を伴うもの
の，環境税(environmental tax)を課したり，補助金を出したり，排出権取引➡　**Topic ⑫**
を行ったりすることが有効な手段となる。

光害の様々な影響

解　答

問1　ア

問2　街灯の光が上向きに放射されると，大気中に散乱し，反射し地面を照らす光害。(36字)

問3　エ. negligible — sensitive

問4　人工的な夜空の明るさの下で，岸辺に移動する頻度が下がり，腐りかけの海藻を食べる機会を逃すということ。(50字)

問5　ウ. compass

問6　光害が夜行性の生物に影響するのかどうか，それはいつ，どのようにしてなのかを理解することによってはじめて，私たちはその影響を和らげる方法を見つけることができるのだ。

▶▶▶ **設問解説** ◀◀◀

問1　下線部は「夜間の光はさらに深刻な影響を及ぼしている」という意味。直後の第1段落第5文に「人間」への影響が述べられ，続く第6文以降に「人間以外の生物」への影響が述べられている。具体的には，第7文に「フンコロガシ」について，第2段落第2文に「クマノミ」，続く第3文に「他の魚」について述べられているので，正解はア。

　　ア.「コウモリは蛾を食べているとき，うまく捕食動物から逃れられない」

　　イ.「クマノミは夜間に繁殖する際に問題を経験する」

　　ウ.「フンコロガシは混乱してどこに行くべきかわからなくなる」

　　エ.「魚は自分を捕食する他の魚によって食べられる危険性が高くなる」

　　□ effect「影響」

問2　下線部(2)を含む文の前半は「このような形態の光害は人工的な夜空の明るさとして知られている」という意味。したがって，「このような形態の光害」を答えればよい。下線部を含む第3段落第1文に「街灯の光が上向きに放射されると，大気中に散乱し，反射し地面を照らす」と述べられているので，この内容をまとめる。

　　□ artificial「人工の」　　　□ skyglow「(光害による)夜空の明るさ」

問3　空所(3a)を含む文の前半に「人間は夜間に物を見ることにはうまく順応してい

ない」と述べられているので,「人間への夜空の明るさの影響は<u>無視できるほど
のもの</u>」となることがわかる。続く空所(3b)を含む文は But で始まっているこ
とから「海や海岸の生物の多くは影響に<u>敏感である</u>」とわかる。したがって,
正解はエ。

ア.「魅力的な」──「鈍感な」イ.「取るに足らない」──「抵抗力のある」

ウ.「目に見えない」──「引きつけられて」エ.「無視できるほどの」──「敏感な」

問4 研究方法として,下線部(4)を含む文の前の第4段落で「夜間に餌を探して動き
回る道しるべとして月を利用する」ハマトビムシを使ったことが,また下線部
(4)を含む文では,「人工的な夜空の明るさの影響を再現」したことが述べられて
いる。研究結果については,第5段落第2・3文に「満月と比べて,人工的な
明るさの下では,動きが不規則になった」とあり,さらに第6段落第1文に
「移動する頻度が下がり,餌を食べる機会を逃すことになった」と述べられてい
る。設問の指示に「具体的に」とあるので,「どこに移動するのか」については
第5段落第2文 migrate towards the shore から,「何を食べるのか」につい
ては第4段落第3文 feed on rotting seaweed から補って答えること。

☐ study「研究」

問5 空所(5)を含む文の直前の第6段落第2文に「ハマトビムシが迷わず進むために
月を利用する」と述べられていることから,「月や星を<u>羅針盤</u>として使う」こと
がわかる。したがって,正解はウ。

ア.「双眼鏡」イ.「磁石」ウ.「羅針盤」エ.「望遠鏡」

問6 only のついた副詞句が文頭に出ているため倒置が起きている。and は if,
when, how を結び,if, when, and how light pollution affects nocturnal life
が understanding の目的語となる名詞節。なお,only + 副詞(句・節)は「…し
てはじめて,…してようやく」と意味を取るとよい。

☐ light pollution「光害」　　　☐ affect「に影響を与える」　　　☐ nocturnal「夜行性の」

☐ moderate「を和らげる」　　　☐ impact「影響」

要　約

現在,夜空はますます明るくなっており,世界各地で見られる光害は,人間だけでなく夜行
性の生物に少なからぬ影響を与えている。我々は生態系への光害の影響を理解し,和らげる対
策を早急に講じる必要がある。(97字)

― 第 1 段落 ―

¹Electric light is transforming our world. ²Around 80% of the global population now lives in places where night skies are polluted with artificial light. ³A third of humanity can no longer see the Milky Way. ⁴But light at night has deeper effects. ⁵In humans, nocturnal light pollution has been linked to sleep disorders, depression, obesity and even some types of cancer. ⁶Studies have shown that nocturnal animals modify their behavior even with slight changes in night-time light levels. ⁷Dung beetles become disoriented when navigating landscapes if light pollution prevents them from seeing the stars. ⁸Light can also change how species interact with each other. ⁹Insects such as moths are more vulnerable to being eaten by bats when light reduces how effective they are at evading predators.

¹電気による光は私たちの世界を変えつつある。²世界の人口の約80％が，今では夜空が人工の光で汚染されている場所に住んでいる。³人類の3分の1はもはや天の川を見ることはできない。⁴しかし，夜間の光はさらに深刻な影響を及ぼしている。⁵人間の場合，夜間の光害は睡眠障害，うつ病，肥満，さらには一部の種類のガンとも関連づけられてきた。⁶研究によると，夜行性の動物は夜間の光のレベルがわずかに変化しただけでも行動を変えることがわかっている。⁷フンコロガシは，光害によって星が見えなくなると，あたりを移動する際に方向感覚を失ってしまう。⁸光はまた，生物種の間の相互作用の仕方も変えてしまうことがある。⁹蛾のような昆虫は，光のせいで捕食動物から逃れることがうまくできなくなると，コウモリに食べられる恐れが高まるのだ。

1 □ electric light「電気による光」　　□ transform「を変える」

2 where 以下は places を修飾する関係副詞節。

　　□ around + 数詞「約…」　　□ global「世界の」　　□ population「人口」

　　□ pollute「を汚染する」

3 □ a third of A「Aの3分の1」　　□ humanity「人類」　　□ no longer「もはや…ない」

　　□ the Milky Way「銀河，天の川」

5 and は sleep disorders，depression，obesity，even some types of cancer を結んでいる。

　　□ humans「人間」　　□ be linked to A「Aと関連している」

　　□ sleep disorder「睡眠障害」　　□ depression「うつ（病）」　　□ obesity「肥満」

　　□ cancer「ガン」

6 □ modify「を変える，修正する」　　□ behavior「行動」　　□ slight「わずかな」

7 when navigating＝when they are navigating

　□ disoriented「方向感覚を失った」　　□ navigate「を通り抜ける／を操縦する」

　□ landscape「風景」　　□ prevent A from *doing*「Aが…するのを妨げる」

8 □ species「(生物の)種」　　□ interact with A「Aと互いに作用し合う」

　□ each other「お互い」

9 □ insect「昆虫」　　□ A such as B「たとえばBのようなA」　　□ moth「蛾」

　□ be vulnerable to A「Aに影響されやすい，傷つきやすい」　　□ bat「コウモリ」

　□ reduce「を減らす」　　□ effective「効果的な」　　□ evade「から逃れる，を避ける」

　□ predator「捕食動物」

---

　[1]Relatively little is known about how marine and coastal creatures cope. [2]Clownfish exposed to light pollution fail to reproduce properly, as they need darkness for their eggs to hatch. [3]Other fish stay active at night when there's too much light, emerging more quickly from their hiding places during the day and increasing their exposure to predators. [4]These effects have been observed under direct artificial light from coastal homes, promenades, boats and harbors, which might suggest the effects of light pollution on nocturnal ocean life are quite limited.

　[1]海や海岸の生き物がどう対処しているかについては，比較的わずかなことしか知られていない。[2]光害にさらされたクマノミは，卵が孵化するには暗さが必要なので，うまく繁殖できない。[3]魚によっては，光がありすぎると，夜間も活動的なままになり，昼間に身を隠している場所から普段よりも速く出てしまい，捕食動物に身をさらすことが増えてしまう。[4]こうした影響は，海岸沿いの家，遊歩道，ボートそして港から発せられる人工の光に直接さらされている場所で観測されており，このことは夜行性海洋生物への光害の影響は，かなり限られていることを示唆しているかもしれない。

1 □ relatively「比較的」　　□ marine「海の」　　□ coastal「沿岸の」　　□ creature「生き物」
　□ cope「対処する」

2 exposed to light pollution は clownfish を修飾する過去分詞句。to hatch は目的を表す副詞用法の不定詞句で，for their eggs は意味上の主語。

　□ expose A to B「AをBにさらす，触れさせる」　　□ fail to *do*「…しない，できない」

　□ reproduce「繁殖する」　　□ properly「適切に」　　□ darkness「暗さ」

　□ hatch「孵化する」

3 emerging 以下は分詞構文。and は emerging more ... the day と increasing their ... to predators の2つの分詞句を結んでいる。

□ active「活動的な」　　□ emerge「現れる」　　□ quickly「速く，すばやく」

□ hiding place「隠れ場所」　　□ during the day「日中，昼間に」

□ exposure to A「Aにさらされること，触れること」

4 and は coastal homes, promenades, boats, harbors を結んでいる。which は These effects ... and harbors の内容を補足説明する非制限用法の関係代名詞節。

□ observe「を観察する」　　□ direct「直接の」　　□ promenade「海岸遊歩道」

□ harbor「港」　　□ suggest (that)節「…ということを示唆する」　　□ limited「限られた」

━━

─── 第3段落 ───

[1]However, when light from street lamps is emitted upwards, it's scattered in the atmosphere and reflected back to the ground. [2]Anyone out in the countryside at night will notice this effect as a glow in the sky above a distant city or town. [3]This form of light pollution is known as artificial skyglow, and it's about 100 times dimmer than that from direct light, but it is much more widespread. [4]It's currently detectable above a quarter of the world's coastline, and from there it can extend hundreds of kilometers out to sea. [5]Humans aren't well adapted to seeing at night, which might make the effects of skyglow seem negligible. [6]But many marine and coastal organisms are highly sensitive to low light. [7]Skyglow could be changing the way they perceive the night sky, and ultimately affecting their lives.

[1]しかし，街灯の光が上向きに放射されると，大気中に散乱し，反射し地面を照らす。[2]夜間に田舎で屋外にいる人なら誰でも，遠くの都市や町の上空の明るさとしてのこの影響に気づくだろう。[3]このような形態の光害は，人工的な夜空の明るさとして知られており，直接光による光害と比べると明るさが100倍ほど劣るのだが，はるかに広い範囲に拡散する。[4]それは現在，世界の海岸線の4分の1の上空で見られ，そこから数百キロ沖の海にまで及ぶこともある。[5]人間は夜間に物を見ることにはうまく順応していないので，夜空の明るさの影響は無視できるほどのものと思われるかもしれない。[6]しかし，海や海岸の生物の多くは微光に対して非常に敏感である。[7]夜空の明るさはそういう生き物が夜空を知覚する方法を変え，最終的にはその生命に影響を与えていることもありうる。

1 and は scattered in the atmosphere と reflected back to the ground を結んでいる。

□ street lamp「街灯」　　□ emit「を発する，放出する」　　□ upwards「上向きに」

2 out in the countryside at night は anyone を修飾している。in the sky above a distant city or town は a glow を修飾している。

□ countryside「田舎」　　□ notice「に気づく」　　□ glow「明るさ，鮮やかさ」

□ distant「遠くの」

3 that＝the form of light pollution

□ be known as A「Aとして知られている」　　□ about＋数詞「約…」　　□ dim「薄暗い」

□ widespread「広範囲にわたる」

4 □ currently「現在（は）」　　□ detectable「検知できる，見抜くことのできる」

□ a quarter of A「Aの4分の1」　　□ coastline「海岸線」　　□ extend「広がる，伸びる」

□ hundreds of A「何百ものA」

5 which 以下は Humans aren't ... at night の内容を補足説明する非制限用法の関係代名詞節。

□ be adapted to *doing*「…するのに適応している，順応している」

6 □ organism「生物」

7 and は changing the way they perceive the night sky と affecting their lives を結んでいる。

□ the way S V ...「…する方法，仕方」　　□ perceive「を知覚する」　　□ ultimately「最終的に」

─ 第4段落 ─

¹We tested this idea using the tiny sand hopper, a coastal crustacean which is known to use the moon to guide its nightly food-seeking trips. ²Less than one inch long, sand hoppers are commonly found across Europe's sandy beaches and named for their ability to jump several inches in the air. ³They bury themselves in the sand during the day and emerge to feed on rotting seaweed at night. ⁴They play an important role in their ecosystem by breaking down and recycling nutrients from stranded algae on the beach.

¹私たちは，夜間に餌を探して動き回る道しるべとして月を利用することで知られている，海岸に生息する甲殻類であるとても小さいハマトビムシを使ってこの考えを検証した。²ハマトビムシは体長1インチにも満たないが，ヨーロッパ全域の砂浜でよく見られ，空中に数インチもジャンプする能力があることから，そのような名前がついている。³昼間は砂の中にもぐり，夜になると腐りかけの海藻を餌にするために姿を現す。⁴海岸に打ち上げられた藻類から栄養素を分解し再利用することで，その生態系において重要な役割を果たしているのだ。

1 using 以下は分詞構文。the tiny sand hopper と a coastal crustacean は同格の関係。

which 以下は a coastal crustacean を修飾する関係代名詞節。

□ test「を検証する」　　□ tiny「とても小さい」　　□ guide「を誘導する，案内する」

□ nightly「夜の」　　□ food-seeking「餌を探す」

2 and は found across Europe's sandy beaches と named for ... the air を結んでいる。

□ less than A「A未満，A以下」　　□ inch「インチ」（長さの単位）

□ commonly「普通に，一般に」

3 and は bury themselves in the sand during the day と emerge to feed on rotting seaweed at night を結んでいる。

□ bury *oneself*「隠れる」　　□ feed on A「Aを食べて生きている」

□ rotting「腐りかけの」　　□ seaweed「海藻」

4 breaking down と recycling が and で結ばれ，nutrients from stranded algae on the beach が共通の目的語となっている。

□ play a ... role in A「Aで…な役割を果たす」　　□ ecosystem「生態系」

□ break A down「Aを分解する」　　□ recycle「を再利用する」　　□ nutrient「栄養素」

□ stranded「岸に打ち上げられた」　　□ algae「藻類」

--- 第5段落 ---

¹In our study, we recreated the effects of artificial skyglow using a white LED light in a diffusing sphere that threw an even and dim layer of light over a beach across 19 nights. ²During clear nights with a full moon, sand hoppers would naturally migrate towards the shore where they would encounter seaweed. ³Under our artificial skyglow, their movement was much more random.

¹私たちの研究では，光を拡散する球体に入れた白色 LED ライトを使い，人工的な夜空の明るさの影響を再現し，それが19日にわたって，夜間の海岸に均一で薄暗い光の層を投げかけるようにした。²満月が出ている晴れた夜ならば，ハマトビムシは海藻が見つかりそうな岸辺に向かって自然に移動するだろう。³私たちの人工的な明るさの下では，彼らの動きははるかに不規則だった。

1 using 以下は分詞構文。that 以下は a white LED light を修飾する関係代名詞節。

□ recreate「を再現する」　　□ diffusing「拡散する」　　□ sphere「球体」

□ even「均一な」　　□ layer「層」

2 where 以下は the shore を修飾する関係副詞節。

□ full moon「満月」　　□ naturally「自然に」　　□ migrate「移動する，移る」

□ encounter「に出くわす」

― 第6段落 ―

[1]They migrated less often, missing out on feeding opportunities, which due to their role as recyclers, could have wider effects on the ecosystem. [2]Artificial skyglow changes the way sand hoppers use the moon to navigate. [3]But since using the moon and stars as a compass is a common trait among a diverse range of sea and land animals, including seals, birds, reptiles, amphibians and insects, many more organisms are likely to be vulnerable to skyglow. [4]And there's evidence that the Earth at night is getting brighter. [5]Scientists found that Earth's artificially lit outdoor areas increased by 2.2% each year.

[1]ハマトビムシは移動する頻度が下がり，餌を食べる機会を逃すことになったが，これは，彼らには栄養素を循環させる生物としての役割があるために，生態系により広範囲にわたる影響を及ぼしかねないだろう。[2]人工的な夜空の明るさはハマトビムシが迷わず進むための月の利用の仕方を変えてしまう。[3]しかし，羅針盤として月や星を利用するのは，アザラシ，鳥類，爬虫類，両生類，昆虫も含めて様々な海洋動物や陸上動物の間に共通する特性なので，はるかに多くの生き物が夜空の明るさに対して脆弱である可能性が高い。[4]しかも，夜間の地球がより明るくなっているという証拠がある。[5]科学者たちによると，地球上の人工の光で照らされた屋外の範囲が，毎年2.2%増加していることがわかったのだ。

1 missing out on feeding opportunities は分詞構文。which は They migrated ... feeding opportunities の内容を補足説明する非制限用法の関係代名詞。
　□ miss out on A「Aを逃す，経験しそこなう」　　□ feeding opportunity「餌を食べる機会」
　□ due to A「Aのために，Aの理由で」　　□ role「役割」
　□ recycler「再利用する者，再処理する者」

2 to navigate は目的を表す副詞用法の不定詞句。

3 1つめの and は the moon と stars を結んでいる。2つめの and は sea と land を結んでいる。3つめの and は seals, birds, reptiles, amphibians, insects を結んでいる。
　□ trait「特性」　　□ a diverse range of A「多種多様なA」　　□ including A「Aを含めて」
　□ seal「アザラシ」　　□ reptile「爬虫類」　　□ amphibian「両生類」
　□ many more＋複数名詞(A)「はるかに多くのA」　　□ be likely to do「…する可能性が高い」

4 that 以下は evidence と同格の名詞節。
　□ evidence「証拠」　　□ bright「明るい」

5 lit は outdoor areas を修飾する過去分詞。

□ artificially「人工的に」　　□ lit＜light「を照らす」　　□ outdoor「屋外の」

□ area「範囲，地域」　　□ increase by A「Aだけ増える」

- ・・

― 第7段落 ―

^{1}As researchers, we aim to uncover how light pollution is affecting coastal and marine ecosystems, by focusing on how it affects the development of different animals and interactions between species. ^{2}Only by understanding if, when and how light pollution affects nocturnal life can we find ways to moderate the impact.

^{1}研究者として，私たちは光害がどのように海岸や海の生態系に影響を及ぼしているのかを，様々な動物の成育と生物間での相互作用に光害がどのように影響を及ぼすのかに焦点を当てることによって，明らかにすることを目指している。^{2}光害が夜行性の生物に影響するのかどうか，それはいつ，どのようにしてなのかを理解することによってはじめて，私たちはその影響を和らげる方法を見つけることができるのだ。

1 1つめの and は coastal と marine を結んでいる。2つめの and は the development of different animals と interactions between species を結んでいる。

□ researcher「研究者」　　□ aim to *do*「…することを目指す」　　□ uncover「を暴露する」

□ focus on A「Aに焦点を当てる」　　□ development「成長，成育」

□ interaction「相互作用」

Topic ⑪　環境汚染

従来からある大気汚染(air pollution)，水質汚染(water pollution)，土壌汚染(soil pollution)などの問題に加えて，本問で論じられている光害(light pollution)や，観光地の観光客が過剰になり環境や社会に悪影響を及ぼす現象をいうオーバーツーリズム(overtourism)，都市部が周囲の地域よりも気温が高くなる現象をいうヒートアイランド現象(urban heat island)，プラスチック製品が環境中に放出され，海洋生物の死傷や生態系の破壊，人体への健康被害などを引き起こす現象をいうプラスチック汚染(plastic pollution)，人工衛星やロケットの破片など人間の活動によって宇宙空間に放出された廃棄物である宇宙ゴミ(space debris [junk])などの新たな環境問題が注目を集めるようになっている。また，こうした問題に関しては，従来の環境問題と異なり，単一の対策では解決が難しいという特徴があり，持続可能な開発(sustainable development)を目指した包括的な取り組みとの関連で取り上げられることも多い。

地球温暖化

解答

問1　イ. helpful and necessary

問2　地球の過去100万年にわたる温度変化。（18字）

問3　莫大な数の木々やそこに棲むあらゆる生物を滅ぼす森林火災の話を聞くことがよくある。

問4　イ. evolve

問5　過去の災害を研究することによって，人類がもし生き残るつもりであれば，今日の環境で起きている大きな変化は人類に変化を余儀なくさせるであろうということは予測できる。

問6　地球温暖化によって，病気の原因となるバクテリアなどが繁殖することで，進化に時間を要する人類のような大型種にとっては好ましくないから。（66字）

▶▶▶ 設問解説 ◀◀◀

問1　空所(1)を含む文は「しかし，この気温上昇は地球が誕生して以来生じた多くの激しい変化のうちのほんの１つであって，後でわかるように，これらの変化の中には生命にとって（　1　）ものさえあるのだ」という意味である。続く第3段落では「小惑星の激突」，第4段落では「氷河時代における寒冷化」，また第5段落では「森林火災や火山噴火」といった具体例を挙げ，地球が被った変化について言及されているが，いずれも人類にとって恩恵があったと述べられていることから，正解はイ。

　ア.「致命的で悲劇的な」イ.「有益で必要な」ウ.「興味深いが不要な」エ.「きわめて重要だが恐ろしい」

問2　they は下線部(2)を含む文の前半部の主語 These changes in temperature「このような気温の変化」を指している。「このような」とは，その前の文で述べられた「過去100万年にわたり，氷河時代の間に何回か地球の温度が低下した」ということである。したがって，この内容を制限字数内でまとめる。

問3　全体の文構造は we(S) hear(V) stories of forest fires(O) である。which 以下は forest fires を修飾する関係代名詞節。and は destroy の目的語である huge numbers of trees と all the ... they contain を結んでいる。that they

（＝trees）contain は all the animal life を修飾する関係代名詞節。

□ forest fire「森林火災」　　□ huge numbers of A「莫大な数のA」

□ contain「を含む」

問4 第6段落第4文に「その当時はほとんどの生物にとって酸素は有毒であった」と述べられている。したがって，有毒な酸素濃度が0％から21％に上昇するにつれて，生物が何を余儀なくされたのかを考えればよい。後ろの文には「死んだ種もあったが，適応し我々の祖先となる種もあった」ことが述べられているので，正解はイ。

ア.「死ぬ」イ.「進化する」ウ.「繁殖する」エ.「退却する」

問5 形式主語構文で，that the ... to survive が predict の目的語となる名詞節である。occurring in today's environment は the big changes を修飾する現在分詞句。if they are to survive の be to *do* は条件節で意図・目的を表し，「…するつもりなら，…するためには」という意味。

例　Keep my advice in mind if you are to achieve success.

「成功したいのであれば私の助言を心に留めておきなさい」

□ disaster「災害」　　□ predict「を予測する」

□ force O to *do*「Oに…することを強いる」

問6 Unfortunately は「不幸なことに，残念ながら」という意味の文修飾の副詞であり，下線部(6)を含む文では「温暖なところで繁殖する生物には病気を引き起こすバクテリアなどが含まれている」ことが「不幸なこと」だと筆者は言っている。その理由としては，後ろの文で述べられているように，「このことが進化に時間を要する人類のような大型種には不利である」からである。よって，この内容を地球温暖化と関連させて，制限字数内でまとめればよい。

要約

　地球がその長い歴史の中で被ってきた様々な災害は一部の種には生存に有利なものであり，別の種には不利なもので絶滅に至ることもあった。現在の地球温暖化は，人為的であるという点で過去の災害とは異なるが，病気の原因となるバクテリアが繁殖することで，進化に時間を要する人間にとっては不利なものとなるかもしれない。(150字)

▶▶ 構文・語句解説 ◀◀

― 第1段落 ―

¹Almost everyone has heard about global warming and how it could cause damage to our environment. ²Recent measurements of the oceans show that this warming is causing the sea level to rise by several millimeters every decade. ³Many island nations are

concerned that within a century or so their homes will disappear under water. ⁴Moreover, this rise in temperature together with pollution and the loss of natural habitat is said to be causing a huge loss in the diversity of life on Earth.

¹地球温暖化，そしてどのように地球温暖化が我々の環境に被害を引き起こすのかということについてほとんど誰もが聞いている。²最近の海洋測定によると，この温暖化によって10年に数ミリずつ海面が上昇している。³1世紀かそこらのうちに自分たちの家が海面下に姿を消してしまうのでは，と懸念している島国は多い。⁴さらに，汚染と自然の生息地の喪失を伴うこの気温の上昇は，地球の生物の多様性が大いに失われつつある原因だと言われている。

1 ☐ global warming「地球温暖化」　　☐ cause A to B「A〈被害など〉をBにもたらす，与える」
2 ☐ measurement「測定」　　☐ cause O to *do*「Oに…させる，Oが…する原因となる」
　 ☐ sea level「海水面」　　☐ rise by A「Aだけ上昇する」　　☐ millimeter「ミリメーター」
　 ☐ decade「10年」
3 ☐ be concerned that 節「…を心配している」　　☐数詞＋or so「…かそこら」
4 ☐ moreover「そのうえ」　　☐ together with A「Aと一緒に」　　☐ pollution「汚染」
　 ☐ habitat「生息地」　　☐diversity「多様性」

──── 第2・3段落 ────

¹When we think of changes like this, we call them disasters, and believe that they are exceptional events in the life of our planet. ²This rise in temperature, however, is just one of many drastic changes in the Earth's existence, and as we shall see, some of these changes are even helpful and necessary for life.

³Perhaps the most famous disaster in the Earth's existence occurred 65 million years ago when it is thought that an asteroid hit the Earth, causing the dinosaurs to go extinct. ⁴Although this was a disaster for the dinosaurs, it turned out to be good news for humans. ⁵It is almost certain that if the asteroid had not struck the Earth, you would not be reading this passage now. ⁶This shows us that disasters can sometimes have a happy ending.

¹我々はこのような様々な変化を考えるとき，それらを災害と呼び，地球の歴史では異例の出来事であると考える。²しかし，この気温上昇は地球が誕生して以来生じた多くの激しい変化のうちの1つにすぎず，後でわかるように，これらの変化の中には生命にとって有益で必要なも

のさえあるのだ。

³おそらく地球が誕生して以来の最も有名な災害は6,500万年前に起こったもので，そのとき小惑星が地球に衝突し，恐竜が絶滅することになったと思われている。⁴これは恐竜にとっては災害ではあったが，人類にとっては望ましいことであるとわかった。⁵もし小惑星が地球に衝突していなければ，あなたが今この文章を読んでいないのはほぼ確実である。⁶このことから，災害は時にはハッピーエンドになることもあるとわかる。

----

1 they は changes like this を指す。

the life of our planet の life は「存続，期間」という意味で，全体としては「地球の存続期間」ということ。

□ exceptional「例外的な」

2 as は some of ... for life を補足説明する関係代名詞。

□ drastic「激しい，徹底的な」

3 □ causing 以下は連続・結果を表す分詞構文。　　□ dinosaur「恐竜」

□ go extinct「絶滅する」

4 □ turn out to be C「Cだと判明する，結局 C になる」

5 if the ... passage now は条件節が仮定法過去完了，主節が仮定法過去の文。

□ strike「に衝突する」　　□ passage「文章」

6 □ have a happy ending「ハッピーエンドになる」

第4段落

¹Although global warming has become a real concern, it is interesting to note that over the past one million years, the Earth's temperature has cooled down several times during ice ages. ²These changes in temperature were also disastrous for some species, but they may have actually helped humans spread around the world. ³When the glaciers grew in size, the level of the sea fell and this may have made it possible for humans to reach new lands. ⁴For example, perhaps early Asians crossed into North America via a land bridge which no longer exists.

¹地球温暖化は現実に懸念されるものとなったが，過去100万年にわたり，氷河時代の間に何回か地球の温度が低下したことに注目するのは興味深い。²このような気温の変化は種によっては悲惨な場合もあるが，地球の温度変化のおかげで実際に人類は世界中に広がっていくことができたのかもしれない。³氷河が大きくなったとき海水面は低下し，これによって人類は新しい陸地に到達することが可能になったのかもしれない。⁴たとえば，おそらく大昔のアジア人は，

今ではもはや存在しない陸橋を経て北米大陸へと渡っていったのであろう。

1 □ concern「懸念」　　□ note that 節「…に注目する」　　□ cool down「さめる，涼しくなる」
　 □ ice age「氷河時代」
2 □ disastrous「悲惨な」　　□ species「(生物の)種」　　□ help O *do*「Oが…するのに役立つ」
　 □ spread「広がる」
3 □ glacier「氷河」
4 □ cross「を横断する」　　□ via A「A経由で」　　□ land bridge「陸橋」

— 第5段落 —

¹Smaller disasters, such as forest fires and volcanoes, may also be helpful. ²Often we hear stories of forest fires which destroy huge numbers of trees and all the animal life that they contain. ³When this happens we feel it is a shame that so much nature has been lost. ⁴However, it is now known that fires are actually necessary. ⁵Without fires, the tallest trees take all the sunlight, which creates very little diversity. ⁶However, diversity is important in any ecosystem. ⁷Without diversity, one disease could easily kill most life. ⁸Erupting volcanoes are another type of disaster which often causes death and destruction, yet once again, they bring great benefits. ⁹The soil around volcanoes is usually very rich, which improves the quality of life for farmers and those living near them.

¹森林火災や火山噴火というもっと小規模の災害も役に立つことがある。²莫大な数の木々やそこに棲むあらゆる生物を滅ぼす森林火災の話を聞くことがよくある。³こういうことが起きると，そんなに多くの自然が失われたのは残念なことだと感じる。⁴しかし，火災は実際には必要であることが今では知られている。⁵火災がなければ，最も高い木々がすべての日光を独り占めし，そのために多様性はほとんど生まれなくなる。⁶しかし，多様性はどんな生態系においても重要なのである。⁷多様性がなければ，１つの病気でほとんどの生命がすぐにでも死んでしまいかねない。⁸火山噴火もしばしば死や破壊を引き起こす別の種類の災害だが，この場合もまた大きな恩恵をもたらす。⁹火山の周囲の土壌はたいてい非常に肥えていて，農夫や火山の近くに住む人々の生活の質を向上させているのだ。

1 □ volcano「火山」
3 □ it is a shame that 節「…は残念なことだ」
5 which は直前の文 the tallest ... the sunlight を補足説明する非制限用法の関係代名詞。
6 □ any A「〈肯定文で〉どんなAでも」　　□ ecosystem「生態系」

7 Without diversity に条件の意味がある仮定法過去。

8 □ once again「もう一度」　　□ benefit「恩恵」

9 which は直前の文 The soil ... very rich を補足説明する非制限用法の関係代名詞。

those living ... の those は「人々」という意味。

□ soil「土壌」

─ 第6段落 ─

¹Perhaps the greatest disaster for life in the existence of the Earth is one that we seldom think about. ²Two billion years ago, there was no oxygen on the Earth, and all forms of life consisted of creatures so tiny that they would be invisible to the human eye. ³Gradually, these creatures began producing oxygen as a waste product, just as plants do now. ⁴However, at that time, for most life, oxygen was poisonous. ⁵As oxygen increased from 0% of our atmosphere two billion years ago, to the present 21%, species were forced to evolve. ⁶Naturally, many species must have died in the poisonous atmosphere; however, some managed to adapt, and these were our ancestors. ⁷While it may seem difficult to believe that oxygen can be poisonous to life, this shows us how disasters can produce strange and unpredictable results.

---

¹おそらく地球が誕生して以来，生命にとっての最大の災害は，めったに考えることがないものであろう。²20億年前，地球にはまったく酸素がなく，あらゆる生命体は人間の目には見えないほどの小さな生物から成り立っていた。³これらの生物は徐々に，今日，植物が行っているのとまったく同じように，廃棄物として酸素を排出し始めた。⁴しかしその当時はほとんどの生物にとって酸素は有毒であった。⁵大気中の酸素が20億年前の０％から現在の21％へと増加するにつれて，種は進化を余儀なくされたのである。⁶当然ながら，有毒な大気中にあって多くの種が死んだに違いない。しかし，どうにか適応した種もいて，これらが我々の祖先となったのである。⁷酸素が生物にとって有毒なものになりえるとは信じがたいようだが，このことからも災害が奇妙で予測不可能な結果をどのようにして生み出すのかがわかる。

---

1 one は a disaster の代用。　　□ seldom「めったに…ない」

2 so tiny ... human eye は creatures を修飾する形容詞句。なお，so ... that〜構文になっていることにも注意。

□ billion「10億」　　□ oxygen「酸素」　　□ consist of A「Aから成り立つ」

□ invisible「目に見えない」

3 just as plants do now の as は様態を表し「…ように」という意味。

122

do は produce oxygen as a waste product の代用。

□ waste product「廃棄物」

4 □ poisonous「有毒な」

5 □ atmosphere「大気」　　□ the present A「現在のA」

6 □ naturally「〈文修飾で〉当然のことだが」　　□ must have *done*「…したに違いない」

　　□ manage to *do*「何とか…する」　　□ adapt「順応する」　　□ ancestor「祖先」

7 how 以下は show O₁ O₂「O₁〈人〉に O₂ を示す」の O₂ に当たる名詞節。

　　□ unpredictable「予測できない」

--- 第 7 段落 ---

¹The present disaster, which is happening before our eyes, is interesting because it is being caused by humans. ²Unlike past disasters, global warming is unique in that it is not natural. ³At this point, no one knows what the outcome of this environmental destruction will be. ⁴By studying disasters in the past, it is possible to predict that the big changes occurring in today's environment will force humans to change if they are to survive.

¹現在，我々の目の前で起こっている災害が興味深いのは，人類によって引き起こされているからである。²過去の災害とは違って，地球温暖化は，それが自然に起こっているものではないという点で他に例を見ない。³現時点では，この環境破壊の結果がどうなるのか誰にもわからない。⁴過去の災害を研究することによって，人類がもし生き残るつもりであれば，今日の環境で起きている大きな変化は人類に変化を余儀なくさせるであろうということは予測できる。

2 □ unique「独特な，特異な」　　□ in that 節「…という点で」

3 □ outcome「結果」

--- 第 8 段落 ---

¹This discussion of disasters is probably both good news and bad news. ²The good news is that in all previous disasters, no matter how destructive they have been, some form of life has always survived. ³This means that there is a very good chance that global warming caused by humans may even be beneficial for some microscopic forms of life which can evolve quickly. ⁴Unfortunately, species that thrive in warmth include things like bacteria that can often cause disease. ⁵This leads us to the bad news, which suggests that this present disaster is almost certainly bad for large species, like humans, which cannot evolve quickly. ⁶With temperatures rising so quickly, humans may not be able to adapt

quickly enough to the new conditions on Earth.

¹災害に関するこのような議論はおそらく，よい知らせでもあり悪い知らせでもあろう。²よい知らせというのは，以前の災害においてはすべて，それらがいかに破壊的であったとしても，何らかの生命体が常に生き残ってきたということである。³このことは人類によって引き起こされた地球温暖化が，素早く進化できる，顕微鏡でしか見えないような微小な生命体にとって有益とさえなる可能性がとても高いことを意味する。⁴不幸なことに，温暖な気候で繁栄している種には，しばしば病気の原因となるバクテリアのようなものが含まれている。⁵このことは人類にとって悪い知らせとなる。それは，この現在の災害が素早く進化できない人類のような大型種にとってよくないのはほぼ間違いない，ということを示唆している。⁶気温がそれほど急速に上昇していけば，人類は地球の新たな状況に十分速く適応できないかもしれない。

2 no matter how ＋ 形容詞 ＋ S V は譲歩を表し「どれほど…しても」という意味。
　□ previous「以前の」　　　□ destructive「破壊的な」
3 □ caused by humans は global warming を修飾する過去分詞句。
　□ chance that 節「…する見込み，可能性」　　　□ beneficial「有益な」
　□ microscopic「顕微鏡でしか見えないほど微小な」
4 □ thrive「成育する」
5 which cannot evolve quickly は large species を修飾する関係代名詞節。
　□ lead A to B「AをBに至らせる」
6 With は付帯状況の with で with A *doing* で「Aが…である状態で」という意味。

— 第9段落 —

¹Although it seems cruel to say so, the extinction of humans would probably be good news for our planet. ²Our selfish behavior, which has led to the extinction of so many species, is obviously not good for life. ³The present disaster caused by humans may just be part of a cycle of destruction and rebirth that our planet has experienced for billions of years.

¹残酷なことを言うようだが，人類の絶滅はおそらく地球にとってはよい知らせであろう。²それほど多くの種の絶滅をもたらした人類の利己的な行為は，生物にとってよくないものであることは明らかである。³人類によって引き起こされた現在の災害は，地球が数十億年にわたって経験してきた破壊と再生というサイクルの一部にすぎないのかもしれない。

1 □ cruel「残酷な」　　□ extinction「絶滅」

2 □ selfish「利己的な」　　□ lead to A「Aに通じる」　　□ obviously「明らかに」

3 that our ... of years は a cycle of destruction and rebirth を修飾する関係代名詞節。
　　□ cycle「サイクル，周期」　　□ rebirth「再生」　　□ billions of A「何十億ものA」

Topic ⑫　地球温暖化

　二酸化炭素(carbon dioxide)やメタン(methane)などの温室効果ガス(greenhouse effect gas)の大気中への放出に伴い地球の気温が上昇し，このことが世界各地での気候変動(climate change)や自然災害(natural　disaster)の増加につながっていると考えられている。気候変動の防止，適応，緩和を目指す気候変動枠組み条約に基づき，各国は温室効果ガスの排出削減目標(emission reduction target)を設定・更新し，対策・施策を実施している。しかし，地球温暖化(global　warming)の進行を防ぐ取り組みは，各国の経済の発展段階や環境問題に対する意識の違いから，合意形成が困難であり，必ずしも十分な効果が上がっていない。さらには，再生可能エネルギー(renewable　energy)の利用，エネルギー効率(energy　efficiency)の向上，脱炭素化(decarbonization)による低炭素社会(low-carbon society)や脱炭素社会(decarbonized society)への移行なども今後の課題である。

遺伝子

問1　人間のクローン作製に反対する者は子供がひどい欠陥を持って生まれるという危険性を強調する傾向があるが，クローンの技術がいったん完成されれば，様々な点で悪用されるのではないかという恐れもある。

問2　エ．there is much less opposition

問3　無害なウィルスに正常な遺伝子を付着させ，患者に感染させることで，欠けていたり欠陥があったりする遺伝子を修復する技術。（58字）

問4　このおかげで生活様式や食事を適切に変えることで，予防措置を講じることができる一方また，保険会社は危険度の高い被保険者を特定する機会が得られる。

問5　イ．paid no attention to

問6　ア．totally dependent on

問7　イ

問8　ウ．to technological development and profits rather than to safety and social responsibility

▶▶▶　設問解説　◀◀◀

問1　前半部は the risks of children being born with severe defects の being born が受動態の動名詞であり，直前の children が動名詞の意味上の主語であることを見抜くことがポイント。but 以下では，that the ... various ways が a fear と同格の名詞節である。なお，once perfected は once it（＝the technique) is perfected と補うことができ，will be ... various ways を修飾する副詞節である。

□ opponent「反対者／敵」　　□ tend to *do*「…する傾向がある」

□ emphasize「を強調する」　　□ risk「危険性」　□ defect「欠陥」

□ once S V...「…するやいなや，いったん…すると」　　□ perfect「を完成させる」

□ abuse「を悪用する」

問2　空所(2)を含む文の however に着目すれば，その前後には逆接の内容がこなければならない。前の文には「人間のクローンについては危険性や不安があり，反対する人がいる」ことが述べられているので，「動物のクローンについて」は

126

どのようなものであるのかを考える。

ア.「より強い反感がある」イ.「誰もがその考えに強く反対している」ウ.「政府によって禁止されている」エ.「反対ははるかに少ない」

問3 下線部(3)を含む文の前半は「同様の技術がすでに犬に利用されている」という意味である。直前の文には「フィラデルフィアの研究者は無害なウィルスに正常な遺伝子を付着させ，その後，患者に感染させてそうした遺伝子を修復する方法を発見した」と述べられているので，「同様の技術」とはフィラデルフィアの研究者が発見した方法のことである。したがって，この内容をまとめる。

問4 While は対比を表し「…だが一方」という意味。this は直前の文内容「研究者は今では欠けている遺伝子や欠陥のある遺伝子を特定できるので，病気の徴候が現れるずっと前に病気を予言することが可能である」ということを指している。明示しなくてもよいが，無生物主語であるため主語を副詞的に訳出すると自然な日本語になる。by making ... or diets は take preventive action を修飾する前置詞句。主節は it(＝this)(S) gives(V) insurance companies(O₁) the chance ... bad risks(O₂) という構造。なお，bad risks の訳出に注意しなければならない。ここでは「(保険会社にとって)危険度の高い被保険者」という意味である。

□ enable O to *do*「Oが…するのを可能にする」　□ take action「措置を講じる」

□ preventive「予防の」　□ appropriate「適切な」　□ diet「(日常の)食事／規定食」

□ insurance company「保険会社」　□ chance to *do*「…する機会」

□ identify「を特定する，確認する」

問5 下線部(5)の直前の also に着目する。前の文には「遺伝子組み換え生産物の安全性に疑問を呈する人に対して，普通の食品とまったく変わらないと業界や行政側から保証された」ことが述べられている。したがって，「環境への影響についての様々な疑問も」どのように対処されたのかを考えればよい。

□ brush A aside「Aを無視する，軽くあしらう」

ア.「について真剣に話し合われた」イ.「に関心は払われなかった」ウ.「について熟考された」エ.「が慎重に考慮された」

問6 空所(6)を含む文のコロン(：)以下は仮定法過去で「もしそのような種子が発展途上国に売り込まれると，農業従事者は全面的に米国の農業関連産業(　6　)ことになるだろう」という意味である。条件節内の「そのような種子」とは，その前の文で述べられた「遺伝子操作によって，翌年使うために種子を作物から採取する必要のない種子」のことである。したがって，この種子が発展途上国に輸出された場合，どのような結果になるのかを考えればよい。

ア.「に全面的に依存する」イ.「をかなりよく知る」ウ.「から完全に自由になる」

エ.「よりとても優れている」

問7 下線部(7)を含む文のコロン以下に「益虫の消失」と「除草剤に強い雑草の繁茂」について述べられ，続く第7段落第2文に「抗生物質の有効性の低下」について述べられているが，イの「土壌流出」についての記述はない。したがって，イが正解。

問8 コロン以下の a system ... はその前の the system ... and environment を言い換えたものである。したがって「人間の健康と環境を賭することも認める仕組み」とは何が優先される仕組みであるかを考えればよい。「健康や環境を危険にさらし，それらを犠牲にし，発展と利益を優先する仕組み」であることは明らか。解答する際には，それぞれの選択肢の中の相関表現に注意すること。
ア.「科学技術開発と利益よりむしろ安全や社会的責任(が優先される)」
イ.「安全や社会的責任も科学技術開発と利益もどちらも(優先され)ない」
ウ.「安全や社会的責任よりむしろ科学技術開発と利益(が優先される)」
エ.「科学技術開発と利益よりむしろ安全や社会的責任(が優先される)」

要　約

　遺伝子工学はクローン作製，遺伝子治療，遺伝子診断など様々に応用されているが，抱えている問題点も多い。とりわけ遺伝子組み換え食品については，環境に対する影響を含め，一般大衆の関心が高い。(94字)

▶▶▶ **構文・語句解説** ◀◀◀

── 第1段落 ──

[1]The natural curiosity of scientists has often led them into controversial areas. [2]When that curiosity is backed up by the resources of rich drug companies and is directed towards the secrets of life itself, however, it becomes a potential time bomb. [3]Genetic research is racing ahead without giving society time to establish the parameters of acceptability.

---

[1]科学者には生来の好奇心があるために論議を呼ぶ領域に入り込むことが多かった。[2]しかし，そのような好奇心が裕福な製薬会社の資金で支援され，生命自体の謎に向けられる場合には，好奇心は時限爆弾になりかねない。[3]遺伝子研究は許容範囲を確定する時間を社会に与えないまま先走っている。

1□ natural「生来の，生まれつきの」　　□ curiosity「好奇心」

□ lead A into B「AをBに至らせる」　　□ controversial「議論の余地のある」

2 □ back A up「Aを〈経済的に・精神的に〉支援する，支持する」

□ resources「資産，資金」　　□ secrets「〈複数形で〉神秘，謎」

□ a potential time bomb「潜在的な時限爆弾」ここでは，非常に恐ろしいものになる可能性があるという意味で用いられている。

3 □ genetic「遺伝子の」　　□ race「全速力で進む」　　□ acceptability「受容性」

- -

━━ 第2段落 ━━

¹Cloning is one of the most controversial aspects of genetic engineering. ²When an animal is cloned, a twin is created. ³So far, the process has succeeded only with sheep, mice, cows and pigs, but several researchers have announced plans to clone human beings. ⁴This has already been made illegal in Germany, and is likely to be banned in all Western countries soon. ⁵Opponents of human cloning tend to emphasize the risks of children being born with severe defects, but there is also a fear that the technique, once perfected, will be abused in various ways, together with a sense that the creation of life is something sacred, and should be left to God. ⁶Where the cloning of animals is concerned, however, there is much less opposition. ⁷American scientists managed to clone a gaur, an endangered Asian species of ox, by implanting a gaur embryo into the womb of a cow. ⁸Although the baby died two days later, its birth was hailed as a major breakthrough which could benefit not only endangered species such as pandas and tigers but even species which have already died out. ⁹When the last bucardo (a mountain goat) died recently, scientists removed some cells in order to produce clones. ¹⁰Some Japanese researchers are even more ambitious: they hope to clone a mammoth, using DNA extracted from cells taken from a frozen mammoth carcass in Siberia or Alaska and inserted into the womb of a living elephant.

¹クローン作製は遺伝子工学において最も議論を呼んでいる分野の1つである。²ある動物のクローンが作製されれば双子がつくられることになる。³今までのところクローン技術はヒツジ，ハツカネズミ，ウシ，ブタに関して成功しているだけだが，クローン人間を作製する計画を発表した学者もいる。⁴これはドイツではすでに非合法とされ，やがてはすべての西洋諸国で禁止されるだろう。⁵人間のクローン作製に反対する者は子供がひどい欠陥を持って生まれるという危険性を強調する傾向があるが，クローンの技術については，生命の創造は神聖なもので神に任されるべきものだという意識に加えて，いったん完成されれば，様々な点で悪用されるのではないかという恐れもある。⁶しかし，動物のクローン作製に関する限り，反対ははるかに

少ない。⁷アメリカの学者は絶滅の危機に瀕したアジア種の雄牛ガウルの胚を雌牛の子宮に着床させて，うまくガウルのクローンを作製した。⁸その子牛は2日後に死んだが，その誕生自体はパンダやトラのような絶滅の危機に瀕した種ばかりでなく，すでに死滅した種にも利益となるかもしれない大躍進であると受け入れられた。⁹先ごろ最後のブカルド（野生ヤギ）が死んだとき，科学者はクローンを作製するために数個の細胞を取り出した。¹⁰日本の科学者の中にはなおいっそう野心を抱いている者もいる。彼らはシベリアあるいはアラスカの凍ったマンモスの死体から採取された細胞より抽出し，生きたゾウの子宮に挿入する DNA を使い，マンモスのクローンを作製したいと思っているのだ。

1 □ clone「クローンを作る，を無性生殖させる」　　□ genetic engineering「遺伝子工学」

3 □ so far「これまで，今まで」

4 □ illegal「非合法の」　　□ ban「を禁止する」

5 is something sacred と should be left to God が and で結ばれている。

　□ together with A「Aと一緒に」

　□ a sense that 節「…という意識」that 以下は a sense と同格の名詞節。

　□ sacred「神聖な」　　□ leave A to B「AをBに任せる」

6 □ where A be concerned「Aに関する限り」

7 a gaur と an endangered Asian species of ox は同格の関係。

　□ manage to *do*「何とか…する」　　□ endangered「絶滅の危機に瀕した」

　□ implant「を着床させる」　　□ embryo「胚」　　□ womb「子宮」

8 which could ... died out は a major breakthrough を修飾する関係代名詞節。which have already died out は species を修飾する関係代名詞節。

not only X but (also) Y「XだけでなくYも」の X に endangered species, Y に species which ... died out がきている。

　□ hail O as C「OをCとして受け入れる，認める」　　□ breakthrough「画期的な出来事」

　□ die out「絶滅する」

9 □ cell「細胞」

10 using DNA ... living elephant は clone a mammoth を修飾する分詞構文。

extracted from ... or Alaska と inserted into ... living elephant の2つの分詞句が and で結ばれており，DNA を修飾している。

　□ even＋比較級「いっそう…」　　□ ambitious「野心的な」　　□ extract「を抽出する」

　□ insert A into B「AをBに挿入する」

第3段落

¹Another use of genetic engineering is in gene therapy.　²Many diseases occur because

a particular gene is missing or defective. ³Researchers in Philadelphia have found a way to restore such genes by attaching normal genes to a harmless virus and then infecting the patient. ⁴A similar technique has already been used to cure a certain kind of blindness in dogs and may easily be adapted to cure humans too.

¹遺伝子工学のもう1つの利用が遺伝子療法における利用である。²特定の遺伝子が欠けていたり欠陥があったりするために起こる病気は多い。³フィラデルフィアの研究者は無害なウィルスに正常な遺伝子を付着させ，その後，患者に感染させてそうした遺伝子を修復する方法を発見した。⁴同様の技術はすでに犬においてある種の失明を治療するために利用されているし，人間を治療するためにも応用されることになるだろう。

1 □ gene therapy「遺伝子療法」
2 □ missing「欠けている／行方不明の」　　□ defective「欠陥のある」
3 □ restore「を修復する」　　□ attach A to B「AをBに付着させる」
　　□ harmless「無害な」　　□ virus「ウィルス」　　□ infect「に感染させる」
4 to cure ... in dogs は目的を表す副詞用法の不定詞句。
　　□ certain A「あるA」　　□ may easily「おそらく…だろう」　　□ adapt「を応用する」

- 第4段落 -

¹Now that researchers can identify missing or defective genes, it is possible to predict illnesses long before symptoms appear. ²While this enables people to take preventive action, by making appropriate changes to their lifestyles or diets, it also gives insurance companies the chance to identify bad risks. ³An above-average risk of breast cancer, for example, can be discovered through genetic testing; and some insurance companies now insist that female applicants reveal the results of such tests, and raise their fees to cover the increased risk. ⁴Once insurance companies demand such information as a matter of course, potential employers will no doubt follow suit, rejecting high-risk job applicants.

¹研究者は今では欠けている遺伝子や欠陥のある遺伝子を特定できるので，病気の症状が現れるずっと前に病気を予言することが可能である。²このおかげで生活様式や食事を適切に変えることで，予防措置を講じることができる一方また，保険会社は危険度の高い被保険者を特定する機会が得られる。³たとえば，乳ガンになる危険性が平均以上あれば，遺伝子検査で発見することができる。そして今や，保険会社の中には，女性の保険加入希望者にそのような検査結果

を明らかにすることを強く求め，増大する危険率をカバーするため保険料を上げるところもある。⁴ひとたび保険会社がそのような情報を当然のこととして要求すれば，雇用主になりえる人は先例にならって危険度の高い求職者をきっと拒否するだろう。

1 □ now that S V ...「今や…なので」　　□ predict「を予言する」
　 □ long before S V ...「…するずっと前に」　　□ symptom「症状」

3 insist that ... such tests と raise their ... increased risk が and で結ばれている。
　 □ above-average「平均以上の」　　□ breast cancer「乳ガン」
　 □ genetic testing「遺伝子検査」　　□ insist that 節「…するように要求する」
　 □ female「女性の」　　□ applicant「保険加入希望者」　　□ fee「保険料，料金」

4 rejecting high-risk job applicants は分詞構文。
　 □ as a matter of course「当然のこととして」
　 □ potential「潜在的な」potential employers とは「この先，雇用をする立場となる人」のこと。
　 □ no doubt「疑いなく，確かに」　　□ follow suit「先例にならう」

第5段落

¹Of all the applications of genetic engineering, the one which has most outraged the public is the genetic modification of food crops and livestock. ²In 1996, the first genetically-modified tomatoes reached the market. ³This was followed by potatoes and other crops such as corn, soybeans and rapeseed containing genes enabling them to kill insects or to withstand heavy doses of herbicides; and by genetically altered livestock, such as pigs with genes that made them grow bigger and heavier, cows genetically altered to produce more milk, and salmon with growth-accelerating genes. ⁴A few people questioned the safety of these products and were assured by industry and government officials that they were absolutely no different from ordinary food products. ⁵Questions about their effects on the environment were also brushed aside. ⁶By 1999, the US Food and Drug Administration had approved 44 genetically modified crops, including a third of all corn and a half of all soybeans grown in the US.

---

¹遺伝子工学のあらゆる分野の中で，一般大衆を最も憤慨させているのは食用作物や家畜の遺伝子組み換えである。²1996年に最初の遺伝子組み換えトマトが市場に登場した。³この後，殺虫能力があり，多量の除草剤にも耐えられる遺伝子を含むジャガイモ，その他トウモロコシ，ダイズ，ナタネが続いた。さらに，より大きくより重く育つようにする遺伝子を持つブタ，もっと多く乳が出るように遺伝子操作された雌ウシ，成長促進遺伝子を持つサケのような遺伝子

操作された家畜類が続いた。⁴このような生産物の安全性に疑問を呈する人は少数ながらいたのだが，それらは普通の食品とまったく変わらないと業界や行政側から保証された。⁵環境への影響についての様々な疑問も軽くあしらわれた。⁶1999年までには米国食品医薬品局は米国産トウモロコシ全品目の３分の１と大豆全品目の半分を含む44種類の遺伝子組み換え作物を認可した。

1 □ the one which ... の one は application の代用。　　□ outrage「を憤慨させる」

　 □ modification「修正，変更」genetic modification とは，遺伝子組み換えのこと。

　 □ livestock「家畜」

3 containing genes ... of herbicides は potatoes and ... and rapeseed を修飾する現在分詞句。enabling them ... of herbicides は genes を修飾する現在分詞句。to kill insects と to withstand heavy doses of herbicides が or で結ばれている。

　 and by genetically altered ... の and は followed by potatoes ... に続く by 以下を結んでいる。

　 □ S be followed by A「Sの後にAが続く」　　□ soybean「ダイズ」　　□ rapeseed「ナタネ」

　 □ withstand「に耐える」　　□ dose「１回分／(薬の)服用量」　　□ alter「を変える」

　 □ salmon「サケ」　　□ growth-accelerating「成長を促進する」

4 questioned the safety of these products と were assured ... food products が and で結ばれている。

　 □ question「を疑う，に疑義をさしはさむ」

　 □ assure O that 節「O〈人〉に確かに…だと言う，保証する」　　□ absolutely「絶対に」

　 □ be no different from A「Aとまったく違いがない」

5 □ effect on A「Aへの影響」

6 □ the US Food and Drug Administration「米国食品医薬品局」

　 □ approve「を認可する，を是認する」　　□ including A「Aを含めて」

── 第6段落 ──

¹In Europe, however, there was growing resentment at the way GM foods had been forced on the public. ²Consumers began demanding labels that allowed them to distinguish between GM and non-GM products; when the Americans refused to sell them separately, British supermarkets stopped buying their corn and soybeans. ³Environmentalists wanted proof that modified crops would not harm other species; on the contrary, they heard reports from Cornell University of a drastic decline in the monarch butterfly population related to pollen from GM corn. ⁴Then came the announcement that US agribusinesses had developed a 'terminator' gene which could be inserted into their seeds to ensure that farmers could not follow the traditional practice of taking seeds from their

own crops for use the following year. [5]Development agencies were furious: if such seeds were marketed to developing countries, farmers would become totally dependent on American agribusinesses. [6]The resulting bad publicity led to a hasty denial by the producers of any plan to market such seeds.

---

[1]しかし，ヨーロッパでは遺伝子組み換え食品を一般大衆に強要してきたやり方にますます憤りが募っていた。[2]消費者は遺伝子組み換え食品と非遺伝子組み換え食品とを区別できるようなラベルを貼るよう要求し始めた。アメリカ人がそれらを別々に売るのを拒否したとき，イギリスのスーパーマーケットはアメリカ産トウモロコシとダイズの購入を止めた。[3]環境保護論者は遺伝子組み換え作物が他の種の害にはならないという証拠を要求した。それどころか，遺伝子組み換えトウモロコシの花粉に関わったオオカバマダラチョウの棲息数が激減したというコーネル大学の報告を耳にしたのである。[4]その後，米国の農業関連産業が「ターミネーター」遺伝子を開発したという発表があった。それは種子内に挿入されて，翌年使うために種子を農業従事者が自分の作物から採取するという従来の慣行に従わなくてよいようにする遺伝子である。[5]開発に携わる機関は激怒した。もしそのような種子が発展途上国に売り込まれると，農業従事者は全面的に米国の農業関連産業に依存することになるだろう。[6]結果として生じた悪評のせいで，そのような種子を市場に出そうという計画も開発者が急遽取り止めることになった。

1 □ resentment「憤慨」　　□ the way S V ...「…する仕方」
　 □ force A on B「AをBに押しつける」
2 □ distinguish between A and B「AとBを区別する」
　 □ refuse to *do*「…することを拒む」
3 that modified ... other species は proof と同格となる名詞節。
　　□ environmentalist「環境保護論者」　　□ on the contrary「それどころか」
　　□ drastic「猛烈な」　　□ decline in A「Aの減少」　　□ population「個体群，集団」
　　□ related to A「Aに関連している」　　□ pollen「花粉」
4 □ Then came the announcement that ... は，the announcement が主語，came が動詞。that 以
　　下は the announcement と同格の名詞節。　　□ ensure that 節「確実に…であるようにする」
　　□ follow「〈例・慣習など〉に習う，従う」　　□ practice「慣習」
5 □ furious「激怒した」　　□ market「を市場に出す」
6 □ publicity「評判」　　□ lead to A「Aにつながる」　　□ hasty「急いだ，迅速な」
　　□ denial by A of B「AによるBの否定」

[1]The harmful effects of genetically modified crops on the environment are gradually appearing: the disappearance of benevolent insects; the growth of herbicide-resistant weeds; the contamination of nearby organic farms. [2]Health problems have also surfaced, including a reported increase in allergies and a decrease in the effectiveness of antibiotic drugs. [3]If, as seems likely, more serious problems develop in due course, there will be huge lawsuits, and some biotech companies may go bankrupt. [4]However, the system which has allowed them to gamble with our health and environment will remain: a system in which priority is given to technological development and profits rather than to safety and social responsibility.

[1]遺伝子組み換え作物の環境に対する悪影響は徐々に現れてきている。益虫の消失, 除草剤に強い雑草の繁茂, 近隣の有機農場の汚染である。[2]健康問題もすでに表面化し, その中にはアレルギーの報告数が増加したこと, 抗生物質の有効性が低下したことが含まれている。[3]起こりかねないことではあるが, より深刻な問題がそのうち発生すれば, 大きな訴訟問題にも発展するだろうし, 倒産するバイオ企業も出てくるだろう。[4]しかし, 人間の健康と環境を賭することも認める仕組みは依然として存在するだろう。つまり安全や社会的責任よりもむしろ科学技術開発と利益のほうが優先される仕組みである。

1 ☐ benevolent「有益な」　　☐ insect「昆虫」　　☐ herbicide-resistant「除草剤に強い」
　☐ weed「雑草」　　☐ contamination「汚染」　　☐ nearby「近くの」
　☐ organic farm「有機農場」
2 ☐ surface「〈問題・秘密などが〉表面化する」　　☐ allergy「アレルギー」
　☐ effectiveness「有効性」　　☐ antibiotic drug「抗生物質」
3 as seems likely の as は more serious ... due course を補足説明する関係代名詞。
　☐ in due course「やがて, ついには」　　☐ lawsuit「訴訟」
　☐ biotech「バイオテクノロジー, 生命(生物)工学」ここでは形容詞的に用いられている。
　☐ go bankrupt「破産する」
4 ☐ gamble with A「A を賭けて一か八かの冒険をする」　　☐ remain「とどまる, 居残る」
　☐ priority「優先順位」

　ヒトゲノム(human　genome)計画が完了し、遺伝情報(genetic　information)を基にした様々な分野の科学がさらに発展しようとしており、特にゲノム編集(genome　editing)技術の進歩には目を見張るものがあり、今後もその進歩がさらに期待される。その一方で、遺伝子組み換えやゲノム編集で生じた生物や食品に関する安全性や倫理性への懸念、人工多能性幹細胞(iPS 細胞)などの再生医療(regenerative　medicine)や人工授精などの生殖補助技術に関する倫理的・社会的な問題も多く、無秩序な遺伝子の操作は人類の未来にとって必ずしも明るいものではない。先端技術や先端医療を扱った文章では、その功罪、特に倫理上の問題点を論じたものが多い。

脳死

▶▶▶ **設問解説** ◀◀◀

問1 空所(1a)には，形容詞＋(1a)＋S V という語順から，ア.as かエ.though が入り，譲歩を表す副詞節になる。

空所(1b)には doctors are ... new one と we have ... decide death が「医者が患者の心臓を機械的に動かし続けることや，悪くなった心臓を新しい心臓に取り替えることができるようになったので，我々は死を判定する部位として脳に目を向けるようになった」という意味でつながるように，原因・理由を表す接続詞ア.as かウ.now that が入る。

空所(1c)の直後には in the first condition という前置詞句が続いている。様態を表す接続詞の as の後ろでは，主節と共通する語句が省略され as＋前置詞句の形で用いられることがある。また，the first condition とは，第6段落第2文の「動くことはできないが，呼吸をし，心臓は依然として血液を送り続けている患者」の容態のことなので，ア.as を入れると，「1番目の容態のように，脳に救いようのない損傷を受けた人の場合，生命維持装置を取り外すことは脳死という結果になるであろう」となり文意も成立する。

空所(1d)には，Until a ... for donation と the patient ... donor card が「たと

え患者が臓器を提供する意思を表明していたり，ドナーカードを所持していたとしても，脳死を宣告されるまでは，臓器提供のために臓器を保存するいかなる処置もなされるべきではない」という意味でつながるように，譲歩を表す接続詞が入る。ここでは空所(1d)以下の内容が確定した事実ではないので，イ. even if が入る。

　以上より，(1a)にはエ. though，(1b)にはウ. now　that，(1c)にはア. as，(1d)にはイ. even if が入る。

問2　So complex and painful は so ... that〜「非常に…なので〜する，〜するほど…」の構文の so ... の部分が強調のため文頭に移動したもの。このように S be　so ... that〜のときに So ... be　S　that〜の語順になることが多い。surrounding such an event は主語の the medical and ethical questions を修飾する現在分詞句。

　例　So terrible was the concert that half the audience left.
　「そのコンサートはあまりにひどかったので聴衆の半分が帰ってしまった」that 以下の構造は，it が形式主語で真主語は to overlook 以下。the fact の後ろに続く that 節は the fact と同格の名詞節である。
　□ complex「複雑な」　　□ painful「面倒な，痛ましい」　　□ medical「医学の」
　□ ethical「倫理上の」　　□ overlook「を見落とす」

問3　下線部(3)は第2段落第1文の a single, simple medical understanding of death を指しており，この内容はコロン以下に述べられている。

問4　下線部(4)は「脳死の概念」という意味。第3段落第1文には「医者が①患者の心臓を機械的に動かし続けることや，②悪くなった心臓を新しい心臓に取り替えることができるようになったので，死を判定する部位として脳に目を向けるようになった」と述べられている。さらに，①については第4段落第1文に the invention of life-support machines that could keep the heart beating とあり，②については第5段落第2文に A　dying　person　may　be　a　potential donor of vital organs such as the heart or lungs とあり，これらが脳死という概念が生まれた背景にあることがわかる。したがって，この2点を制限字数内でまとめればよい。
　□ concept「概念」　　□ brain death「脳死」

問5　空所(5a)(5b)を含む文の the traditional way of thinking about death とは，第2段落で述べられた「心臓の停止」と「呼吸の停止」によって死を判断する，脳死の概念が生まれる以前の考え方のことであり，this kind of machine とは life-support machine that could keep the heart beating のことである。したがって，「機械的に心臓を動かされている患者」は従来の考え方では「死んでいな

い」ことになる。よって，空所(5a)には still　alive が入る。また，空所(5b)を含む部分の後ろには，前の節の内容を補足的に説明する非制限用法の関係代名詞があり，「周囲の状況を認識することも，愛する者を識別したり愛する者に反応を返したりすることも，あるいは思考や感情を持つことも二度とないということを意味する」と述べられていることから，空所(5b)には cannot が入る。

問6　not only X but also Y「XだけでなくYも」のXとYに evident を修飾する副詞句がきている。また，X では for　doctors　treating　brain-damaged　patients と for families ... one's condition が and で結ばれている。

　　□ distinction「区別」　　　□ loved one「愛する者，最愛の人」

　　□ condition「容態，健康状態」　　□ supply A for B「AをBに提供する」

　　□ organ「臓器，器官」　　　□ transplant「移植／を移植する」

問7　空所(7)を含む文は仮定法過去である。どのような場合に「生命維持装置を止めて，移植のため臓器を摘出することを決断する基準が，あいまいで主観的なものとなり，頻繁に変わってしまう可能性がある」のかを考える。

　　ア.「脳死についての明確なガイドラインがなければ」

　　イ.「臓器提供者よりも潜在的な受容者が多ければ」

　　ウ.「臓器移植に関する厳しい制約にもかかわらず」

　　エ.「臓器移植技術の進歩のおかげで」

要　約

　生命維持装置の発明と臓器移植の実用化に伴い，心臓と呼吸の停止による従来の死の判定基準に加えて，脳死をもって人の死とする新たな死の定義が生まれた。ただし，各方面から批判も多く，脳死に関する明確なガイドラインが必要である。(109字)

▶▶▶ 構文・語句解説 ◀◀◀

― 第1段落 ―

¹Natural and inevitable though it may be, death confuses us nowadays. ²All too often, dying seems like a mysterious process full of difficult decisions, like the dilemma Michele Finn faced after she decided to have her severely brain-damaged husband's feeding tube withdrawn, allowing him to die.

---

¹死とは自然で避けられないものではあるが，今日我々は死に困惑している。²脳に重度の損傷を負った夫の栄養管を取り外してもらい，夫を死なせてあげようと決意した後でミシェル・フィンが直面したジレンマのように，死ぬということは，困難な決断の多い不可解な過程のよ

うに思えることがあまりによくある。

1 □ inevitable「避けられない」　　□ confuse「を困惑させる」

2 full of difficult decisions は a mysterious process を修飾する形容詞句。Michele 以下は the dilemma を修飾する関係代名詞節。allowing 以下は連続・結果を表す分詞構文。
　□ all too「あまりに…」　　□ face「に直面する」　　□ have O *done*「Oを…してもらう」
　□ feeding tube「栄養管」　　□ allow O to *do*「Oが…するにまかせる」

─── 第2段落 ───

[1]So complex and painful are the medical and ethical questions surrounding such an event that it is easy to overlook the fact that, until recently, we had a single, simple medical understanding of death: we accepted that people died when their hearts stopped beating and they stopped breathing. [2]It is the absence of those signs that doctors still use to decide death about 90 percent of the time in hospitals today. [3]Since the late 20th century, though, medical advances have undermined this simple understanding and forced physicians to look beyond the heart for an additional means of defining the end of life.

[1]そのような出来事を取り巻く医学上や倫理上の問題はとても複雑で面倒なものなので，最近まで死に対しては唯一の単純な医学上の理解しかなかったという事実を見落としやすい。つまり，心臓が脈打つのを止め，呼吸が停止したとき人は死ぬということを認めていたのである。[2]今日病院でおよそ9割の場合医師が死を判定するのにいまだに用いているのは，そうした徴候の欠如なのである。[3]もっとも，20世紀終盤以来，医学の進歩によってこうした単純な死の理解は後退し，医師は心臓以外に命の最期を定義するさらなる手段を探し出さなくてはならなくなったのである。

2 It is the absence of those signs that ... は強調構文。the absence of those signs は「心臓と呼吸の停止」ということ。
　□ absence「欠如」　　□ sign「徴候」
　□ about 90 percent of the time「およそ9割の場合」A of the time で頻度の副詞句になる。

3 □ though「もっとも，しかし」　　□ undermine「を徐々に衰えさせる」
　□ force O to *do*「Oに…することを強いる」　　□ beyond A「A以外に」
　□ additional「追加の」　　□ define「を定義する」

¹Now that doctors are able to keep a patient's heart beating mechanically or replace a damaged heart with a new one, we have turned to the brain as a place to decide death. ²The brain cannot be transplanted or replaced by any machine; without a working brain, people cannot breathe or maintain their blood pressure; they also lose the traits that we commonly associate with humanness, such as their ability to communicate, as well as any awareness of their surroundings. ³Although widely accepted in medical practice, the concept of brain death has spawned a host of medical, legal, ethical and philosophical debates, and recently has come under attack by different religious or political groups. ⁴Some say that defining death should not be left to physicians, that the death of the brain is not the same as the death of a person; others resist any definition of death that is based on science and technology.

¹今や医者が患者の心臓を機械的に動かし続けることや，悪くなった心臓を新しい心臓に取り替えることができるようになったので，我々は死を判定する部位として脳に目を向けるようになった。²脳は移植できないし，機械と取り替えることもできない。脳が機能しなければ，人は呼吸することも，血圧を維持することもできない。また，意思の伝達を図ることができることや，周囲の状況を何らかの形で認識するといった，我々が普通に人間らしさと結びつけて考える特性を失ってしまう。³医療においては広く認められているものの，脳死の概念は医学，法律，倫理，哲学各方面で多くの論争を生み，最近では様々な宗教団体や政治団体から非難されるようになっている。⁴死を定義することは医師に任せてしまうべきではない，脳死は人の死と同義ではないとする意見もある。また科学技術に基づいたいかなる死の定義にも反対する者もいる。

1 □ keep O *doing*「Oが…したままにしておく」　　□ mechanically「機械的に」
　□ replace A with B「AをBと取り替える」　　□ turn to A「Aに目を向ける」

2 □ blood pressure「血圧」　　□ trait「特性，特色」
　□ associate A with B「AをBと結びつけて考える，AでBを連想する」
　□ humanness「人間らしさ」　　□ A's ability to *do*「Aが…できること」
　□ X as well as Y「XもYも／YだけでなくXも」　　□ surroundings「周囲の状況」

3 Although widely accepted ... = Although it is widely accepted ...
　□ medical practice「医療（行為）」　　□ a host of A「多くのA」　　□ legal「法的な」
　□ philosophical「哲学的な」　　□ debate「論争」　　□ come under attack「攻撃を受ける」
　□ religious「宗教の」

4 □ leave A to B「AをBに任せる，ゆだねる」　　□ physician「医師，内科医」
□ resist「に反対する，抵抗する」　　□ definition「定義」
□ be based on A「Aに基づいている」

- 第4段落 -

[1]The first challenge came in the late '50s with the invention of life-support machines that could keep the heart beating. [2]According to the traditional way of thinking about death, patients who are supported by this kind of machine are still alive, but they cannot recover from severe brain damage, which means they will never again be aware of their surroundings, recognize or respond to their loved ones, or have any thoughts or emotions.

[1]1950年代後半に，心臓を動かし続けることができる生命維持装置の発明とともに最初の難題が生じた。[2]死についての従来の考え方によると，この種の装置によって生命を維持している患者はまだ生きていることになるが，重度の脳の損傷から回復することはない。つまり，周囲の状況を認識することも，愛する者を識別したり愛する者に反応を返したりすることも，あるいは思考や感情を持つことも二度とないということである。

1 □ challenge「難題，課題」　　□ invention「発明」　　□ life-support machine「生命維持装置」
2 □ recover from A「Aから回復する」　　□ recognize「を識別する」
□ respond to A「Aに反応する」

- 第5段落 -

[1]There is a second challenge arising from the medical and technological advances. [2]A dying person may be a potential donor of vital organs such as the heart or lungs. [3]If a surgeon operates quickly enough, a heart that has stopped in one body can be removed and transplanted into another, where it can return to normal working — possibly for many years. [4]The stopping of the heart, then, is not a satisfactory way of deciding death.

[1]2つめの難題は医学と技術の進歩によって生じる。[2]瀕死の患者は，心臓や肺などの生命維持に不可欠な器官の臓器提供者になりえる。[3]外科医が早急に手術を行えば，ある肉体の中で停止した心臓を摘出して，別の肉体に移植することができるのであり，そこでその心臓はひょっとすると何年も再び正常に動き続けることもある。[4]したがって，心臓の停止は死を判定する十分な方法ではない。

1 □ arise from A「Aから生じる」

2 □ potential「潜在的な」

  □ donor「臓器提供者，ドナー」donor から臓器を提供される人は recipient。

  □ vital「生命の維持に必要な／不可欠の」   □ lung「肺」

3 where 以下は another を修飾する関係副詞節。

  □ surgeon「外科医」   □ operate「手術をする」   □ remove「を取り除く」

  □ possibly「ひょっとすると」

4 □ satisfactory「十分な，満足な」

- 第6段落 -

¹It is important to understand that brain damage is not an all-or-nothing state, though. ²Some patients cannot move but can breathe or their hearts still keep pumping. ³Others have lost any brain working, and can be maintained solely by machines. ⁴The distinction between the two conditions is important: withdrawing life support in a hopelessly brain-damaged person, as in the first condition, will result in brain death, but that person is not actually brain dead at the time the decision is made; in the second condition, the patient is already brain dead.

¹しかし，脳の損傷は白黒のはっきりした状態ではないということを理解しておくことが重要である。²動くことはできないが，呼吸をし，心臓は依然として血液を送り続けている患者もいる。³一方で脳の機能を完全に失い，ただ機械によって生命を維持しているだけの患者もいる。⁴この2つの容態の間の区別は重要である。1番目の容態のように，脳に救いようがない損傷を受けた人の場合，生命維持装置を取り外すことは脳死という結果になるであろうが，その決定が下された時点ではその人は実際には脳死状態にはない。しかし2番目の容態では，患者はすでに脳死状態にある。

1 □ all-or-nothing「白黒のはっきりした，すべてか無かの」

2 □ pump「ポンプのように働く」

3 □ solely「ただ，もっぱら」

4 the decision is made の直前に関係副詞の when が省略されている。

  □ withdraw「を取り外す，引き抜く」   □ result in A「Aという結果になる」

¹The importance of this distinction is evident not only for doctors treating brain-damaged patients and for families who need to understand their loved one's condition, but also in the question of supplying organs for transplant patients. ²Since transplantation techniques were first developed, it has been clear there would be more potential recipients than donors. ³The primary responsibility of the potential donor's medical team is proper care of that patient and the patient's family. ⁴Until a patient is declared brain dead, absolutely no steps should be taken to preserve organs for donation, even if the patient has declared his or her wishes to donate organs or carries a donor card. ⁵Without clear guidelines for brain death, the basis for deciding to stop life-support machines and to remove organs for transplant would be vague, subjective, and likely to change often.

¹この２つの容態の区別の重要性は，脳に損傷を負った患者の治療にあたる医師や，愛する者の容態を理解する必要のある家族にとってだけでなく，臓器を移植患者に提供する問題においても，明白である。²臓器移植技術が最初に開発されて以来，提供者よりも潜在的な受容者の方が多くなるということは，はっきりとしていた。³潜在的提供者を引き受ける医療班の最も重要な責任は，提供者とその家族に対する適切なケアである。⁴たとえ患者が臓器を提供する意思を表明していたり，ドナーカードを所持していたとしても，脳死を宣告されるまでは，臓器提供のために臓器を保存するいかなる処置もなされるべきではない。⁵脳死についての明確なガイドラインがなければ，生命維持装置を止めて，移植のため臓器を摘出することを決断する基準が，あいまいで主観的なものとなり，頻繁に変わってしまう可能性がある。

2 □ transplantation「臓器移植」

3 □ primary「最も重要な，主要な」

4 □ declare O C「OがCであると言明する」　　□ absolutely「絶対に」
　□ take steps to *do*「…する処置をとる」
　□ preserve「を保存する」　　□ donation「臓器提供」　　□ donate「を提供する」
　□ donor card「ドナーカード，臓器提供承諾カード」死後の臓器提供に同意したことを示す携帯用のカード。

5 □ the basis for A「Aの基準」　　□ vague「あいまいな」　　□ subjective「主観的な」
　□ be likely to *do*「たぶん…するだろう，…する可能性がある」

　脳死(brain　death)は，脳全体のすべての機能が非可逆的に停止した状態をいう。人工呼吸器の出現により，脳死後も心臓を動かし続けることができるようになったことで，心臓や肝臓など新鮮でないと移植できない臓器の臓器移植(organ　transplantation[transplant])の道が開けた。一方で，脳死を確実に診断する方法と基準，および脳死を即個体の死と見なしえるか否かについて，種々の意見がある。また，臓器の提供者(donor)が被提供者(recipient)に対して不足しており，臓器や組織の一部を人工的に培養する再生医療(regeneration)が注目されている。

20世紀最大の発見

解 答

問1 人類が大人になったことを印すのが，他の何よりも，我々が無知であることに気づいたことである。

問2 イ. discoveries of the vastness of the universe

問3 エ. nothing

問4 この写真には数千の銀河の像が含まれており，それぞれの銀河が何千億もの恒星と惑星系から成り立っている。

問5 ア. finite — infinite

問6 イ. drives

問7 前世紀の初めに知っていたことと比べて，知識が拡大したために知っていることが増えたと同時に，無知の範囲がさらにはっきりと認識されたために知っていることが少なくなったとも言えること。

▶▶▶ **設問解説** ◀◀◀

問1 主語の this を強調した強調構文である。the coming of age は come of age「大人になる，成年に達する」という表現が名詞化したもので，「大人になること」という意味。また，our species「我々の種」とは「人類」ということ。this は前の our awareness of it を指し，この it はさらに前の文の Our ignorance を指す。

　　　□ more than anything else「他の何よりも」　　□ mark「を印す，特徴づける」

問2 空所(2)を含む文が，前の疑問文によって提起された「我々が無知であることの確認がどのように生じたのだろうか」という問題に対する答えとなるように空所に入るものを考える。第5〜9段落では「宇宙には膨大な数の銀河や恒星があることが発見される」に至って，「人間が最終的な知識を得ることは不可能であることを認識した」と述べられている。

　　　ア.「DNA の構造の発見」

　　　イ.「宇宙が広大であることについて発見が次々となされたこと」

　　　ウ.「地球が宇宙の中心であるという考え」

　　　エ.「星の動きの説明」

問3 空所(3)を含む文は，前の文と共に，第6段落第1文の主節の内容「宇宙の内容

を残らず列挙することができると我々は信じることができた」を補足したもの。ここでの a complete catalog of its contents was possible とは「宇宙についてすべてを知ることができる」ということである。したがって,「宇宙には人間の頭で理解できないものは<u>ない</u>」となるように,エを選ぶ。

問4 前半は In this photo(副詞句) are contained(V) the images of several thousand galaxies(S) という構造。場所・方向を表す副詞(句)が文頭に置かれると,その後に V S という語順が続くことがある。後半は意味上の主語を伴った分詞構文である。

例 In the distance could be seen the snow-capped mountain range.
「遠くに,雪を頂いた山並みが見えた」

□ contain「を含む」　　□ image「像,映像」　　□ galaxy「銀河,星雲」
□ consist of A「Aから成り立つ」　　□ hundreds of billions of A「何千億ものA」
□ planet system「惑星系」

問5 空所(5a)(5b)を含む文は「知識が増えるほど,無知であることを認識するようになる」ことを述べた Karl Popper の言葉の引用の一部である。また,この文の this はダッシュ以下を指しているので,空所を含む部分は「我々が無知であること」の要因となる事実である。したがって,「我々の知識は<u>有限である</u>が,<u>無知は無限である</u>」となるように,アを選ぶ。

問6 空所(6)を含む文は強調構文で,the latter frame of mind「後者の心持ち」とは第11段落第4文で述べられた「我々が無知であるという認識に対して,さらなる発見の機会であると奮い立つ」ような心持ちのことである。よって,このような心持ちが科学をどうするのかを考えればよい。第12段落第2～4文の Heinz Pagels の引用では,「複雑さや矛盾を受け入れることが探求には必要であり,絶対的真理の追究を放棄することで科学が進歩を遂げるようになった」と述べられている。したがって,正解はイ。

ア.「を単純化する」イ.「を推し進める」ウ.「を否定する」エ.「と矛盾する」

問7 下線部(7)は「今や我々は,前世紀の初めに我々が知っていたことと比べて,より多く,そしてよりわずかに知っている」が直訳。know more and less に関して,その理由が直後のコロン以下に述べられているので,この内容を含めて下線部をまとめればよい。なお,our inventory of knowledge has been greatly expanded「我々の知識の目録が大いに拡大された」とは「知識の範囲が大幅に増加した」ということである。

　20世紀最大の科学上の発見は，人間が無知であることを発見したことであった。この背景には，宇宙の広大さの発見と共に人間がすべてを知ることができないという認識があった。一方で，無知であるということは，新たな発見の機会があるということであり，これが科学の進歩につながるのである。(135字)

▶▶ 構文・語句解説 ◀◀

── 第1段落 ──

¹What was the greatest scientific discovery of the 20th century? ²Nuclear energy? ³The structure of DNA? ⁴The theory of digital computation? ⁵The Big Bang? ⁶It was an exceptional century of discovery. ⁷How do we choose one discovery over any other?

¹20世紀最大の科学上の発見とは何だったのだろうか？²核エネルギーだろうか？³DNA の構造だろうか？⁴デジタル処理の理論だろうか？⁵ビッグバンだろうか？⁶20世紀は他に例のない発見の世紀であった。⁷他のいかなる発見にも勝る発見を1つどのように選ぶのであろうか？

2 □ nuclear energy「核エネルギー」
3 □ structure「構造」
4 □ digital computation「デジタル処理，デジタル式計算法」
5 □ the Big Bang「ビッグバン，宇宙爆発起源論」宇宙の初めに起こったとされる大爆発。
6 □ exceptional「例外的な」
7 □ choose A over B「Bに優先してAを選ぶ」

── 第2・3段落 ──

¹The physician Lewis Thomas made a choice. ²He bluntly asserts: "The greatest of all the accomplishments of 20th-century science has been the discovery of human ignorance."

³The science writer Timothy Ferris agrees: "Our ignorance, of course, has always been with us, and always will be. ⁴What is new is our awareness of it, and it is this, more than anything else, that marks the coming of age of our species."

¹医師のルイス・トーマスは選択した。²彼は単刀直入に断言する。「20世紀の科学のあらゆる成果の中で最も偉大なものは，人間が無知であることの発見であった」
³サイエンス・ライターのティモシー・フェリスも同じ意見である。「もちろん，我々が無知

であることは常に我々と共にあったし，今後も常にそうであろう。⁴新しいことは，我々がそのことに気づいたことであって，人類が大人になったことを印すのが，他の何よりも，このことである」

1 □ physician「医師，内科医」

2 □ bluntly「単刀直入に，遠慮なく」　　□ assert「と断言する」

　 □ accomplishment「成果，業績」

3 always will be＝always will be with us

<hr>

― 第4段落 ―

¹It is an odd, unsettling thought that the greatest discovery of the last century should be the confirmation of our ignorance. ²How did such a thing come about? ³The discovery of our ignorance followed inevitably from discoveries of the vastness of the universe.

¹前世紀の最大の発見が，我々が無知であることを確認することというのは奇妙で，不安にさせる考えである。²そのようなことがどのように生じたのだろうか？³我々が無知であることの発見は，宇宙が広大であることについて発見が次々となされたことから必然的に生じたのである。

1 □ odd「奇妙な」　　□ unsettling「不安にさせるような」　　□ confirmation「確認」

2 □ come about「生じる」

3 □ follow from A「Aから結果として生じる」

　 □ inevitably「必然的に」

<hr>

― 第5段落 ―

¹I begin my course in astronomy at Stonehill College holding in my hands a 16-inch clear acrylic celestial globe spangled with stars. ²A smaller terrestrial globe is at the center, and a tiny yellow ball representing the sun circles between Earth and sky. ³This tidy cosmos of concentric spheres was invented thousands of years ago to account for the apparent motions of sun, moon, and stars, and for that task it still works pretty well.

¹私は，星がちりばめられた16インチの大きさの透明なアクリル製の天球儀を手にして，ストーンヒルカレッジでの天文学の講座を始める。²より小さな地球儀が中心にあって，太陽を表

す小さな黄色い球体が地球と空の間を回っている。³同心の天体からなるこの整然とした宇宙は、太陽と月と恒星の見かけの動きを説明するために、何千年も前に発明されたもので、そのような役目には今でも十分使えるのである。

1 holding 以下は同時動作を表す分詞構文。

　□ course「講座」　　□ astronomy「天文学」

2 □ represent「を表す」　　□ circle「回る，旋回する」

3 that task は to account for the apparent motions of sun, moon, and stars を指す。

　□ tidy「整然とした」　　□ cosmos「〈秩序ある体系としての〉宇宙」　　□ sphere「天体，球」

　□ account for A「Aを説明する」　　□ apparent「見かけの」　　□ motion「動き」

　□ work「機能する」　　□ pretty well「かなりうまく」

- -

── 第6段落 ──

¹When we thought we lived in such a universe, we could believe that a complete catalog of its contents was possible. ²The universe was proportioned to the human scale, created specifically for our home. ³Presumably, since it was made for us, the universe contained nothing beyond the understanding of the human mind.

¹我々がそのような宇宙で生きていると考えたとき、その内容を残らず列挙することができると信じることができた。²宇宙は人間の尺度に合わせられており、我々の生きる場のために特に創造されたのだ。³我々のために作られている以上、宇宙には人間の頭で理解できないものは何一つないであろう。

1 □ catalog「一覧，カタログ」　　□ content「内容，中身」

2 created 以下は，主節の内容を補足説明する分詞句。

　□ proportion A to B「AをBに合わせる，調和させる」　　□ scale「尺度，規模」

　□ specifically「特に」

3 □ presumably「たぶん，どうも…らしい」　　□ mind「知力，頭脳」

- -

── 第7段落 ──

¹Then, in the winter of 1610, Galileo turned his newly-crafted telescope to the Milky Way and saw stars in uncountable numbers, stars that served no apparent purpose in the human scheme of things since they could not be seen by human eyes. ²It was an ominous hint of the cascading discoveries to come.

¹その後，1610年の冬，ガリレオは新しく作った望遠鏡を天の川に向けて，無数の星を，人間の目に見えない以上，人間が関与している世界においては特に目的を果たしていないように思われる星を見た。²それは，その後来たるべき数々の発見の不穏な前兆であった。

1 stars that … human eyes は stars in uncountable numbers と同格の名詞句。

☐ turn A to B「AをBに向ける」　　☐ in uncountable numbers「無数の[に]」

☐ serve「を果たす」　　☐ the scheme of things「物事のあり方，成り立ち」

2 ☐ ominous「不穏な，不吉な」　　☐ hint「かすかな兆候，気配」

☐ A to come「来るべきA」

- -

第8段落

¹I end my astronomy course with the Hubble Space Telescope's Deep Field Photograph, a 10-day exposure of a part of the dark night sky so tiny that it could be covered by the intersection of crossed pins held at arm's length.　²In this photo are contained the images of several thousand galaxies, each galaxy consisting of hundreds of billions of stars and planet systems.　³A survey of the bowl of the Big Dipper at the same scale would show 40 million galaxies.

¹私はハッブル宇宙望遠鏡による深探査写真で天文学の講座を終える。その写真は，腕を一杯伸ばして持った交差させたピンの交点で覆うことができるほど小さな，暗い夜空の一角を10日かけて露出したものである。²この写真には数千の銀河の像が含まれており，それぞれの銀河が何千億もの恒星と惑星系から成り立っている。³北斗七星の鉢状の部分を同じ倍率で調査すると，4千万もの銀河が見えるであろう。

1 a 10-day 以下は the Hubble Space Telescope's Deep Field Photograph と同格の名詞句。so tiny that … は so … that〜「非常に…なので〜する，〜するほど…」の構文で，a part of the dark night sky を修飾している。

☐ Hubble Space Telescope「ハッブル宇宙望遠鏡」1990年，アメリカがスペースシャトルを使って地球周回軌道に打ち出した口径2.4メートルの反射望遠鏡。地球の大気の影響を受けないので高解像度撮影が可能。　　☐ exposure「露出，露光」　　☐ intersection「交点」

☐ cross「を交差させる」　　☐ at arm's length「手を伸ばしたところに」

3 ☐ survey「調査」

¹Galaxies as numerous as snowflakes in a storm! ²Each with uncountable planets, strange geographies, perhaps life forms, intelligent beings. ³To live in such a universe is to admit that the human mind singly or collectively will never be in possession of final knowledge.

¹吹雪の中の雪片と同じくらいの数の銀河！²それぞれの銀河には無数の惑星，見知らぬ地形，ひょっとすると様々な生命体があり，知的存在もいるかもしれない。³そのような宇宙で生きているということは，人間の知性が単独であるいは集団として，最終的な知識を持つことは決してないことを認めることである。

1 □ numerous「多数の」　　□ snowflake「雪片」

2 □ geography「地形／地理学」　　□ intelligent being「知的存在」

3 □ collectively「集団的に」　　□ in possession of A「Aを所有して」

¹Ferris quotes the philosopher Karl Popper: "The more we learn about the world, and the deeper our learning, the more conscious, specific, and clear will be our knowledge of what we do not know, our knowledge of our ignorance. ²For this, indeed, is the main source of our ignorance — the fact that our knowledge can be only finite, while our ignorance must necessarily be infinite."

¹フェリスは哲学者のカール・ポパーの言葉を引用している。「世界について多くを知れば知るほど，そして我々の学識が深まれば深まるほど，我々が知らないことを認識すること，つまり我々が無知であることの認識がますます意識され，特定され，明らかになるであろう。²というのも，実際のところ我々が無知であることは次のようなことが主な要因なのである。すなわち，我々の知識は有限なものにしかなりえないのに対して，我々の無知は必然的に無限のものにならざるをえないという事実である」

1 The more ... our ignorance は The ＋比較級 ...，the ＋比較級〜「…すればするほど，ますます〜」の構文。前半部分は the more we learn about the world と the deeper our learning が and で結ばれており，our learning の後ろに is が省略されている。後半部分はＣＶＳの語順にな

っている。

our knowledge of our ignorance は our knowledge of what we do not know と同格の名詞句。

　□ quote「の言葉を引用する，を引き合いに出す」　　□ specific「特定的な，明確な」

2 □ source「要因，源泉」

- -

── 第11段落 ──────────────────────

¹How do we react to this new and humbling knowledge?　²That depends, I suppose, on our temperaments.　³Some of us are frightened by the vast spaces of our ignorance, and seek refuge in the human-centered universe of the acrylic star globe.　⁴Others are inspired by the opportunities for further discovery, for the new vistas that will surely open before us.

¹この新たな屈辱的な認識に我々はどのように対応するのだろうか？²それは気質によって決まるのではないかと思う。³我々が無知であることの広大さに恐れをなし，アクリル製の天球儀の人間中心の宇宙に逃げ込む者もいる。⁴さらなる発見の，間違いなく我々の前に広がるであろう新たな展望の機会に奮い立つ者もいる。

1 □ react to A「Aに対応する，反応する」　　□ humbling「屈辱的な」

2 □ depend on A「Aによって決まる，A 次第である」　　□ temperament「気質」

3 □ seek refuge in A「Aに逃げ込む」　　□ human-centered「人間中心の」

4 for the ... before us は for further discovery を言い換えたもの。

　□ inspire「を奮い立たせる」　　□ vista「展望」

- -

── 第12段落 ──────────────────────

¹It is the latter frame of mind that drives science.　²The physicist Heinz Pagels wrote: "The capacity to tolerate complexity and welcome contradiction, not the need for simplicity and certainty, is the attribute of an explorer.　³Centuries ago, when some people suspended their search for absolute truth and began instead to ask how things worked, modern science was born.　⁴Curiously, it was by abandoning the search for absolute truth that science began to make progress, opening the material universe to human exploration."

　　¹科学を推し進めるのは後者の心持ちである。²物理学者のハインツ・ペイゲルズは次のように書いた。「単純さや確実性を求めるのではなくて，複雑さを受け入れ，矛盾を歓迎する能力が

探求者の属性である。³何世紀も前に，一部の人が絶対的真理の追究をひとまず取りやめ，代わりに物事がどのような仕組になっているのかを問い始めたとき，近代科学が誕生した。⁴奇妙なことに，絶対的真理の追究を放棄することによって，科学が進歩を遂げるようになり，物質的宇宙を人間の探求の対象としたのである」

2 the capacity ... welcome contradiction, not the ... and certainty は not X but Y「Xではなく Y」が Y, not X の語順になったもの。

- □ capacity to *do*「…する能力」　　□ tolerate「を許容する，に耐える」
- □ complexity「複雑さ」　　□ contradiction「矛盾」　　□ attribute「属性，特性」
- □ explorer「探求者」

3 □ suspend「を一時停止する」　　□ search for A「A の追究」　　□ absolute「絶対的な」

4 it was by abandoning the search for absolute truth that ... は強調構文。opening 以下は連続・結果を表す分詞構文。

- □ curiously「〈文修飾で〉奇妙なことに」　　□ abandon「を放棄する」
- □ material「物質的な」　　□ exploration「探求」

第13〜15段落

¹The discovery of our ignorance should not be conceived as a negative thing. ²Ignorance is a vessel waiting to be filled, permission for growth, a foundation for the electrifying encounter with mystery.

³Now we can claim with optimism that we know both more and less than we knew at the beginning of the last century: more because our inventory of knowledge has been greatly expanded, less because the scope of our ignorance has been even more greatly realized.

⁴Timothy Ferris writes: "No thinking man or woman ought really to want to know everything, for when knowledge and its analysis is complete, thinking stops."

---

¹我々が無知であることの発見は否定的なものであると捉えるべきではない。²無知とは満たされることを待っている器であり，成長の承認，神秘との電撃的な出合いの基盤である。

³今や我々は，前世紀の初めに知っていたことと比べて，知っていることが増えたと同時に少なくなったと楽観して主張することができる。増えたというのは，我々の知識の目録は大幅に増加したからであり，少なくなったというのは，我々の無知の範囲がさらにはっきりと認識されたからである。

⁴ティモシー・フェリスは書いている。「ものを考える人であれば本当にすべてを知ろうと願

ってはならない。というのも知識とその分析が完全なものになるとき，思考は停止するからである」

1 □ conceive O as C「OがCであると考える」

2 □ vessel「器，容器」　　□ foundation「基盤」　　□ electrifying「電撃的な」

3 □ claim that 節「…であると主張する」　　□ optimism「楽観(主義)」

　□ inventory「在庫目録」　　□ expand「を拡大する」　　□ scope「範囲」

4 □ analysis「分析」

Topic ⑮　科学論

　科学論は入試では頻出のトピックの1つである。代表的な論点としては次のものを押さえておきたい。①科学は，仮説(hypothesis)を設定し，観察(observation)や実験(experiment)による検証を通じて客観性(objectivity)を確証し，法則(law)として確立されるという手順で進められ，新たな仮説に対しては，反証(disprove)することが科学者の責務である。その意味では科学は絶対的真理に到達することはなく，常に自己修正的に進む過程であるとする論点。②一見無秩序に見えるものの中に，隠された秩序を見い出し，複雑・多様なものを単純な原理に還元しようとするのが科学であるとする論点。③人間を苦役から解放し，豊かな社会の土台を築いたという科学の功績と，セキュリティーを脅かし，自然環境の破壊をもたらしたという科学のマイナス面に対して，科学を制御することができるのはそれを用いる人間であり，社会であるとする論点。④科学の行き過ぎた専門分化に対していかに統合することが可能になるかという論点。⑤科学以外の分野，宗教や哲学，芸術などとの類似点，相違点から科学を捉える論点などがある。本問は，「人間が無知であることを認識したことが20世紀最大の科学上の発見である」という論考であるが，科学に対する捉え方として，①の論点が基本にある。